writings from the

Beaver Trail

by
Residents of the Albany-Rensselaer Area
Editors Florence Boochever and Raymond H. Jackson

ALBANY PUBLIC LIBRARY
161 Washington Avenue
Albany, New York 12210

ERASTUS CORNING, 2ND
MAYOR
WILLIAM L. KEEFE
EXECUTIVE ASSISTANT

CITY OF ALBANY
STATE OF NEW YORK
OFFICE OF THE MAYOR
12207

Congratulations on publishing an anthology of writings by senior citizens.

Many of those writings that have never been published are better than some that have.

I hope and believe that this anthology will bring to light poems and prose which will give joy and new insight to a lot of people and justifiable pride on the part of those who have created them.

Sincerely yours,

MAYOR

CONTENTS

PREFACE

Writings from the Beaver Trail

by Residents of the Albany-Rensselaer Area

This anthology of hitherto unpublished prose and poetry by senior citizens has been sponsored by the Albany Public Library, headquarters of the Upper Hudson Library Federation which serves Albany and Rensselaer counties. The writings not only record past history and customs—they have provided a creative activity for the leisure years.

Contributions were solicited through letters to senior citizen centers, retirement apartments, nursing homes, churches and synagogues, and notices were sent to newspapers, radio and television stations. The responses were phenomenal.

Gloria Freedman, Special Services Librarian, was in charge of the project. The selection committee included writers, retired but active, teachers and librarians. Professor Raymond H. Jackson was appointed associate editor; his help has been invaluable. Other hard working admirable committee members were: Patrick Glavin, Louise Gunn, Eleanor Huba, Rose Panitch, Rebecca Richter, Arthur D. Rosenberg, and Mildred Zimmermann. Assisting were staff members Michael Catoggio, Fran Lewis and Marguerite Mullenneaux; also student Marie Irwin, now a graduate of SUNYA School of Library and Information Service. Edgar Tompkins, Director of the Albany Public Library, and the Upper Hudson Library Federation has supported the Anthology project with his usual whole-hearted cooperation.

We thank Arthur D. Rosenberg who sparked the idea for the Anthology; Patrick Glavin for suggesting as motif the beaver, official State animal and native to our region; Sister Mary Charles Lilly for the charming drawings;

Robert L. Ewell for designing the cover and makeup throughout; Mary Carolyn Powers for taping this volume for the blind and physically handicapped; also, the New York State Library, and the following cooperative agencies: Albany City Arts Office; Albany Nursing Home; Ann Lee Home; Child's Hospital Nursing Home; Good Samaritan Nursing Home; Guardian Home; Highland Retirement Center; Institute of Gerontology at the School of Social Welfare, SUNY, Albany; Jewish Community Center and Teresian House.

How delightful that in this audio-visual age, the love of the written word persists. Webster tells us that the word "anthology" derives from the Greek: *anthos* flower + *logia* collecting. We are grateful to the citizens of our area for sharing with us the flowers of their minds.

— Florence Boochever
Editor

I. MEMOIRS

ALBANY GUARDIAN HOME RESIDENTS REMEMBER
INSIDE AND OUTSIDE ALBANY

. . . . I was a young teacher in 1914, teaching German, and I was advised to take some German courses in Berlin during my summer vacation. This I did. While I was there, war broke out. I was in a nightclub in the city when newsboys came in with "Extras" announcing the beginning of World War I. It had begun between Austria and Serbia and soon Russia and Germany declared war.

Many of the Americans in Germany rushed to our embassy in Berlin. I had to have my passport signed by our ambassador, Mr. Gerard. Mrs. Gerard was helping in the emergency, and it was through her that I was able to get my name on a list of Americans who were to sail from Rotterdam, Holland.

The Ambassador in Holland, Mr. Van Dyke, sent a train to meet us at the border. There were five hundred in our group. The regular time for going from Berlin to Rotterdam was fifteen hours. It took us thirty hours. I did not have my hat and coat off for two days. We arrived in Rotterdam about three o'clock in the morning. I remember that the Red Cross nurses met us and served coffee and doughnuts.

When we boarded the ship in Rotterdam, we were assigned to cabins with six bunks. The cabins were very clean, but there were no sheets or pillow cases. The trip took nine days, three more than the usual crossing time, because the North Sea was already in the war zone. One of the Allies' warships followed us out of the Channel for a whole day. Then we were on our own.

I had tried to contact my parents from Europe but letters were forbidden. On the ship coming home I was allowed to send a wireless message which was relayed from Newfoundland to New York and from there to Albany. My message said, "I will be in New York about midnight." It was midnight when they received the message. Were they happy to hear from me! My father came down to New York to meet me the next day.

That was a great experience for a twenty-two-year old.

. . . . I attended State College when it was a Normal School located on Willett Street. We went to the Presbyterian Church for English and German and to Trinity Methodist Church on Lancaster Street for History and Math. I happened to be in the first class that graduated from State College after it was moved to Western Avenue.

—*Florence Chase*

. . . . I first came to Albany in 1932 to take a course in child care at what was then the Albany Infant Home. It is now St. Catherine's Child Guidance Center. The Albany Infant Home was a shelter for single mothers, and it was an ideal spot because it was connected with the Brady Maternity Hospital and the mothers could stay at the Infant Home where living quarters were provided and then go to the hospital to deliver the babies. The Brady Hospital was a memorial built by the Anthony Brady family. It was told that when Mr. Brady was approached for a donation to help build the hospital, he said he would give the whole hospital as a memorial to his family. This was a beautiful hospital and very modern for its time.

In 1932 the Albany Infant Home had approximately a hundred children from four days to six years of age. It was a charming place operated by the Sisters of Charity who have always had a reputation for caring for children. The work was satisfying and the atmosphere always cheerful. In those days infant formulas were mixed individually. There were no prepared cereals such as pablum nor were there commercial baby formulas.

Some days were especially great because an adoption would have been arranged and the happy new parents would come to get their baby. That was a great experience for all of us at the Home. I worked there for many years after my training was completed.

My life was rather circumscribed in those years of my training. Going downtown was our recreation. At that time downtime Albany was a most interesting place with its shops, movies and nice restaurants.

—*Mary Cummings*

. . . . I recall that when I first came to Albany in 1915, I was impressed by so many cobblestone streets. I had never seen anything like that. It hadn't been too many years before that they had had horsecars on those same streets. Right across from the New York State Library there were strange little shops crowded together, not appropriate neighbors for the State Capitol at all. Now, of course, it is a beautiful small park for the capitol. Later, I remember they were preparing to build the Governor Smith Building and they had to move Fort Frederick across the street on the corner of State Street. They had a big construction company supervising the move. It was very exciting to see the Fort being taken across the street and placed there on the corner. I know that the first construction company that was hired to build the Governor Smith Building found that there was so much quicksand they could not continue and another firm had to take over. The second firm drove down piles many feet into the ground before they were able to find a solid foundation on which to build. That was a big event when the Governor Smith Building was completed.

When I came to the State College it was located on Western Avenue. It had been moved from Willett Street a few years before. In 1917 we had the first Moving Day that had ever been celebrated. Milne High School was connected with the college and that was where we did our practice teaching. Many times in the evening we would go down to the State Library to study and to make our preparations for the next day. The park nearby was a beautiful place and we had no fear of going there at that time. Things have changed considerably now. I remember for one assignment we were told to sit in the park and close our eyes and imagine what it would be like to be blind.

When I taught in Schenectady our club would take trips down the Hudson River. In those days the Hudson River boats were really something. We would go down to Kingston and have our picnic there and return the same day. I remember there was a retired river boat captain who lived down at Van Vie's Point. I think his name was Welch, at least I know he was Belle Welch's father. After he retired he used to watch for the boat and he would wave a huge white tablecloth at us as the boat sailed by. For years those Hudson River Dayboats were a very popular means of travel to New York City and people made good use of them. It was a sad day for us when those boats were taken off. It had been an ideal way to travel to Kingston or New York City from Albany.

—*Florence Jennings*

My father was born in the old Albany Academy in Capitol Park, Albany. His father was then the caretaker and the family lived upstairs. As time went on, my grandfather had to go to fight in the Civil War and all the brothers and sisters came home to the Academy to live because they could live there more cheaply. There were no doles given out for the families of men in the service and they had to get along the best way they could. I heard my father say that at every meal they had to eat a bowl of cornmeal mush before they could have even one piece of bread. For the rest of his life he would never eat a bowl of oatmeal because, as he said, he had enough of such things when he was a child. While the family was still living at the Academy, my grandfather came home from the Civil War. Lincoln's body was brought to Albany on its funeral procession via the New York Central railroad to its final resting place in Springfield, Illinois, and my grandfather was chosen as one of the Honor Guard.

My grandfather on my mother's side was born in England as were my grandmother and my mother. My grandfather settled in Slingerlands and worked for Goldring Florists. After two years, my grandmother came over with the rest of the family. The oldest daughter had just been married and spent her honeymoon on the ship. Her husband said that he spent most of the time on his honeymoon running around the ship trying to round up his young in-laws, seven boys and four girls. My father took over the florist business from his father-in-law and it has stayed in the family. My niece now runs The Garden Gate Florist in Crescent. The florist business has been a part of my life for all of my life.

I was born in Albany in 1900 in our home on New Scotland Avenue when New Scotland Avenue was really country. Our pavement was a plank road, planks on one side and just plain dirt road on the other. I remember many times when I was young going to something in the city and coming home after a storm, taking my shoes off and walking barefoot because I didn't want to get my shoes muddy. The road went out to Slingerlands. There was a tollgate near my home. That was about where Ramsey Place is now. You could walk through the tollgate free, but a vehicle, a horse and carriage, had to pay toll. Of course there were almost no automobiles at that time.

I went to School 4 which was at the corner of Madison Avenue and Ontario Street. There wasn't any school bus; we walked home for lunch unless it was very bad weather and then we took our lunch to school. No lunches were served in the schools at that time. Sometimes when the weather was bad in the winter my father would hitch up the horses and come over after school to get a load of youngsters and take them home. We had no public transportation on New Scotland Avenue so we had to walk over to Madison Avenue and Quail Street to get the trolley car.

When I was young, downtown Albany was flooded every spring. That was before the Sacandaga Project. Many times I went down as far as State and Broadway and saw people going around in row boats. That was really quite a sight for us who lived in the country on the heights of New Scotland Avenue. Another impressive time in my childhood was the day of the fire in the State Capitol. A large part of it was burned and the teachers let us out of school to see the fire.

As I grew older and had a boy friend, one of our chief enjoyments was to take a boat ride to Troy. On the boat there was a nice old pianist who played, "I'm Forever Blowing Bubbles." We would ride up to Troy for five cents and ride back for another five cents. It was lovely and sometimes we would stay on and take two round trips or we would take a special moonlight trip.

In the summer, our Sunday School would have a picnic. Our church, sometimes with other churches, would rent a boat, a barge or a tugboat and we would go down the river to a place called Marina Park. The barge would moor there for the day and we would get off with our lunches to spend the whole day having fun. The Park had a Ferris wheel and many things to entertain us. That annual event was a big occasion. We would also go to Hudson and Catskill on the Albany to New York City day boat and return the same evening on the "up-boat."

All in all, my youth spent in Albany in the early 1900s was a very enjoyable time in my life.

— Dorothy Anthony

ANN LEE HOME RESIDENTS RECALL THEIR PAST THE DEPRESSION EXPERIENCE:

" . . . of course we were little children and then when the depression come nobody wanted to go and get the food. They only allowed so much money for food: $3.65 a week. And you had to get the coal by the bags and the little wood by the bags and nobody in my family wanted to go. I said Well I'm not going to go hungry and I'm not going to let nobody else go hungry so I went . . ."

Edith Bartuk

"My father was in politics in Cohoes, great Republicans by the way. Everything was Republican through here. This was died-in-the-wool Republican

(Laughs). They used to holler: 'Shoot the rat, shoot the cat, shoot the dirty Democrat!'. Then we had to run or fight!'' (Laughs).

"The depression, oh boy, I don't know whether I had a good time or a bad time, but I didn't suffer. But I seen these young people on the road, handsome young men, and young girls would go to the hospital when they were in trouble from, well, you know, the boys meet the girls and you hobo and you live a different life . . . ''

Robert Carney

"Say you'd walk to such a place, maybe twenty miles or thirty-five miles. You'd go there and when you get over there you'd meet somebody who'd gone before you and he'd say 'Well that job is filled up, for God's sake go home!' ''

Jack Gavin

'' . . . Friend of ours had a car and he was bootlegging down from Canada. Cadillac car, coming down through and they were chasing him, I guess, pretty hot. He hit an old feller with a horse. Didn't kill him, but I guess it killed the horse. By luck he got out with the car, hid it. He had a lot of friends in Mechanicville and he hid the car!''

Warren Jones

About Al Smith . . .

"I think everybody loved him, everybody loved him. You know, he was just like one of the regular people. Like they're all talking about their Alma Mater sitting in the lounge at Fort Orange. Somebody asked Al: 'Al, what's your Alma Mater?' And Al said: 'FFM.' They said: 'Whats' that?'—Fulton Fish Market!' (Laughs) You couldn't help but love him!''

Kevin Root

"The Government didn't do nothing for you. You either went to jail if you wasn't working or just sit around and starve, that's all."

Barney Smith

About Raids on Speak-easies . . .

"A lot of it was set up, and you could tell that after the raid was over. Because you got out, didn't have to pay nothing to get out, no fines or nothing like that—just the humiliation of going to jail, that was all. . . . Rich people went and half of them didn't go to jail. They'd take them in the patrol wagon to the station house. When they got to the station house, they took them inside, and let them out!"

William Winn

N.B. In order to protect total privacy and the confidentiality of the participants' interviews, only pseudonyms have been used here.

AN ALBANY COOPERAGE RECALLED

I came to Albany about forty-five years ago. At that time my father-in-law, Isador Becker, was in the wooden barrel business, which is a cooperage. He was born in Warsaw and when he came to this country, he had a family of six children to support and coopering was the first thing he could put his hands on. He worked very hard, had one or two helpers—it was possible to get them at that time but it's a lost occupation now.

The business was located in a great big yard on the lower south end of Cherry Street near Arch Street. The men worked out in the open all year long, regardless of weather. They would build a fire in a metal drum or something and warm their hands whenever they got cold. Neighbors on Cherry Street named Cone were very nice to the workers, called them in to their home and gave them a hot cup of tea. My husband always remembered them. It was a rough business in an isolated area, established about sixty years ago.

At that time nothing was known about steel drums. The chemical manufacturers all used wooden barrels. There was a great demand for them by the Italian people when it came time to put up wine. It was a terrific business. A man had to understand how to put the barrel together because it would leak if it wasn't done right. There were ten gallon, thirty gallon and fifty gallon barrels made of white oak sent up from the South. The fifty gallon barrels were about 3 feet high.

My husband Milton was the oldest of the five boys; the only daughter Sharon lives now in Catskill. The boys used to help in the business for a while until they were old enough to move away to their own professions. Abe worked on the truck delivery. He and Ben were twins, but Ben never had a part in it. He went to college and became a school principal.

Milton worked at Zuckerman's Bakery before he went to grammar school. He got up at five or six in the morning to help and they'd give him a loaf or two of bread to bring home to the family for breakfast. He went to School 14 at night and when he got a little older, he worked for Western Union as a delivery boy. When he was through with high school, he had a craving for the banking business and started working for the State Bank of Albany and became a teller. He felt that this area was not broad enough for the banking business so he went to New York, attended school at Columbia University, and graduated from the American Institute of Banking at Columbia. He worked with Manufacturers Trust in Brooklyn for a while and was a bank manager in New York, but his father wanted him up here. In those days the warmth of your family was so important that there were no questions asked. If his father wanted him to come, he came.

This was in the early '30s just before the depression. I wanted him to go back into the bank business but he stayed here. He took an old Mack truck and one day he said "I'm going out for barrels," and he did, and worked hard at it. Thank God he became very successful. We were known as the National Cooperage Company.

After a while the wooden barrels went out and they went into metal drums. We used to buy them secondhand and we had a reconditioning plant and put the metal drums through a certain process that was the new method of the barrel business. We didn't make the wooden drums any more because the profession of the cooperer went out. We had to buy the finished barrel from liquor stores.

They came from Kentucky and we would have them sent up during the wine season. There was a tremendous demand. The Italian people were interested in barrels that held liquor previously because they made a better wine. It was interesting and humorous to watch them because they would pull the round cork out of the side of the barrel and put their noses right in the barrel. If it smelled of good liquor, they said, "This is it." When the liquor was soaked right into the wood, it would make excellent wine and we sometimes received samples that were beautiful.

I worked in the business for a while and it was really hard work, but it was interesting. I used to go out in the yard and pick out the various barrels and have good conversations with the people who came in. When the children were real young, I had an extension, and would answer the phone; but when they were grown, I worked in the office, did everything and made myself useful. After my husband died, I kept up the company for two years and then sold it.

There were a few companies after ours but there aren't many barrel people now. There is just one company in Watervliet. They just do metal barrels. The big thing is reconditioning metal drums.

Bess Becker
(Interviewed by Eleanor Koblenz on tape
at the Jewish Community Center)

OLD ARBOR HILL

It was good to be a boy in the Arbor Hill section of Albany during the first decade of the present century. It was good for here within walking, skipping or running distance was everyting needed to satisfy the adventurous spirit of youth.

The field of operations of a boy at such a time was roughly marked by bodies of water. To the north, the Erie Canal, to the south (if he chose to wander a bit) the Normanskill Creek, to the west, Little's Lake and to the east, the Hudson River. Within this territory were the open fields for a game of "One-O-Cat," narrow alleys in which to run and hide when engaged in the pastime known as "Cops and Robbers." Then, for a winter activity there were the steep hills for sledding. Yes, there in Old Arbor Hill was just about everything a younger fellow might want to fill in his spare time.

In that era there were no Boy Scout Troops for a boy to join where he could be taught the lore of the out-of-doors by understanding leaders. There was however a book written by Daniel Carter Beard that could be borrowed at the Pruyn Library from which an eager student could glean such knowledge as "How to Build a Catamaran," "How to Mark a Woodland Trail," "How to Build Figure 4 Trap." These were some of the fascinating "How To's" in Mr. Beard's book.

As a result of this reading many a strange craft was launched and sunk in the pond near the Shaker's settlement and the route through the woods between the Northern Boulevard and Little's Lake was clearly marked by tree nicks and small piles of stones.

And what nuggets of knowledge these boys shared, much of which is forever lost to mankind. They knew for instance:

That a horse chestnut that had been soaked in vinegar overnight when held at the end of a string, through a hole bored in it, would not split when knocked by another chestnut, similarly strung, that had not been so conditioned.

That the proper way to approach an afternoon of swimming in the fingers of water that projected from the Erie Canal in the Lumber District was to hitch a ride on the back of the horse car that served the area.

That the most important player on the sandlot baseball team was not the pitcher, the catcher or the long ball hitter but the player who could knit the cover on a ball made of cord that had been wound around a rubber "Chunk."

That if one's taste wearied of the jaw breakers, known as Jackson Balls (three for a penny) one could always switch to the licorice balls, same price, sold at Leddy's candy store on North Pearl Street near the old St. Joseph's Academy.

That one cure for summertime boredom was to collect a handful of blue clay from Hunter's brickyard (off Van Voert Street), then to scatter it impartially about the neighborhood. A glob of this stuff would stick to anything and was sure to awaken the wrath of all whose property had been so decorated.

Yes, those Arbor Hill boys knew all of these things and much more, facts that linger only in the memories of those who romped her streets and fields so long ago.

Perhaps we of an older generation should feel a twinge of envy for today's young people and all the wonders of the atomic age that lie before them. But perhaps we can take a degree of consolation from the fact that many of the sights, sounds and smells that we recall will have no duplication in the years ahead.

The sight of Buffalo Bill at the opening of his Wild West Show in Peacock Park in North Albany. The old Plainsman himself, on his white steed before a canvas backdrop, his sombrero and the left front leg of his horse lifted a salute. Here was the embodiment of every boy's dream of the Wild West.

The sound of the steam whistle on the locomotive hustling the Twentieth Century train up Bull Run on its way west, the glow from its open firebox painting the underside of an overhanging cloud a deep red.

The clean smell of freshly cut lumber piled high in the Lumber District or the tantalizing smell from the "Steam Bakery" on the corner of Livingston Avenue and North Pearl Street.

Guess the action in the Arbor Hill of those days was somewhat different from that of the present. It is hoped that the youth of this generation will carry into their age memories as rich as are those of the boy who lived there in the dim and distant past.

—*John S. Bantham*

LUCY ADAMS

To trace my mother's ancestry would not be difficult, for she always enjoys telling about her forefathers. To get your attention she will start off by saying, "Do you know where the Saratoga Depot is?"

To which I answer that I do.

She continues with, "That is where my father lived." My grandfather ran a large hotel known as the "Adams House" which was located where the depot is now. I saw a picture of it once. It had rows of trees leading to the entrance and was surrounded by vast, well-kept grounds. My grandfather was considered a well-educated man. A college man was quite a rarity in those days. He visited France and soon became able to talk fluently in French.

It was in France that he met my grandmother. (Here I sigh and wish some author could hear of this neat little plot and weave it into a story.) And then she continues to talk of her grandmother. Somehow, I have always believed that this little French lady who always said her prayers in Latin was one of the greatest influences in my mother's life. She could sew and mend beautifully. After her husband died, she lived with her children, staying at each home only as long as they could keep her busy with sewing and when the sewing would be finished she would pack her little bag and go on to the next. My mother was named Lucy after her and with the last name Adams there was formed a combination which has always sounded pretty to me—Lucy Adams

Just a curious fancy, no doubt, but whenever I hear that name, "Lucy Adams," a picture of a dark-haired, pretty, young girl in a large hoopskirt flashes across my mind. And this is "Lucy Adams."

—*Sister Catherine Isabel*

I REMEMBER ALBANY . . .

When one walks along North Pearl Street in Albany, the capital of the Empire State, there seems to be nothing but empty buildings. The sidewalks are covered with ice and snow making walking almost impossible. It looks like a ghost city, especially at night when the few stores are closed. Oh yes, there are a few stores, the Rite Aid Pharmacy, Sherry's, Adams Jewelry Store, Earl's Bakery Shop, Lodge's, and the Grand Cash Market. People drive up in their cars, make their purchases, and drive away.

It was not always like this; there was a time when there wasn't an empty store on Pearl Street from State to Clinton Avenue. People could spend an entire day, going through the stores or just window-shopping, having something to eat, and going to the theater. Whitney and Myers Department stores (Dry Goods stores they were called at one time) stood side by side but each did a thriving business. You could buy anything from a spool of thread to a houseful of furniture and have it delivered. Even the five-and-ten cent stores would deliver if you bought five dollars worth. No one carried shopping bags in those days.

Across the street from Whitney and Myers was Drislane's grocery. They had every kind of food anyone had every heard of, both domestic and imported; also, liquor and cigars. They had their own bakery; their pies and cakes were better than many homemade ones. Fruits and vegetables were perfect and theirs was the first store in the city to have fresh strawberries in the spring and to get watermelons, even before the fourth of July when most stores had watermelon. When you bought a pound of fresh-ground top round steak for hamburger, you always got a piece of suet to cook it in. When you bought a piece of soup meat, the butcher threw in a marrow bone to give it flavor, and there was always an extra bone or a piece of liver if you said you had a dog or a cat.

Few people carried home their own groceries and there were no shopping carts. At the desk you received what was known as a traveler, with your name and address on it, and going from one counter to another, you picked out the things you wanted, went back to the desk where it was added·up and you paid for it and received a duplicate so you could check your order when it arrived to see if everything was there. If anything was missing it was sent to you without question.

Upstairs over Drislane's was Professor Campbell's Dancing Academy and you walked two long flights to get there. On Friday afternoon there was a class for little children, some of them no more than four or five years of age. On Friday evening there was a class for teenagers. There was no sneaking off in dark corners, no drinking, no smoking, no petting. These were the rules and if one was broken, the pupil was dismissed from the class and it was hard getting back. Most of the mothers were there to help keep the youngsters in order. The children were taught the waltz, the two-step and the polka. They were also taught to be ladies and gentlemen. Professor Campbell took great pride and joy in his pupils. The boys had to have a clean white handerchief so their hands would not soil the girls' pretty dresses. On special occasions like closing for the season, the boys had to wear white gloves.

There were also special classes for beginners and even private lessons if one preferred; and there were some for older people and one for young married couples. Professor Campbell was liked by everyone and his methods seemed to be very popular even if he was so strict. After the dancing lessons everyone went over to Huyler's candy and ice-cream store next door to Myers. There were other candy stores and ice-cream stores along Pearl Street but none of them could compare to Huyler's. Their ice-cream sodas were made with two scoops of ice cream. The sundaes were topped with whipped cream, chopped nuts and a cherry, and a glass of carbonated water was served with it — all for a nickel. For fifteen cents you could get a banana split with three scoops of ice cream, two or three kinds of fruit, whipped cream, nuts and a cherry.

The ten-cent stores had soda fountains and lunch counters and in Kresge's was a doughnut machine where you could buy doughnuts right out of the hot fat if you wanted them plain. If you wanted the sugared ones you had to take the cool ones. There was also a soft ice-cream machine, vanilla or chocolate, right as you came in the door at Kresge's.

On Pearl Street and Maiden Lane were sandwich shops with golden brown roast turkeys in the windows and inside homemade soup, salads and sandwiches of all kinds, but the most popular were the turkey or cold cornbeef on rye with potato chips and pickle. No one liked the hot corn beef better. Calories? Cholesterol? Who ever heard of such things? Places to eat and the bakeries were always crowded. Hagaman's Bakery was up at 1080 Madison Avenue but they had a branch on Maiden Lane and VerPlanck's was up on Clinton Avenue next to the Grand Theater.

The best dressed women shopped at Muhlfelder's. When you first stepped inside the door, you were greeted by a beautiful array of handkerchiefs, linen, silk, cotton with flowers, lace and embroidery, priced from ten cents to a dollar. Over at the left was the glove counter and more handkerchiefs, some as much as five dollars. All but the very cheapest were given to you in a folder with a paper doily in it, sprinkled sachet underneath. There were long gloves, short gloves, cotton gloves, silk gloves, and of course kid gloves. Black, white and brown were best selling but there were many other colors to match a dress or coat. The kid gloves were eased on your fingers one by one by the clerk. You were always sure of a perfect fit at Muhlfelder's. In winter there were fur-lined gloves if you didn't have a muff.

Muhfelder's also had a complete line of costume jewelry, cosmetics, exquisite underwear of silk and lace, and in the back of the store, hats with ribbon and lace and flowers and feathers, not cheap but so beautiful that there are no words to really describe them. You sat at a dressing table with a three-part mirror so you could see all sides and a clerk tried one after another until one or two were exactly right for you. Then you would try some beautiful hatpins and veiling and when everything was satisfactory, the clerk would put in an elastic to help hold it securely at the windy corner of State and Pearl while you waited for a trolley. The next day your purchase would be delivered in a bandbox. Downstairs were shoes and budget-priced dresses and upstairs, better dresses, coats and furs.

On the corner of Broadway and Maiden Lane was a hat shop, not so fancy, but with hats for everyday use at one, two and three dollars. Then there was Van Heusen and Charles with Lenox and Haviland china, silver, jewelry, rugs, etc. The New York Central Railroad Station was the most beautiful in the State outside of New York City. It is still standing on Broadway but is going to wrack and ruin. There is a lot of talk about making it this or that but nothing is done. Once upon a time it was a busy place, trains going to Buffalo, Binghamton, New York, and stopping at all places in between that were of importance. There were locals to Altamont and Rensselaer for people who worked in Albany and Rensselaer. But more than passengers used the depot and waiting room. It was a pleasant place to go and watch people going here and there, to meet friends, to have lunch in the beautiful restaurant with delicious food at reasonable prices, or just to rest after a shopping tour. It was a godsend for people living alone in rooming houses with no friends or relatives.

The Leland Opera House and the Majestic Theater were on South Pearl Street, The Empire Theater on State Street just above Pearl showed burlesque. Now and then there was Ladies Day and the admission fee was ten cents. No lady would think of going alone. The Grand Theater was on Clinton Avenue between North Pearl Street and Broadway. Here were shown the latest moving pictures and outstanding vaudeville acts. It was grand in every way, with beautiful chandeliers and carpets, and tapestries on the walls. The Strand Theater was where First Church parking lot and Clee Park area are now located. Pictures like "The Birth of a Nation," "The Ten Commandments," and "Ben Hur" were shown here. It was a sad day for Albany when this beautiful theater was torn down. In a way, it was no one's fault and in another way, it was everyone's fault. People no longer went to the movies but stayed home to watch their new TV sets.

Friday evening, October 23, 1931, was a gala occasion for Albany. It was opening night of the Palace Theater. Every one of the 3,659 seats was occupied. The varied program included RKO Pathe News, vaudeville and Ann Harding and Leslie Howard in "Devotion." In accordance with time of day or where you sat, admission prices ranged from twenty-five to seventy-five cents. In 1960 the theater was remodeled and the seating capacity reduced to 2,775 seats in order to give the patrons more leg room, and a new oversized screen was installed. The theater was reopened on October 28, 1960, the feature picture, "Midnight Lace," starring Doris Day and Rex Harrison. Under each seat was a wire frame where men could put their hats. In the wintertime many people, especially those with children, would buy an extra ticket for a seat on which to put coats and hats.

Up on Washington Avenue next to the Armory was Harmanus Bleecker Hall. Here appeared the most outstanding actors and actresses in show business, among them, Eddie Cantor, Al Jolson, and Will Rogers. In the summer Bert Lytell and his wife, Evelyn Vaughn, were here in a stock company, a different play each week at reasonable prices. Of all these theaters, only the Palace remains, but the memory of the others lingers in the hearts of many older Albanians.

There were no taxis in those days and only a few automobiles. The two-car family was unheard of. Women drivers? Who ever heard of such a thing? Trolley cars answered the needs of the people. Women shoppers usually went home just before the stores closed so as to have a seat instead of standing in the aisles holding on to a strap. In the summer there were open trolleys and it was a happy time riding around the Belt Line. It took thirty-five minutes and the cooling breeze was delightful, especially in the evening.

The Tulip Festival has been going on for a long time. At first they used to crown the Queen on the Capitol steps and once they had it on the park lake. Each of the girls came down the lake in a rowboat, dressed as a shepherdess and was met by Mayor Corning as she came ashore. Now the ceremony is held on the old croquet grounds in Washington Park. The Capitol steps have been used for band concerts and many other occasions. Armed Forces Day in 1959 saw many an event on the steps and in the park.

Where the Alfred E. Smith State Office Building now stands, there was an apartment house. A young man twenty-five years of age with a team of horses moved it. It was jacked up on wooden horses and moved inch by inch across

State Street to its new foundation. At first no one would move in—not even the former tenants—because it was expected to collapse any minute, but it is still standing there to this day.

At one time there were many rows of three-story and basement houses, sometimes several all alike, with party walls, one wall between two houses. On Hamilton Street, beginning at Swan, was a row of red brick houses with brownstone steps and vestibules. In the wintertime when the vestibule doors were closed it made the front halls dark but it kept out a lot of cold. There were front and back parlors with sliding doors in between, marble mantelpieces in both rooms, and beautiful chandeliers with gas mantels. Some were later wired for eletricity and others were discarded and hauled off to the dump. What a pity! The windows had indoor wooden shutters which folded back into the window frames. Off the back parlor was a butler's pantry with a sink and cupboards to the ceiling. As some people used the back room for a dining room, there was a dumbwaiter to bring food up from the kitchen. There were bells on each floor and a speaking tube to the kitchen as most people had servants. In back of each house there was a small yard separated by high wooden fences. Each yard had a woodshed with coalbins and ashcans. All the houses had coal furnaces, and during the winter bringing in scuttles of coal for the furnace and the kitchen stove was no fun. An alley ran in back of the yards where coal was delivered and ashes removed each week.

These houses had been built for one family, but as families became smaller and taxes became higher, many changes had taken place and by 1913 only a few were occupied by one family. The one on the corner, 282, had an apartment on the third floor, 284 was a boarding house. The last two in the row, 292 and 294, were still occupied by one family, the others were rooming houses. Mrs. Harris lived at 284 and her basement dining room contained two long tables. She had twelve to fifteen regular boarders, but if she had a little advance notice, could serve four or five more. There were linen tablecloths and napkins and everyone had a napkin ring because a napkin had to last for one day at least and the tablecloth for several days. There was a dish in the center of the table and when anyone got a spot on the tablecloth he had to put a coin in the dish—ten cents for a small spot, twenty-five for a large. Once a man spilled a half cup of coffee that cost him fifty cents. Two people solved the problem by putting squares of white oilcloth under their plates.

Mrs. Harris' meals were without equal: chicken dinner with baking powder biscuits, roast beef with Yorkshire pudding. Her mustard pickles and brandied peaches, lemon meringue pie, hot apple pie and homemade ice cream were worth coming back for, even if one had to pay the entire cost of getting the tablecloth laundered.

These houses are no more. As with many of the lovely houses of Albany, no one cared enough to fix the roofs or mend the chimneys until at last it was too late and there was nothing to do but tear them down. Albany was a beautiful city in those days. The stores and theaters were filled with people. One could safely walk the streets night or day. So come what may, I'll close my eyes and remember her that way.

— Beatrice S. Crannell

OLD DAYS REMEMBERED

Prior to May 1907, my father, John Laird Cochran, was employed in the bookkeeping department of the Milburn Wagon Company at 108-110 State Street. The major business was with wagons, carriages, and harness. The four-story building was on the right side of State Street, if you went down hill from the Capitol. There were a large plate glass window and platform outside and tapered steps. There was a life-size gray stone horse in the window, to which many wagons and carriages were attached at different times and different harness and other equipment used.

When parades going down State Street were held, my sister and I were allowed to sit in the wagon high above the pedestrians' heads on the street and view the entire performance. At one time I was lifted onto the horse. The stone body was cold and slippery. I clutched the harness, I pretended to enjoy but was pleased to return to the security of the wagon. This was a "not-too-often happening" and a great pleasure long remembered.

I do not recall the time span of this experience — only the fearful endangerment. At 94-96 State Street before Pearl Street was reached, the Richard Healy Company selling furs had its store. It had a wide entrance, and standing in the middle of the space between two large glass windows was a huge, white bear with arms upstretched, claws showing, mouth open, tall and threatening on two hind feet. I would walk at curb-side rather than admit I was afraid, and if avoidance were at all possible, would not walk on that side of the street.

My grandfather, George N. Cozine, owned and operated the Albany Paper Box Manufactory at "Steamboat Square," 283-291 Broadway, together with Richard B. McMillan. It was a four-story building with a saloon at one end and

"Peoples Line" office on the other. Delivery was made in a one-horse, closed wagon for products, with a drop curtain to keep the driver's seat dry in inclement weather. When we were children, we spent many happy hours with the piles of colorful scrap paper, making mats, doll furniture, etc., in a world of make-believe.

Much later in my childhood my mother was employed by bringing home collars and cuffs to turn, press and bring back to a factory in the Arch Street area. To expedite the pickup and delivery we were left in a little park called "Riverside" halfway between the riverboat docks and the bridge to Rensselaer. The park had a 5-to 6-foot concrete wall enclosure with steps leading from Broadway. There were trees and benches and usually other children to play with. Watching the boats and eating lunch was a "happy-stance" long remembered.

I also recall along State Street the so-called "Nipper," a present-day discard by the R.C.A. Company. A huge replica of a dog, he would sit by the doorway and curve his head for all to know he was listening for his "Master's Voice." Sometimes he was not so white and occasionally had peeling spots. At holiday time, he wore a wreath about his neck. He was beloved by many a passerby, especially the children.

— Alice C. Eschenbecker

MOTOR TRIP — 1910

It was in the summer of 1910 that Uncle Charlie bought his first Model T. We kids hadn't yet heard the expression "status symbol," but we felt it put us a cut above our friends to have an uncle who owned an automobile.

Uncle Charlie and Aunt Lib planned a trip through the "North Country," from which Aunt Lib hailed. Since it was unheard of in those days to let a back seat go empty, Aunt Lib packed in my mother, my brother and me. There were a few inches left — so we had with us a cousin, many times removed, a pesky kid named Elsworth. My poor mother — she must have suffered on that trip, for my brother devoted himself wholeheartedly to heckling Elsworth.

My mother and Aunt Lib were well covered in dusters and "automobile bonnets." They must have been roasting as was Uncle Charlie in his duster and driving cap. Of course, we had luggage all over the car, plus a big hamper of lunch. We started off with puffs and snorts from the motor on the dusty road to adventure. It was hot — it was dusty — it was dirty. We had to make frequent stops at springs to drink the cool water — then at tree-secluded spots to handle the results of our drinks.

My brother Charlie teased — Elsworth cried. Mama lambasted Charlie. Uncle Charlie drove — Aunt Lib told him he was going in the wrong direction. The sun shone down — we perspired (we called it sweat) — we kids got hungry — Aunt Lib said we had to wait. Oh, the joys of a motor trip!

Then the sky darkened — could such a day change to rain? It could, and it did. We stopped to put the side curtains down. The dust began to turn mud as the rain pelted down. The car labored — it balked, then stopped. My mother prayed, and Uncle Charlie swore. We kids cried, and Aunt Lib berated Uncle Charlie: it was his fault; he wanted rain; he had taken the wrong road. And why did he need an automobile? The Weavers didn't have one, and they had more money than Uncle Charlie.

While we were mired in the mud, we ate our lunch, which perked us up a little. The rain had stopped, so we all got out and pushed. When you get three adults and three kids at the back of the car on a muddy road, you have a real mess. But somehow we got going again.

That trip from Wynantskill to Johnstown took two days (we stopped overnight in Schenectady). We stayed a few days and returned home. On our return, a news item appeared in the local paper to the effect that we had "toured the Adirondacks."

We now make that trip in an hour. But nothing now can equal the thrill of our first trip in the Model T.

— Georgiana Cole Halloran

MY UNCLE GEORGE AND AUNT GEORGIE

My father's family was a large one. They were brought up in Bentley Hollow, in the vicinity of the present Sacandaga Reservoir. His father was a farmer but never made much more than a living for he was not satisfied with farming. I really think he thought it beneath him, for he was an intellectual man, despite the fact that he had had little education.

My grandmother died young, and not long after her death, the members of the family left home to settle in different localities. My father went first to Troy and later moved to Cohoes where he spent the rest of his life.

Uncle George located in Johnstown, a glove center. The glove business then was booming. He went to work in a glove shop, and when he had learned the business, started a shop of his own. Uncle George was one of those men who make a financial success of every undertaking.

I was the youngest of our family when I began visiting at Johnstown, Uncle George had built a little compound at the corner of Market and Court Streets. On the corner facing Market was his big house, next to a two-story dwelling. On Court Street there were three more two-family houses. Situated in the center of these five buildings was the glove shop. The tenants all worked in the glove shop—men did the cutting and women the sewing and turning. Besides the workers in the shop, some work was done by women at home. My two older cousins delivered gloves and picked them up when finished. In this way they got to know the people in the outlying area, and this was a factor of Uncle George's success when he went into politics. He was a supervisor for his county for many terms.

He was a shrewd businessman. His customers numbered all the better Fifth Avenue stores, as well as small shops on the East Side in New York. He made frequent trips for orders, and on one of these, one of his East Side customers who often matched wits with him complained about a shipment being inferior. Uncle George asked if he wanted to keep the goods at half price, or return them for replacement. The customer kept the gloves. Soon after, he sent an order for twelve dozen gauntlets. Uncle George shipped him twelve dozen beautiful gauntlets—all for the right hand! There was no complaint—the man realized he had gotten what he ordered—and he ordered twelve dozen left-hand gauntlets. In Uncle George, he had met his match.

There was a casual manner of bookkeeping in Uncle George's family. His safe was his pockets. When rents came in, if he took them, they were added to his roll of bills (he never bothered to count it.) If Aunt Georgie or the boys took it, it was pushed under the tablecloth—Aunt Georgie's safe. Everyone who came to the house knew that the bumps in the tablecloth covered money, but I never heard of their losing anything.

Once my mother took us children to Johnstown for a visit. Arriving, we saw posters indicating it was Fair Day. We went in the house (all three doors were unlocked) and found nobody there. We went to the shop and that, too, was empty. What a dream for a thief! The house had money under the tablecloth and in dresser drawers. The shop had expensive leather and fur pelts, linings and bindings. But the Coles and their tenants were enjoying the Fair. We finally met them there.

Another venture that Uncle George engaged in was buying unclaimed railroad merchandise from receivers in bankruptcy proceedings and salvage from fires. Once he bought a case of apples and stored them in his heated basement. The basement was a huge, wonderful place—you never knew what you were going to find there. The apples lasted too long—until the house, from basement to attic, was permeated with the smell of apples. I don't know how he finally did get rid of them.

Another time he brought home several cases of fleece-lined underwear. We always shared in what he had, so we kids wore the underwear. They were fine in winter—but come spring, they itched beyond human endurance—and we were reminded in school many times to "sit still."

Once he bought up the contents of a store that went into bankruptcy. I remember two items that came to us through that deal—my mother got two net shirtwaists and I got a doll the size of a four-year-old child, with a bisque head "eyes that opened and closed" (which was a novelty then) and a flesh-colored china body, with movable arms and legs.

We took all these things for granted, and it was not until I was mature that I appreciated the wonderful things we received from Uncle George and Aunt Georgie and the good times we had at their house. We never realized, either, that the manner in which they lived and did business was at all unusual.

My mother and Aunt Georgie were very fond of each other and it's a good thing Aunt Georgie was a religious and law-abiding person, for she could get my mother to do anything. Aunt Georgie was a shrewd businesswoman. Like her husband, she was successful in everything she started. And pride was not one of her sins—she used to come down with big packages to sell to Troy stores, and my mother, a timid but loyal soul, would shamefacedly accompany her on her selling trips, embarrassed beyond words at the price haggling—something a true salesman loves.

Aunt Georgie opened a "beauty parlor" in a side addition to her home. She had a very wealthy clientele. One time I called with her at the beautiful home of Mrs. Knox of the Knox Gelatin family. They greeted each other with an embrace, and Aunt Georgie proceeded to do her thing to Mrs. Knox.

In line with her beautician's work, she patented a hair dye which she called "Georgie Cole's Hair Restorer." (I can see the label plainly in my mind's eye.) The formula was made up at the drugstore, and she added various liquids, put it out in pint whiskey bottles, and sold it for 50¢ a bottle. There was a stigma attached to dyeing your hair in those days, and people who bought the dye did it in a surreptitious way, like buying bootleg liquor. My mother had several friends she supplied with the dye and they sneaked out of our house with their packages like fugitives from the law. The dye must have worked, for my mother's hair was a natural dark brown until Aunt Georgie died—then began to gray.

Aunt Georgie's last business venture—and the one on which she really cleaned up—was antiques. Here was one of the ways in which her acquaintance with the farm folks in the Johnstown area paid off. She went from one place to another, and bought anything she wanted at low prices. Most people didn't know the value of antiques then, and they were delighted to get a few dollars for a seemingly worthless piece of furniture. She never cheated anybody—she always paid more than they asked—sometimes even twice as much.

One time she got a call from Troy, telling her that there was to be an antique auction. The contents of the home of a furniture dealer were auctioned. The house had been sold, and the contents had to be removed in a few days. It was a huge house, with a tremendous amount of furniture—far too much to be accommodated in any place she knew of. Undaunted, she got on the telephone and learned that the Palace Theater was closed. She contacted the owner and rented the theater, then had the furniture trucked in.

She had purchased the antiques at a very modest figure, the rent for the theater was low, and she had plenty of time to sell her stock. This she did, a few pieces at a time. This deal brought her a fantastic profit.

The youngest, brother George, learned the antique business from her. He told me that she once said, "On the first sale to a customer, I let him set the price. If he picks up a piece of glassware and asks the price, ask him what he wants to pay. If he says fifty cents, even though you know it's worth lots more, tell him he can have it for ten cents. He'll be delighted, thinking he has put something over on you. And he'll come back and you'll make it up on the next sale."

George still does some buying and selling—antique dolls, old guns, old coins and old documents. After Aunt Georgie's death, all the antiques were sold to settle the estate. The one thing George has of them is a George Washington lamp.

By the time the boys grew up and were ready to choose careers, the era of the small businessman was over. Therefore, none of them followed his father's career in the glove business, although Johnstown is still a glove city.

But the expensive kid leather and soft calfskin gauntlets with fur backs, coming almost to the elbow, were no more. These were his most expensive product, and even in 1910, sold for ten and twelve dollars a pair. So the oldest boy went to work for a small railroad of which he became president in later life. The next, Deb, became a very successful funeral director. And George is a fireman, but still carries on some antique business. He's like his parents—he's always in the right place at the right time—which pays off for him.

Sometimes Uncle George's tenants paid rent—often they didn't. Nothing was ever said if they didn't pay. Uncle George had sort of a "lord of Manor" idea—if they worked for him, they were entitled to rent.

Deb's son is now a partner in his business. Howard lived in Johnstown until two years ago, when, his wife having died a few years earlier, he remarried and moved to Gloversville. The boys have nice summer homes in the country where they used to deliver gloves.

This is part of my family—a colorful part, indeed.

— Georgiana Cole Halloran

B. COOPER ICE AND COAL COMPANY

B. Cooper Ice and Coal Company was founded in 1854 by Benjamin Cooper of Troy, New York, along with John and James Cooper of that city. The main plant was located on the Hudson River bank at Bond Street, north on Turner Street to Glen Avenue. It consisted of a row of wooden frame two-story buildings on the north side of Bond Street from Turner Street west to the Hudson River Bank, where today the Federal Locks and Dam are located. On Bond and Turner Streets, in the Cooper row of frame buildings was the office with the Company Board of Directors Room on the second floor and the general office section on the first floor, along with the wagon scales; and it was here that the bookkeepers would accept the receipts of the day from the drivers or route men. In this section was also the Manager's Office in which were kept his records along with the weather reports received from the United States Weather Bureau. These reports were very important for the ice business.

On the Turner side of the office were located the wagon scales. The scales were inspected by the city and the State. The weighmaster usually was an office helper or a company official. Each ice wagon was driven on the scales empty with its driver and the combined weight was listed in the office. In the early morning the loaded wagons were weighed again before starting on their routes; and on their return at the close of the day, the wagons were weighed again to determine how much ice was sold.

The next building to the office was occupied by a branch of the Albany Ice Cream Company later sold to the Sealtest Ice Cream Company. This branch was managed by Fred Ives of Troy. In front of the building was the office and in the back room was a large box with a tin cover with a rope pulley attached to it and a heavy weight on the floor end to make it possible to lift and close the cover of the ice box. The ice cream was stored in this box in cans and packages packed in crushed ice and rock salt.

The main ice house had ten rooms, twelve, before a fire in 1913. There was a loading dock on the north side of the ice house at Glen Avenue. The main loading dock was on Turner Street almost three quarters of a block south of Glen Avenue, over which was a large roof covering the loading dock area. The wagons would be backed up to the loading dock close together, the wagon hubs almost touching one another. Across from the loading dock on the east side of Turner Street was a two-story red barn in two sections. On the main floor of the north section were stalls on both sides for horses and an opening on the south side to the south section of the barn where a large box stall for sick horses was located. There were also six other stalls. The second floor was used for the storage of hay.

Between the main loading dock and the office was a large paint shop and garage. The north side was the paint shop. All the ice wagons, sleighs, and equipment were painted and lettered in this section. The south side of the building was the garage for two Federal trucks and a Model T Ford runabout with a deck or box on its rear, for the use of the General Manager. The two Federal five-ton trucks were used to supply the ice wagons whenever they ran low on ice. The trucks were used also to deliver big ice boxes used for storage of meat and other perishable food. In the winter the trucks were used to deliver coal.

The ice elevator, used when the ice was harvested off the river, was located on the northwest end of the ice house at the foot of Glen Avenue. The elevator ran on electricity. Above the elevator cage was the gear house from which the gears and huge chains were attached to the elevator. Large levers would start or stop its operation. The heavy chains on both sides of the elevator had 4 x 4 wood bars attached to them, spaced so at least two one-hundred-pound cakes of ice could be placed in each section. A one-hundred-pound cake of ice was about 24 inches wide and 36 inches long by 18 inches to 20 or 22 inches thick. After leaving the ice elevator, the ice would first go through an ice shaver in order to scrape the snow-ice or soft ice off the cakes. The cakes of ice would then slide down the outside of the ice house on the ice runway which ran the length of the west side of the Cooper Ice House from Glen Avenue almost to Bond Street. There was a catwalk along the west side of the runway where, in front of each room opening, a man would be stationed with a pike pole to guide one cake of ice at a time off the runway into the storage room on an ice run. At the end of the runway was a huge pile of ice that was pushed off as not wanted. The one-hundred-pound cakes of ice were placed tightly against each other from wall to wall. One cutting or harvest from the river would only half fill the ice house. On the last layer in each room of the ice house a thick layer of straw covered the ice until it was wanted and then only a small section of the room would be uncovered. About twelve feet was left unfilled above the ice in the room in order to leave an air space.

Ice harvest time was a cold busy time. Often a man with a rope around his waist would float a section of ice to catch on the Federal Dam so on the first cold day the river would freeze early. A careful check was kept on the thickness of the ice. This would be done by chopping a hole in the ice and lowering a rod with a loop on one end of the rod. It had inches marked off from the hooked end of the rod which would show how thick the ice was. When it showed 8 inches or over, the ice elevator was lowered into the river at Glen Avenue and a channel was marked off for two cakes width from Glen Avenue to 102nd Street where Cooper Company would start clearing the snow off the ice field and marking the ice for cutting. If the cold weather held, the ice would be thick enough to cut.

Plowing or scraping the ice was done with wooden plows attached to a team of horses and most times it was necessary for a man to lead the horses. The snow was dumped or unloaded on the west bank of the river. During the work day were usually six to eight teams scraping ice, but on many Sundays there were as many as thirty teams. After the field was scraped, a couple of gasoline saws would mark the ice field and long hand saws would be used to cut the cakes of ice into floats of about twelve cakes each, two cakes wide. Men would use pike poles to float the ice into the channel; another group of men would push the floats down the channel to men on a plank across the channel. These men using a heavy sharp bar would break the ice floats into cakes. Another pair of men with pike poles would push at least two cakes of ice between the section of bars on the elevator. It was necessary for a crew of men to work all night long in keeping the channel open. This was done by pushing the floats of ice back and forth in the channel.

There were about thirty-five routes for the Cooper Ice Company, which covered the city of Troy, village of Green Island and the town of Waterford. In the summer the drivers and their helpers would start loading the wagons at 3:00 a.m. The drivers would load the wagons at the loading dock and the helpers would push the cakes of ice out of the ice house onto the dock. When the wagons were loaded to their roofs, they would first be driven on to the wagon scales to be weighed and then be off to their routes. While on their routes in summer, the wagons were reloaded sometimes twice a day. Many route wagons wouldn't return to their plants until 5:00 or 6:00 p.m. During the year the same drivers would fill large walk-in ice boxes at markets and wholesale meat hourses.

Many times it was necessary to load railroad box cars with ice for the storage of meat and other perishable products. The ice compartments were at each end of the car, and about 4 feet wide. For house deliveries Cooper and Company had a square blue card about 12 inches in size printed in black ink, with the name of the company and telephone numbers in the center of the card. Up until the early 1920s there were two local telephone companies; therefore two numbers were listed. The New York Telephone Company bought out these companies and assigned new numbers for all of their subscribers. The numbers of 25, 50, 75, and 100 appeared on the border or edge of the card and when customers wanted ice, they placed the card in their front windows to show how many pounds they wanted delivered. The route man would know just how to cut the cake of ice for each box, because the ice compartments varied in shapes and sizes.

Each wagon was supplied with a long-handled pike pole, at least two pairs of ice tongs to carry the ice, and an ice shaver to shave or chop it in wooden tubs for deliveries to markets, ice cream stores, saloons and places where crushed ice was needed. The wagon also carried two bags of oats for the horses and a pail of water to be used for them or to clean off a cake of ice. The pails were kept under the wagon on a hook. On the wagons was a weighing scale that was hooked on an angle iron in the rear. It was necessary in the summer to keep the ice covered with a heavy tarpaulin. The Cooper Company route wagons were high with a canvas roof. There was a wooden step in the rear of each wagon, from which the driver would prepare the ice for delivery. The step was also used by all the children along each route to grab a small piece of ice to suck on.

The route man or driver of the ice wagon was an important person to any ice company. It was he who would hitch up the horses to the wagons at the loading dock in the early morning. After he packed the ice on his wagon, he would start out on his route, first stopping on the scales at the office to weigh the load. There he would receive his route book which had his customers listed on each page, along with any special orders from the office such as telephone notes to stop at a new customer, change the size of a cake of ice for a customer, or fill some commercial ice box as it was running low. By the time he drove from the office over Bond Street to River Street, it being a long haul to his respective territory, he would stop at some place for coffee. After completing his route, he would stop first at the office scales to weigh in, then he would back his wagon to the loading dock, unhitch his team, drive the horses into the barn where he would take off the harness and hang it up. The barn man would feed and bed his horses for the night, inasmuch as the driver had to turn in the day's receipts and his route book to the office. Many times this would be about suppertime. Once a week, mostly on Sundays, he had the responsibility of cleaning his horses, occasionally paying the barn man to do it for him.

In the winter he delivered his route by sleigh and many of the drivers would double up their routes because there was not the demand for the ice. A sleigh would be rented out for sleigh rides, and by putting straw on the floor, it made a comfortable seat. The streets and roads were not plowed, and evening rides to Melrose or around the Horseshoe in Pleasantdale back to some hall or hotel for a hot lunch and dance was quite the sport. Many of the drivers would drive their teams up the side of a hardpacked snow drift to tip the occupants out of sleigh into the snow. Oh yes, on these rides it was necessary to wear heavy clothing with blankets to keep warm, but it also served as a padding in case the sleigh tipped over. The drivers in Ice Harvest time on the Hudson River would start walking with their teams up River Street and on the river at 103rd Street to the ice field. After a day's work at four o'clock, they would start back to the barn. Half of the drivers were needed for ice deliveries; the rest of them were used in the Ice Harvest.

Cooper Company had many fine horses. At times the company would buy ex-fire horses, especially after the Troy Fire Department became motorized. The fire bells in every section of the city would ring the fire box number for the location of the fire. The route men who had these horses would drop whatever they were doing and run to their teams to hold the reins. But they were not always in time and the team with the ice wagon would be off on a run. After a spell the driver would corral the runaways perhaps with the help of passing teamsters. To add to being a good citizen at the cost of his own time, the drivers would be called upon to hitch their team to the horse-driven Hook and Ladder Companies of the city to assist in pulling the apparatus up the hilly streets.

On winters when it was too warm to cut ice off the river, the Company would buy their ice from ice companies up north. Many times the Cooper Company would cut their own ice up north and pile it up, shipping it to Troy by canal boats in the spring.

The Horton family sold their interest in the B. Cooper Ice and Coal Company to the Stewart Ice Cream Company of Albany in 1922. The Stewart Ice Company tried to keep the business going but after about two years the routes dropped from thirty-five to ten routes. The Stewart Company turned the Cooper Company back to the bank and they in turn got the Shaughnessy Ice Company of Troy to manage it. In another couple of years the Cooper Ice and Coal Company was out of business.

When the Horton family sold the B. Cooper Ice and Coal Company of Troy, it meant the end of a great era of the ice business, and it was the beginning of the electric refrigerators. The ice companies went through Prohibition, fires, and warm winters, but it was impossible to compete with electric refrigeration. Today we have only to open the doors of our refrigeratiors to get all the ice cubes we want, never realizing the hardships, toil and labor our forefathers had to endure. Working through hot summers and very cold winters to earn a living, they pass on a proud heritage.

— Warren D. Horton

OFF BROADWAY: A MEMOIR

None of us was born in a trunk; nor did our names ever glitter in lights. Our family was a long way from Broadway in that little upstate New York town—but we were all stars. And the warmth and glow of show business that we offered made first nighters of all the town folks.

I don't think either of our parents gave a thought to talent—did we have it or didn't we—as we came along, my brother, two sisters, and I. They simply threw us into the water of show business, expecting each to surface in his own way.

Mama started us off, still in the cradle, practicing her dramatic readings on a captive audience who squealed and gurgled in applause. In time we learned the lines ourselves and mimicked her style in exaggerated dramatics.

One would have difficulty surviving the heartbreak enhanced by Mama's reading of "Mother of a Soldier Boy." It ended, "Go, my Boy, where duty calls, and my heart will follow you." It was one of our favorites, and we took turns to see who could cry the best. I often wonder now what our neighbors thought when our wails reached their ears. You may think it's easy, but crying is an art, and our interpretations varied on a scale form one to five with quiet tears at one end and hysteria at the other, but the winner was never in question—crying was my forte.

I became an object of wonder at an early age entertaining company on a regular basis with my wet renditions of "Boohoo Baby." The louder they clapped, the more the tears flowed. My talent grew with me, and later on, I reaped the rewards of perfect indulgence as I hysterically watched little Eva fly up to heaven in the stage version of "Uncle Tom's Cabin."

Another hit of Mama's was a poem, "The Face on the Barroom Floor," a story of a broken-down artist who sketched the face of the woman he loved on the floor of the barroom, and after placing the final touches, he "fell across the picture . . . dead." We could never compete with my brother on this one; the scene was always his. He lurched across the room like a John Wayne imitation, holding the verbal pause between "picture" and "dead" for an eternity. Our eyes were glued to his every movement, our ears keyed for the death rattle. With face contorted, he twirled around, and finally dropped, clutching the picture like a bear pawing its victim.

With his strength running out he mustered a last effort, and the word we were waiting for rasped from his throat like a deathbed secret. As he passed the point of no return, his body quivered, his mouth gaped, his eyes glazed. The ordeal had ended. What a future he might have had in the monster movies to come!

Then there was a play where Mama had the lead role—a father who took over the household for a day to show the little woman how easily it could be done. It ended in disaster—the children had a pitched battle, the washtub overflowed, the dinner burned—but instead of realizing his wife needed help, he vowed never to interfere again. Much of the comedy was lost on us. What we really laughed at was seeing Mama wearing pants.

At another time we laughed at our father dressed as a woman—high heels, lace dress, big flowered hat with puffs of false red hair protruding—in a play called "The Womanless Wedding." The Chamber of Commerce persuaded staid businessmen to take part for charity, to walk through town in costume to the opera house where they played out their roles in the wedding. The town doctor was the bride, tall and thin. He plodded awkwardly through the streets with a real goatee and an overstuffed artificial bosom, head thrust out and down like a crane, as he concentrated on trying to make his big feet walk properly in high heels. The bald wreathed head of the local undertaker, pink to match his dress, bobbed up and down as he scattered flowers to the crowd lining the sidewalk, while a short fat judge skipped along in a bright yellow tutu, balancing the wedding ring on a pillow. My father wasn't exactly a staid businessman but he could sing, and he went as the famous Italian soprano, Galli-Curci, horrifying onlookers as he drew heavily on a long cigarette holder, blowing the smoke wickedly into the crowds.

It was in this same opera house that we were allowed to play while the grownups practiced. The Opera House sounds grand, but it was only as elegant as we made it. The dressing room consisted of four cement walls in the basement, cold and damp, furnished with a distorted mirror in a tarnished frame, and a chair covered in red velvet turned brown with age, proudly displaying their faded glamor like two old troupers in a final performance. But we didn't care. We were a part of the magical Bigtime as we argued over which actress we would be—Corinne Griffith, Norma Shearer, Laura LaPlante, Joan Crawford, the list was endless.

Father was Mr. Showbiz in our town. He sang, he acted, he produced, he directed. And he did them all well. The one thing he couldn't do well was to take care of his family. The emotional feedback from his audience seemed to be enough in payment for him. But when he came home with only a rising vote of thanks for his talents, it wasn't enough for Mama who had to put food on the table. Fortunately, we were able to rely on humor, and when we were wanting, we ridiculed our father, kid-fashion, by holding a private ceremony where one of us as speaker praised his talents, after which we all stood up and shouted, "Thank you, Father!"

"The Alchemist" was a big production song of my father's, a winner every time, guaranteed to draw oohs and aahs from the grownups and terrified cries from the children. As the curtain went up, the soft lights of the semi-darkened stage centered on a bearded man in a long white robe. Long white hair fell over his shoulders as he hovered over the anvil. This was a learned man trying to turn metal into gold. The first line of the song was "The alchemist stood in the weird, red light." Father clipped the last three words, singing in soft stacatto for mood emphasis. Then, when he sang, "of the fiery furnace glare," the flames leaped up and the unsuspecting audience stirred as one, matching the leaping flames with their emotions. I don't know how Father created the effects but I do know it was revolutionary.

The production climaxed with an angel appearing, warning the alchemist there are better ways to spend his talent than in trying to amass great wealth. We must have taken the moral seriously because none of us ever did.

When my father produced and directed a play, he expected my two sisters and me to provide the entertainment between acts. There were times when I felt rebellious, torn between a dignity that was growing and the fun of letting myself go which I was beginning to equate with making a fool of myself. But I stuck with the others as we danced the Charleston like Joan Crawford and harmonized songs the way the Boswell Sisters did.

Once I was a geisha girl in a musical called, "Jappyland." In spite of the title, the performance was a tribute to the Japanese in support of their troubles with the eternal bad guys—the Russians.

Minstrel shows were very popular, featuring musical numbers interspersed with corn, like stage versions of Hee Haw. We blacked up and sang songs with lines like this, "And they taught my Mammy how to use a frying pan, they made it twice as nice as paradise, and they called it Dixieland."

One extravaganza Father produced and directed was the biggest thing since Ringling Brothers, Barnum & Bailey paraded their circus through town. It was inspired by George M. Cohan; my father's motto was "Why not the best?" In the finale, four ladders were spaced evenly across the stage. There were twelve of us who did a military routine as we sang the rousing song, "Bunker Hill, O Bunker Hill." At the end we went up the ladders, three to a ladder, and as we unfurled a piece of cloth we had worn across the front of us as part of our costume, the American flag was formed. The band played while we sang "You're a Grand Old Flag," and the curtain came down amid cheers and applause, only to go up and down, again and again, as we answered the curtain calls. This was heady stuff for a small town, and my heart wasn't the only one beating like a fevered drum.

I look back on those days in that little town—days of inflated patriotism, days before the women's movement and the declared rights of minorities revolutionized our institutions, days with so much to ponder—but all I can see is the glare of the footlights, all I can feel is the joy of a clown, and all I can hear are voices of the past, echoing, "Encore, encore!"

— Eleanor Huba

PLEASANT MEMORIES

I was born in Washington, D.C. on July 10, 1919. My father was a Government Librarian, and although he was a civilian, he worked for three Service Branches: the Army, Marines and the Navy. During the years of World War I, he established libraries in Fort Myers, Camp Quantico and Fort William Henry Harrison. When I was three years old, we moved to Newport, Rhode Island, where he was stationed at the Naval War College. He stayed there until he retired in 1945 or '46.

He was born in Slingerlands, a premature baby, very small, and the doctor old Dr. Adams, said he would put him in a shoebox and bury him in the back garden. My grandmother was a very determined woman. She had already lost one boy and she had no intention of losing this one. She said, "That child is going to live." So, the doctor and my grandmother wrapped the baby, placed him in a shoebox, and put him in the oven. They had fashioned an incubator from the oven of the old coal and wood kitchen stove! He did live, but was quite frail and sickly. Grandmother hovered over him and coddled him, and he survived very well. He attended school in Slingerlands, then went to public school in Albany and on to Cornell University. He attended Library School at Columbia University and obtained his master's degree there.

My mother, Marion Leita Peckham, was born in Utica. She spent wonderful summers on her grandparent's farm where there were always a dozen or so thrashers working the fields. They rose early and had a half day's work done by breakfast-time. Breakfasts were not the skimpy fare of today. There was home-cured ham and bacon, fried potatioes, cereals such as oatmeal and hominy grits, cornbread and/or muffins and/or baked biscuits, yesterday's pork chops, doughnuts and pie. No wonder my mother had to watch her weight all her life! Her father was a conductor on the old Black River Railroad. He kept a diary up until 1922, the year he died. When the Black River Railroad became part of the mighty New York Central, Grandfather Peckham moved his family to Albany and then to Slingerlands where Mother met my father at a fair at the Community Methodist Church. She went to the Female Academy, later named Albany Academy for Girls. After graduating, she taught Drama, German, and of all things, Fudge-Making, which was one of the main forms of entertaining one's beaux of an evening.

My paternal grandparents were of old Dutch stock and owned quite a lot of land. They were charter members of the Dutch Settlers' Society and Grandmother was a charter member of Tawasentha Chapter, D.A.R., organized in 1907. The Blessing Land and Improvement Company sold moldings and made considerable money from it. The old Blessing Homestead is at the corner of Cherry and Orchard Streets in Slingerlands. They maintained large orchards, especially apples and pears, strawberry patches, grapevines, raspberry and currant bushes, besides a large vegetable garden. Today, the land, having been sold off, is laid out in street developments and apartment complexes. Before this, they were mostly dairy farmers. It is said when they came from Holland through what is now New Jersey, they brought the first cows (Jersey, naturally) into this country.

My grandfather was Frederick Slingerland Blessing, and in the Community Methodist Church there are stained glass windows with his ancestors' names, Magdalene Slingerland and Christian La Grange. My grandmother, Arthetta Reed, was born and brought up in Vischer's Ferry. My grandfather used to take his horse and carriage across the Mohawk River on a large type of ferry to "court" her. After they married, they moved to the old home up on the hill overlooking Bridge Street in Slingerlands. In 1913 they moved to 1584 New Scotalnd Road. Grandfather owned the Blessing Coal Company in Delmar and his coalyards were near the Delaware and Hudson Railroad tracks. He also used to sell wood and ice by a horse-drawn wagon. As a small girl I loved to go with him to "the office" and play on the typewriter. Each summer when I arrived for my two-or three-week vacation, Grandfather always had a huge, whole watermelon in the icebox, and it was an icebox—he never owned a refrigerator. After supper he and I would ride to the Delmar Four Corners in his aircooled Franklin. He purchased one of the first of that type car and it semed so big to me. We went to Wager's store for a quart of ice cream, usually vanilla, which was put under sliced fresh peaches for dessert.

His house was a large, three-story Victorian home with lots of "gingerbread" outside and a long porch extending from the front and around to the side door. There was a circular driveway with many stately elm trees on the street side. He had apple and pear trees, a plum and peach, two sour cherry trees, and Grandmother made an excellent cherry pie. Grandfather had lilac trees, icluding a double French white lilac. He also had a "truck garden," grew currants, raspberries and all sorts of vegetables, including asparagus. He had horseradish root and rhubarb, and there was also a large, two-car barn. It had an upper floor where he kept all his tools and an old-fashioned wall telephone which worked by turning a crank at the side. At the time, it was one of the very first telephones to be installed outside of Albany proper. In the doorway to the barn, he built a swing for me. It was made of thick, strong rope and had a wooden plank seat. How I loved it! It would keep me happy for hours. Also in the barn was a large ice chest filled with dried corn for his chickens. Behind the barn he had a hen house and a yard for scratching and pecking. He used to let me go into the coop with him to get the eggs, and I was always very scared. Any clucking or movement, and I was the one who "flew the coop."

The house had a front parlor with the inevitable upright piano, topped by a velvet fringed scarf, and a swivel stool piano bench. Grandmother had an upholstered Boston rocker and in the bay window a large potted palm. On the walls were many religious pictures, so one of my favorite games of make-believe was to play church. I was the parishioners, organist (piano), minister, and when I "passed the plate," I used my mother's old tambourine. I would dress up in Grandmother's castoffs, use scrap paper for money, play hymns on the piano and of course, read from the "Good Book." Also in the front parlor was an old-fashioned Victrola. It stood on a record cabinet and used wooden needles. You pushed a small lever so the record would roll out toward you.

The attic was always fun. It consisted of many small rooms and one large room that covered the entire front of the house. Grandmother made her own soap and there were usually two wooden crates holding cakes full of lye—not very good for the skin—but it did get the clothes clean. I used to pore over the many discarded items up there: old Christmas tree ornaments, copies of the "National Geographic" and "The Christian Advocate," all sorts of pans and tubs, especially old, beautiful copper bathtubs, the kind that used to be brought down in front of the stove on Saturday night and filled with steaming hot water for the weekly bath.

Each evening my grandparents and I would play dominoes from about 7:00 to 9:00 p.m., then everyone went to bed. The day was over! I would be awakened at 7:00 a.m. and have breakfast by myself. My grandparents had eaten about 6:30 a.m. or earlier, and Grandfather had already gone to work. Grandmother used to cook oatmeal or hominy grits, or whatever, in a double boiler on the old coal stove, and usually had fruit to go with it. The cereal was very glutinous and resembled library paste, but it tasted good since I knew no better. Grandfather came at 12 noon sharp for a big, hot dinner, summer and winter; supper was at 5:00 p.m. As my brother, Reed, (Arthur Reed Blessing, Jr.) grew up—he was born in 1925—he joined me summers at Grandfather's until I was well along in high school. By then Grandmother became ill and was bedridden for seven years. She died in September, 1939, and was buried in the Blessing plot in the old cemetery behind the New Scotland Presbyterian Church in New Salem.

I was brought up in Newport, Rhode Island, and came back to visit until 1945 when my father moved to Slingerlands, later retiring to Florida in 1945.

My growing-up years were wonderfully happy. My family was a close-knit one and we did many things together. Grandfather Peckham died in 1922 and my grandmother came to Newport. We lived on the first floor of a large, two-story house with an attic. My parents' bedroom had a lovely sun porch attached to it which overlooked the Bay, and it was nice and cool in the summer. There were two rooms and bath above where Grandmother lived, and she took her meals with us. Dad and Mother belonged to a bridge club—six couples—and the ladies alternated in giving dinners beforehand. Often I was allowed to stay overnight with Grandmother. In her front room she had one of the first types of sofa that opened out to make a bed. I loved to stay up there and she and I would make raw onion sandwiches to eat in bed.

A whole group of us kids grew up together. We attended Callendar School for kindergarten and through third grade. We would take walks in the fall and pick up horse chestnuts. They were beautiful with their shiny, satiny, mahogany covers. On the last day of school, my friend Johnny Watson and I came home and told our mother we hadn't passed. We thought that was a terrific joke to play on them. Fourth through seventh grades were spent in Coggeshell School, eighth at Mumford, and the last four years at Rogers High School. All of these schools were named after prominent people from Newport's past.

I had decided to be a mother after my brother was born. I loved him and everything to do with and for him. I started babysitting when I was eight years old and then branched out through the neighborhood, babysat for everyone and anyone—for free, of course. It never occurred to me that anyone would think to pay me. I was having so much fun. I still do babysit occasionally, only I do get paid now.

Our "gang" put on plays, had a bridge club, did floor shows and ran rummage sales. The "Varsity Drag" was popular at that time, so we would use old lace curtains for costumes and form a chorus line to do the Varsity Drag. Rags were another form of popular music, and when my parents went to New York City one time, they asked me what I wanted them to bring me, and I said, "A record, "Tiger Rag." I had no idea what a rag was. I thought the record was about an animal, the tiger. Father brought the record back to me and I played it for years afterward. It was my very first record and I loved it.

Mother saw to it that I had ballet lessons, ballroom dancing and piano lessons. I always sang. I started in the choir at our church and have continued all my life. In high school and in college I sang in the Women's Glee Club and each Sunday in chapel. After that, for a few years, I sang with the choir at the First Presbyterian Church in Albany, and now I sing in the choir of my own church, Roessleville Presbyterian Church. I took music lessons from Mr. Sneeden Weir at the Albany Institute of Music on Dove Street for about five years and was also a member of the Monday Musical Club. Our family was quite musical. Both my grandmothers played piano as did my mother who also sang. We would all gather around and sing. Father played the violin and the cello, continuing with both instruments for several years.

In high school we had dances each Friday night and sometimes "formals." In spite of the depression, my teen years were happy and carefree. The Duke of Windsor, later King Edward VIII, was much in the news in 1937, the year I graduated from high school. For my Class Day dress, Mother bought me a chiffon over taffeta gown in "Wally Simpson blue," named for a shade favored and worn by Mrs. Simpson, the woman for whom Edward VIII gave up the throne of England.

After high school I went to Cornell University, taking a fairly new course "Hotel and Institutional Management." I was really quite unhappy there. My father paid for my education. He didn't want me to work my way through—but there was a catch to it. He picked the college and the course I was to follow. He wanted to be sure I got a "practical" education. However, I was very shy, away from home for the first time. There I was a small frog in a big pond. (In Newport I had been a big frog in a small pond.) I was class of '41, my father, '15.

After Cornell I went to live with Grandfather Blessing as his housekeeper. He was in his '70s at that time and needed someone to help him in that great big, old house. He paid me $7.00 a week. In my spare time I knitted sweaters for the Navy boys and folded bandages for the Red Cross. In November of 1942, I got a job working in the cafeteria of the New York Telephone Company in Albany. I started out as a dishwasher and graduated to baker. In those days everything was made from scratch, including pie fillings such as chocolate cream, lemon meringue, etc. I went on to become a cashier and then Assistant Supervisor. By 1947, I was Division Dining Room Supervisor and had charge of six cafeterias. In 1950 I was married to Harry Raymond Lawton in the Community Methodist Church in Slingerlands, but stayed on with the Telephone Company until 1952 when I left to await the birth of the first of our four children. My first pay for the Telephone Company was $10.84 a week, but when I left the Company, I earned $400 a month, which was excellent pay for a woman at that time. I had my own apartment while I was working but after my marriage we moved first to 479 State Street opposite Washington Park, bought our home at 67 Rooney Avenue, lived there until 1976 when we moved to the Towers of Colonie where we now reside.

Our family was Presbyterian. In Albany I attended the First Presbyterian Church and the Madison Avenue Presbyterian and am now a member of the Roessleville Presbyterian in Colonie. My church was and is very important to me. I guess I have held just about every position in the church, serving in the Woman's Association, now President, choir, nursery, kindergarten, helping out in plays, suppers and fairs. My husband, four children and daughter-in-law are also practicing Presbyterians.

When I was growing up, the family unit was most important. My father was head of the home and the breadwinner, and as was the custom, my mother did not work outside the home. She was expected to keep house and bring up my brother and me. My parents used to tell us about their childhoods. Mother spoke of roasting potatoes in the leaves in the gutter with her father, and Dad told of his Halloween tricks like putting the old hay wagon up on Uncle Charlie's barn roof. Sunday was our "family day." We did things together—I established this with our children. Often the neighboring children wandering the streets would join us when we played games and went on picnics.

Today's generation doesn't believe there was anything before television; but I can remember our first small table radio, an Atwater Kent, and if you got KDKA-Pittsburgh, it was a personal triumph. My grandfather had a "crystal" set. We bought our first TV set in 1952.

Moral codes were more strict when I grew up, but each generation is different. What we did in our growing-up years must have shocked our grandparents. All in all, this has been a wonderful era in which to live. We've had our wars, our prosperity and our depressions, but think of all the advances in all areas. We have seen many inventions, explorations, advances in science, medicine and new technologies—electricity, modern conveniences and modes of transportation. We have really achieved a more rounded and better way of life. Let us hope and pray that the next generation is able to do as well, if not better.

—Annetta Blessing Lawton

A NINETEENTH CENTURY BOYHOOD

After having made several futile attempts to find a suitable home for me, my mother finally made arrangements with an elderly couple by the name of John and Eveline Clowe. They lived alone in a little house on Swaggertown Road, on about three acres of land that had a small trout stream running along the extreme back end. The Clowe place was situated about six miles north of Schenectady, about two miles from the Glenville Center Methodist Church, and about an equal distance from the Swaggertown schoolhouse.

The house was a story and a half structure of no particular design, having a rather good sized living room and separate pantry, with a not too large bedroom situated off the living room. These two rooms constituted the living quarters for the three of us during the winter season, until I was old enough to sleep by myself upstairs. Heat was supplied by a large kitchen stove which was moved into the living room for the cold season, and back again into the lean-to kitchen for the summer, and from then on until fall we continued to do all our living in that one crudely constructed room.

There was one good sized bedroom finished off upstairs to accommodate visitors. By stepping up one step at the top of the stairway one entered an unfinished attic area showing only the bare studding and rafters. This was where I was assigned my sleeping quarters when I became old enough to sleep alone. I do not know what the pillow was filled with, if I had a pillow, but the mattress was filled with corn husks and there were no springs, just a series of ropes stretched back and forth and fastened to knobs on the railings. There were two windows that always rattled with the wind and were so dilapidated and worn that the snow would drift in on the floor. Many was the time that I jumped out of bed in my bare feet and landed in a miniature snowbank.

Snow storms were very severe in those days and drifts were piled high and heavy. Sometimes the banks remained in our yard blocking sleigh traffic in or out all winter. After a severe storm the farmers would turn out en masse with their teams and heavy bob sleighs, and some only with shovels, to open up the roads. Drifts in our yard were so high that I would dig high tunnels into them and play house standing erect.

As the Clowes had been living all alone for several years, there were, of course, no toys or playthings that would interest a little boy. The only toy I had was a home-made cart that Mr. Clowe fashioned for me. It consisted of two wheels sawed and shaped from a thick piece of board and fastened on a wooded axle. On this was mounted a wooden box, which, together with a tongue or rod about four feet long, completed my first plaything and made me a very happy youngster. There were no other small children closer than a mile or two, so that I was strictly on my own, and grew up entirely among adults.

One of my favorite pastimes during the summer months was to play "House," all by myself, of course. I would go out near the barn, and, with small stones, lay out a plan of living room and kitchen. My greatest thrill in this game was serving the meal. At the table I would arrange the china ware which consisted of small flat stones, pieces of shingle or board. For the cups I usually used old cans. Knives, forks and spoons were fashioned from pieces of wood or twigs. And how real it all seemed. Serving the meal was a delight. I was always the father and did all the serving and passing to my imaginary family. I made great quantities of mud patties which served as pie, cake, griddle cakes or whatever the occasion demanded. My fantasy family consisted of myself at the head of the house, my wife, Annie, and several children.

At the back end of the three acre plot was a small brook with an occasional deep pool from which I provided many a fish dinner for the Clowe family! My equipment consisted of a bent pin attached to a piece of cord which was fastened to a slender sapling or branch cut from a tree. I never owned a real, "honest-to-goodness" fishing pole and line until many years later. For bait I used common earth worms and grasshoppers. Besides catching the fish I was made to clean them as well.

My favorite pet was a gray and white Plymouth Rock hen that I named, "Kirpie." It was the tamest chicken I have ever seen and the most likeable. It might be truthfully said that Kirpie was my first girl friend. It roosted with the rest of the flock on the second floor of the hen house. No matter at what time of day or night, I could go out and call, "Here Kirpie, Kirpie, Kirpie," and that chicken was sure to come walking down the ramp to me. While I dug worms for her, she would stand close by the spade and dash in to grab a tasty morsel as it turned up in the broken earth. She would follow me all around, sit on my shoulder, eat out of my hand while standing on my arm and tell me some tall stories at the same time.

Next door south of us on the same side of the road lived the Streever family. It was to the Streevers that I traveled each day for our supply of milk at two cents a pint. As I grew older, I loved to drive the team out in the meadows as they brought in the hay. Then I learned to ride horseback, and they would send me way out to a distant pasture to bring in the cows for milking. They let me use a gentle gray horse that would gallop along smoothly without bouncing you up and down as most horses do. I rode him bareback, rain or shine, and this was always one of the highlights of my daily living. My first pay job was picking potatoes for the Streevers at two cents a bushel. That afternoon I earned fifty cents and I was a multimillionaire.

I had very little use for spending money out there in the country, but there were times when, if I had a twenty-five cent piece in my pocket, no Rockefeller could have been as rich.

Mrs. Clowe turned over to me several bushes of black currants for my very own project to make out of them whtever I could. When they had become ripened and ready to pick, I filled a fairly good-sized basket, and started on my hike to the city in high hopes of getting at least fifty cents for them at Kreuger Grocery Store. This store was located on lower State Street and was sort of a trading post where farmers would bring in their produce and trade for supplies. By the time I reached the city, the berries had packed down and were deteriorated in the heat. Imagine my disappointment and chagrin when Mr. Kreuger would pay me only thirteen cents for the lot. There went my hopes for two hours of blissful happiness. I had expected to rent a bicycle at twenty-five cents an hour and have such a wonderful time. My heart was just about busted.

On another occasion I did have the twenty-five cents with which I rented a bicycle, and was learning to ride on lower Union Street when I sighted a pair of spirited horses and surrey emerging from what was then one of the "Ellis" mansions. I became confused, lost control and narrowly escaped being trampled by that pair of horses attached to "A Surrey With The Fringe On Top." I shall never forget falling from the wheel and seeing those great horses' hooves menancing me from above. How I escaped unharmed and with the bicycle intact, I have often wondered.

Union Street then was paved with small cobblestones which made bicycle riding rather difficult, especially for a beginner. The city was proud of its horse-drawn street cars as the latest means of transportation. Trains passed through the city at street level and the old Erie Canal came in to the city from the Mohawk River at Aqueduct, then up along what is now Erie Boulevard and continued past the General Electric Company plant as it traveled its course westward to Buffalo. Many were the hours I idled away watching the operations of the canal boats as they stopped to unload or take on merchandise. The boats were pulled along by mules attached to a long tow line, a slow means of transportation compared to present-day methods. My favorite delicacy was cream puffs and, whenever I was in the city and had five cents, I invariably made my way to a bake shop and gladly gave up my nickel for two of those delicious bits of pastry. Boy, they were good!

The only reading matter I had was "The Youth's Companion" which someone had subscribed for me. I had only one book which was given to me by Mrs. Hedden, across the road, on my ninth birthday. All other reading material came from the library at the Church. One book, in particular, that caught my fancy, and I must have read it through a dozen times, was titled, "The Go-Ahead or The Fisher Boy's Motto." It had a fine moral that appealed to a youth, based on honesty, courtesy and perseverance.

The nearest church was at Glenville Center, a good two miles away, and, as the years passed, I would wend my way there each Sunday. I used to think it was a terribly long hill up Bolt Road and it was for a little fellow who had to walk in the hot sun of summer or cold of winter. I had the grandest Sunday School teacher named Rosella Sanders. I really worshipped her, for, in my rather lonely life away from my mother and family, she seemed to fill a need for my little soul. Her family was reputed to be quite well off in "Wordly Goods." I can still envision the Sanders fmily arriving at church in a two-seated surrey drawn by a pair of horses having blankets of loosely knitted cord as protection from the flies.

My education began when I started to attend the little old one-room school known as the "Swaggertown School," situated about two miles from the Clowe home and about four miles north of Schenectady. How well do I remember walking back and forth with my dinner pail in hand. I was always alone for no other children of school age lived out my way. I would often stop along the route home to pick my lunch pail full of berries and was always rewarded by the pleasure and praise with which Mrs. Clowe greeted my efforts.

The school house was typical of those old-fashioned, one-room buildings we read about. It had high ceilings, a massive potbellied stove that would burn either wood or coal. The stovepipe extended straight up to the ceiling, then continued to the end of the room where it met the chimney. The pipe was held in place by wires attached to the ceiling, and where the holding screws were screwed into and through the plaster, much use had broken away some of the plaster, making an easy exit for a colony of wasps that always had possession of the space between the ceiling and the roof. Whenever the room became well heated, the wasps would thaw out and swarm through those openings into the room to make life miserable for the scholars. We all wore short pants, that is, the boys did, reaching just to the knees. Many a time I had a battle royal with one of those critters who persisted in getting inside my pants, and letting me know in emphatic wasp language that "He was there, Charlie."

The scholars took turns bringing in the wood or coal, also the drinking water which was kept in a large covered pail with one community dipper for the use of all. The water was carried from a nearby farmhouse. Plain wooden desks and benches provided the only equipment. Slates and slate pencils were used exclusively, never any paper that I recall.

The School District was governed by one trustee elected annually, who hired the teacher and had complete charge and control of all school matters. There were no recreation facilities of any kind and no playgrounds were provided. In those days the children knew nothing about baseball. Practically the only games they enjoyed were "Pon, Pom Pullaway," "Duck the Grate" and "It" or "Tag."

On extremely hot summer days teacher would occasionally permit the entire group to hold their study periods outside the school building down by the creek where nature had thoughfully provided a lovely rustic setting for just such a purpose. Huge boulders and stones of all sizes and shapes had placed themselves along the sloping banks of the stream to form a natural amphitheater. Here each student would select his favorite spot and proceed to study. It was a novel venture and we all looked forward to it with great anticipation.

As long as it was possible, I traveled about without benefit of shoes or stockings. There comes to mind one morning on my way to school. There was snow on the ground in scattered places and very cold. And, there was a large hole right through the sole of my right shoe. Every time I took a step, part of my bare foot came in contact with the frosty ground. It became so painful that I cried. After a while I figured that, if I walked on my heel, I could avoid the pain and that's how I traveled to school that morning.

I can remember walking home from school when the roads were filled with deep snow. In order to make any progress I had to walk in the narrow tracks made by the horses and sleighs that had previously passed through. If any of my readers have ever tried to do this, you will recall it is quite difficult to hold a balance. I discovered I could maintain my equilibrium much better by running.

On one unusually cold and blustery day I had started home form school but had not traveled very far before I had difficulty keeping my ears warm as I was wearing only a little skull cap. After a time, however, the ears felt really comfortable and I arrived home without any further discomfort. The fire in the old stove was going strong and, soon, I was as warm as toast except that both my ears began to sting and smart and burn. Mrs. Clowe looked at them and said, "Why, Freddie, your ears are frozen solid." She put snow on them and then saturated them with kerosene oil. I went back to school the next day and told the teacher I had frozen my ears. She, thinking that it had just happened, took me outside and applied the snow treatment again. That was plain torture.

Word of this must have gotten to the trustee for, when I was passing his house that night on the way home, he called me in and gave me a heavy winter cap many sizes too large but which well shielded my head and ears from winter's blasts.

The years came and went and my school life at Swaggertown continued on its normal course. Following a brief period of school life in Schoharie County, I found myself one morning entering the Haskell School in Lansingburgh which became my seat of learning for the next four years.

EPILOGUE

I graduated from Haskell School in 1900 and immediately arranged to make my first visit to the scene of my early childhood, the Clowe home. I set sail one morning on the New York Central train for Schenectady. From thence I started on the journey to walk the six miles to my old home.

As I was passing the Schairer farm, a group of people were busy feverishly picking strawberries. A storm was threatening and they were hurrying at all possible speed to get the patch picked over before the rain should come. Martin Schairer hailed me and inquired if I wanted to make some money picking berries at two cents a quart. I was delighted at the chance to make some spending money for my vacation so I readily agreed. That afternoon, working from one o'clock until four, I made $1.02, having picked fifty-one quarts. On the strength of my good showing, Martin asked if I would like to work for a whole month at fifty cents a day and board. I jumped at the offer and, the next morning, began my new and first real job. My duties were varied. I helped to gather, wash and bunch the vegetables, did weeding, picked berries and assisted in loading the wagons for market. The Schairer family peddled their own produce from door to door in Schenectady. I went along and acted as doorbell ringer and delivery boy from wagon to customer. The food was excellent, cooked as only the Germans know how. My room consisted of a bunk in the barn with the hired man. It was not so bad even though the mattress was stuffed with straw.

At the end of the month Martin Schairer gave me $14.00 in cash, the first sizable amount of money I had ever had. I immediately proceeded to spend it all in one place. The hired man had an unusually good bicycle that he wanted to sell and agreed to let me have it, oddly enough, for just $14.00.

There never was a happier youngster than I when I proudly mounted my prized possession and realized it was really mine. Ever since I had seen the first bicycle, the kind with the large wheel in front and the tiny one behind, I had longed for the time when I would have one for my very own. And now, that time had arrived. I really owned a bicycle. How my heart fairly bounded as I peddled along the road and proudly displayed my prized possession before Mr. and Mrs. Clowe.

— Frederick Long

A DEVICE OF THE DEVIL

"A playhouse is a device of the devil, and play-actors are but vagabonds who would steal your silver and perhaps even your wife if given a chance." With these or similar words men of the cloth in the year 1812 warned the good citizens of Albany, New York, against permitting the erection of a theater in their community.

Announcement had been made that such a temple of cultural endeavor would soon be built on the west side of Green Street just south of Hamilton. Almost at once a fanatical opposition was raised. Theaters were condemned as immoral and dangerous not only to the spiritual but also the physical welfare of the residents of the city. The loss of seventy-one lives in a theater fire in Richmond, Virginia, was interpreted as the hand of God showering His displeasure upon an unholy place. Theatrical enterprises everywhere suffered because of this tragic event.

In spite of the opposition, theater people wanted a playhouse in the growing community of Albany. The Hudson River offered the city an easy line of communiation with New York. Because of this, Albany was looked upon as an ideal location to expand and exploit any managerial effort over and above that which might exhaust the potential for profit in the metropolitan area. Those people who usually earned their living in the New York theater but who were temporarily "at liberty" welcomed an opportunity to work so close to their center of operation. Fortunately for all concerned the proposed Albany theater project enjoyed some support from a few influential local residents.

Theatricals were nothing new to Albany. In 1757, during the French and Indian War, a group of British officers stationed at Fort Frederick, which stood to the west of the present-day intersection of State and Lodge Streets, produced a ribald farce, "The Beaux Stratagem." This production, serving to while away the leisure hours of a bored garrison, was the first theatrical performance given north of New York City. The old Dutch burghers of Albany, although not understanding one word of English, packed every show given in the lamplighted barn which served as a theater and which stood at the present intersection of Pine and Lodge Streets. They screamed and howled with laughter, while His Majesty's fine gentlemen cavorted around the stage dressed as pretty ladies complete with hoop skirts and bonnets.

The Reverend Theodoseus Freylinghausen, Dominie of the Dutch Church, fought the project and characterized actors and the people of Albany as "damned souls abandoned to the wiles of the devil." So discouraged and disillusioned did he become that he jumped overboard in a ship bound for his native Holland.

The first professional actors to invade Albany came in 1769. David Douglas, with the permission of His Britannic Majesty's governor, Sir Henry Moore Bart, presented a company of English thespians three times weekly for one month. They performed Otway's "Venice Preserved" in a large room of a hospital quite near the site of the barn which had housed the "Beaux Strategem" production.

The Albany of that day boasted a population of over three thousand but had no newspaper; therefore, very little is known about this professional adventure in theater. We do know Dominie Freylinghausen's condemnation of theatricals twelve years before apparently had some effect. The good Dutch burghers of 1769 frowned upon the presence of these "disciples of the devil" and let the fact be known. Their attitude must have made an impression; it would be sixteen long years before a second troupe of professional actors ventured into Albany.

Late in 1785 the Mayor and the City Council of Albany, New York, granted permission for a touring theatrical company to appear in the city. The group, composed of many players who had worked for the famous Hallam brothers at one time or another, was scheduled to present Shakespeare's "Taming of the Shrew" and a farce comedy, "Cross Purposes," by O'Brien. Once again the hospital at Pine and Lodge Streets was pressed into service as a theater. Members of the company began feverishly to work to convert two rooms for this purpose.

By this time Albany had a newspaper, "The Albany Gazette," and it printed its first theatrical press notices to herald the coming of the players. An enterprising advance man had convinced its editors that "Theatrical presentations are of all others best calculated to eradicate vulgar prejudices and rusticity of manners, improve the understanding and enlarge the ideas." Opposition to the appearance of these players was widespread. Part of this was a suspicion that actors were low persons of no breeding and part because these particular actors were British. In 1785 the deeply felt hatreds of the Revolution were still too fresh in mind. The press notice which had appeared in "The Gazette" was quickly answered, ". . . though suspected of rusticity and want of politeness . . . (the people of Albany) stand in no need of plays and play-actors to be instructed in our duty of good manners."

On December 12, 1785, the Mayor and the City Council in meeting were petitioned to revoke their permission for the players to appear. Sensitivities of some of the residents of the city were inflamed and threats had been made to burn the hospital if the actors weren't prevented from performing. The Mayor and some of the members of the Council felt that having given permission which encouraged the players to spend money and effort to convert the hospital rooms for a theater, the integrity of the city was at stake. After considerable argument, a vote was taken and decision was made to let the actors proceed.

Eighteen active years slipped by. Albany had doubled in population and gained eminence as the capital of the State of New York. In 1803 the Hallam brothers brought a third company of professional actors to appear in the assemlby room of a dance hall at the north end of Pearl Street near Patroon. They presented Sheridan's "School for Scandal" and Goldsmith's "She Stoops to Conquer." Very little is know of these performances except that one of the actors was Joseph Jefferson, grandfather of THE Joseph Jefferson, one of the theater's greats, dean of the American stage and famous for his acting in "Rip Van Winkle" and "The Cricket on the Hearth."

In 1810 still another touring company whose name and repertoire are sealed in the vaults of time appeared in the City of Albany. Its appearance is noteworthy only because John Howard Payne, one-time student at Union College in Schenectady, and destined to gain recognition as a lyricist and author of over sixty plays, was a member of the troupe.

Almost immediately following the announcement of the intention to establish a permanent theater on Green Street in the City of Albany, construction began. It was to be the first real theater in all of upstate New York, and its gradual raising caused great excitement. Each Sunday hell-and-damnation sermons were preached against this "den of the devil" and bitter articles appeared daily in the newspaper. The wisdom of the city fathers was seriously questioned in even allowing professional actors to appear in the city. Although it had presumably been settled twenty-six years before, the reaffirmation of the permit for a traveling company to renovate and appear in the two rooms at the hospital was once more revived.

At a meeting of the corporation board of the city, convened shortly after construction of the Green Street playhouse had started, a motion was made to classify all theatrical performances as "a nuisance." By resolution the law committee was directed to report "whether all public shows and theatrical exhibitions are not contrary to good order and morality, and, therefore, ought to be discontinued."

At the January 20, 1812 meeting, a lengthy report was made on this resolution. John V.N. Yates, city recorder, is credited with writing the report which upheld the legaity of the theater and stated, "that a well-regulated theater, supported by the respectable portion of society, so far from being contrary to good order and morality, must essentially contribute to correct language, refine the taste, ameliorate the heart and enlighten the understanding.".

With a vote of ten to three a resolution was passed by the city officials: "That the board cannot legally interfere, nor would it be expedient for it to pass any laws regulating or restraining theatrical exhibitions in this city." Legal permission to build and operate the Green Street Theater was a triumph over the local censorship movement.

On the evening of January 18, 1813, the doors of the new Green Street Theater swung wide to greet its first audience. P. H. Phelps in his "Players of a Century," published in 1880, describes "Its judicious arrangement and architectural symmetry and splendid decorations, not to mention spacious salons for refreshments helped attract the better people." The "first nighters" were described as being "numerous, respectable and polite." In the opening night program a note announced that as a gesture to the ladies the management had "engaged a strong police force to keep out all ruffians." John Bernard, veteran actor and first manager of the new playhouse, arrived in Albany with a letter of recommendation from an Episcopal clergyman in Boston. Apparently Mr. Bernard was determined to operate a first-class place of amusement.

The opening night audience not only saw "The West Indian" and "Fortune's Frolic" but also was treated to an inaugural address consisting of several hundred lines of poetry composed for this special occasion by the editor of "The Albany Register," Mr. Solomon Southwick.

In the prologue Mr. Southwick promised:
"No vile obscenity . . . in this blest age,
Where mild religion takes her heavenly reign . . . "

Later he continues:
" . . . though 'mong players some there may be found
Whose conduct is not altogether sound . . .
Your remedy is good with such a teacher,
Imbibe the precept, but condemn the preacher."

The editor further stated:
"And lo, where Hudson's wave majestic glides,
O'er fair Albania's plains in vernal tides;
Praised be the gen'rous flame that warms their hearts,
Whose bounty flows to aid the rising arts."

Because the theater opened during the War of 1812, some of its earliest performances were given to benefit "the poor sufferers on the lines" who had fallen victim of the British and the Indians. One of the theater's first apprentice actors had been born in Albany in 1797 but, as a small child, sent to live with his grandmother in Galway. At fourteen he returned to Albany determined to be successful on the stage. For unknown reasons this budding actor's fire for art slowly cooled, while his fire for science burst into flame. He entered Albany Academy which had just occupied the spanking red stone building still standing to this day on Eagle Street. There in 1829 he touched two wires to ring a bell in a distant room, and its ringing echoed and reechoed throughout the world to bring him fame. His name ws Joseph Henry.

Even after its successful opening, the Green Street Theater continued to have much opposition from the straightlaced citizens of Albany and support for it was sporadic. Because of this, operating the theater was a continuous struggle. The 1817 season was a disastrous one; the following year the theater was closed and the building sold. In June of 1818, the spirit of Dominie Theodosius Freylinghausen must have wept with joy; the Green Street Theater, that temple of the devil, was converted to become a Baptist Church.

Thirty-four years slowly drifted down the path of time. In 1852 the Baptist Church gave up the building and it was reconverted to its original purpose by Madame de Marguerites, the abandoned wife of a French nobleman. This distinguished lady gave theater in Albany one of its most picturesque chapters.

Madame presented her theater and drama in her theater on a lavish scale. So that the audience might admire itself between the acts, this eccentric French-woman had two huge mirrors set in the front curtain of the stage.

Not only was Madame de Marguerites the impresario, she was also the leading lady of her company. One of her favorite roles was Little Eva in "Uncle Tom's Cabin," a play which had its first production not too far from the locale of Madame's theater. George C. Howard, popular actor and producer of Troy, New York, in the early 1850s, breathed life into Little Eva as a stage personal-ity. Mr. Howard was rehearsing his wife, Caroline, in one of her most suc-cessful roles, Oliver in "Oliver Twist" by Charles Dickens. Upon the suggestion of one of the other actors in the company, Howard cast his own four-year-old daughter, Cordelia, as Little Dick, the sick pauper who bids a sad farewell to Oliver as the latter runs away from the poorhouse.

Cordelia, dressed in one of her brother's suits, was thoroughly rehearsed in her few lines and simple action. As Oliver entered to make his escape, he discovered Little Dick down stage, right, in front of a mound of dirt wielding a small shovel to dig little graves.

Oliver: "I'm running away, Dick."
Little Dick: "Won't you come back anymore?"
Oliver: "I'll come back and see you someday."
Little Dick: "Good-bye, Oliver."

Opening night Cordelia, her face whitened to simulate a victim of con-sumption, followed directions in complete detail until Oliver's line, "I'll come back and see you someday." At this point Cordelia ad-libbed: "It won't be any use, Olly dear." She broke into the sobs of a broken heart. "When you come back, I won't be digging little graves, I'll be dead in a little grave myself."

Tears not only flowed freely in the audience, they flowed freely backstage as well. Cordelia's family was quick to recognize a natural born actress and immediately determined that such talent should not be wasted.

Harriet Beecher Stowe had already created the perfect vehicle for that talent. Her "Uncle Tom's Cabin" or "Life Among the Lowly," published on March 20, 1852, was enjoying great popularity. In its first year it enjoyed a tremendous sale of 300,000 copies in the United States. In England it eventu-ally sold over a million copies. Immediately Mrs. Stowe was given an opportu-nity to have her story dramatized. Never having seen a play because she believed the theater to be "an instrument of Satan," she refused the offer. She was afraid "it would bring Christians into the theater."

Copyright laws as we know them today did not exist, so Mrs. Stowe's wishes were not respected for very long. Clifton W. Tayleure wrote a dramatization which was produced in New York in August of 1852 and enjoyed a brief run. His version completely ignored both Topsy and Little Eva. They were not ignored for long.

Among Howard's Troy company was his cousin, George L. Aiken, a struggling young playwright. When Caroline Howard suggested Mrs. Stowe's story as an ideal one for both Little Cordelia and their acting company, Aiken adapted it in a week. Because their company was small and lacking in funds, there were no bloodhounds or jubilee singers and it was necessary for some of the actors to "double in brass." What the company lacked in material things, they made up in enthusiasm.

On September 27, 1852, at Pearle's Troy Museum in Troy, New York, the curtain rose on "Uncle Tom's Cabin" with George C. Howard, who wrote all the music, as Saint Clair, Caroline Howard as Topsy, E. K. Fox, Caroline's uncle, as Phineas Fletcher, Mrs. E. Fox, Caroline's mother, as Aunt Ophelia and little Cordelia as Little Eva. Eyes were red, noses were runny and handkerchiefs wet both on stage and off, particularly when Eva died in the third act. But the real flood of tears was prompted by the tableau of the epilogue, "Gorgeous clouds, tinted with sunlight. Eva robed in white is on back of milk white dove, with expanded wings, as if just soaring above. Her hands extended in benediction over Saint Clair and Uncle Tom, who are kneeling and gazing up at her. **Very** slow curtain."

The **very** slow curtain gave Little Eva time to climb off her milk white dove and hurry out to the lobby in time to sell photographs of herself to the departing grief-stricken audience. The production was an instant success and ran one hundred successive nights in Troy. This was a record for the time, not only in Troy, but for the whole United States.

In later years this "great American drama" was offered by as many as twenty-five companies at one time and played in theaters, halls, warehouses, skating rinks, tents and even livery stables. It is said that "Uncle Tom's Cabin" brought more people into theaters than any dozen plays up to that time, and one critic claimed "it influenced more human beings than all of Shakespeare's plays in four centuries."

Before opening at the National Theater in New York City where they enjoyed a run of 325 performances, an unheard of accomplishment for those days, George Howard brought his "Uncle Tom" company to Albany. This is undoubtedly where Madame de Marguerites saw the plan for the first time and decided to adopt it for herself. Madame played Little Eva in spite of her advanced age and corpulence. What's more, the fiery Madame refused to use a curly blonde wig to cover her own graying hair. But people must have loved her in the part; she appeared in it time and time again.

Not all the people of the city shared this love of Madame, her role of Little Eva, or her theater. Growing highly incensed at the immoral aspects of Madame's theater, one group of townspeople organized to drive her and her company out of town. On the evening of the attack the moral gladiators were met by the actors and the stage hands of the company who had armed themselves with swords and battle axes from the theater property room. The battle raged from one side of the stage to the other. The outcome was sometimes in doubt, but the followers of Thespis eventually reigned victorious.

Victory was sweet, but not so long-lived. A few days following the battle on stage, the sheriff arrived to collect the theater's many outstanding debts. Madame was not able to raise the money. The theater was closed by one man, the sheriff.

The Green Street Theater did open again but had a rough struggle for seven years. During that time various attractions played there. Among the productions offered on its stage was "Clari" or "The Maid of Milan" in which Miss Maria Tree introduced the song, "Home, Sweet Home," the only piece still remembered from the pen of John Howard Payne who had played in Albany so many years before. Sir Henry Bishop, a British composer of note, wrote the music for "Home, Sweet Home" in 1821. No copyright laws covered the work and he received only twenty pounds for a song that sold over a hundred thousand copies the first year and has never stopped selling. The lasting popularity of the number was insured when it became a concert favorite of the famous Jenny Lind.

Madame Lola Montez, Irish-born, self-styled Spanish dancer and glamour girl of the 1800s, also played the Green Street playhouse. Madame, known the world over as "the Enchantress" and as an intimate (very intimate) of Alexander Dumas, Franz Liszt and King Ludwig of Bavaria, was an actress, lecturer, and behind-the-scenes politician. She was described as having "a face of great beauty with white skin, a pair of tameless black Spanish eyes which flash fire when she speaks, black hair with ringlets hanging by the side of her face, a nose of pure Grecian cast and cheek bones that are high and give a Moorish appearance to her countenance."

When in Albany Lola performed her "Spider Dance, a provoking and voluptuous routine which gained its appeal form Lola's endeavoring to shake countless India-rubber spiders off her tight-fitting costume. Even Madame Lola's provocativeness couldn't save the failing Green Street Theater. After mortgage foreclosure proceedings in 1859, its doors were closed and the "Device of the Devil" went to hell.

— Charles Leo Miller

NOW AND THEN
Education

I was born at 239 North Pearl Street, Albany, across from a public school and a police station—I had to make my choice. My father had a dairy business on Broadway. This was the era of the "Little Red Schoolhouse" and my early years were spent in a school in Slingerlands which was red brick on the first story and frame on top—which made me possibly a halfbreed.

High school years were spent in the Albany Academy for Girls, located at 155 Washington Avenue. Its chief attraction—noncurricular—is the fact that it was located next to Harmanus Bleecker Hall which at the time had the famous, good-looking Bert Lyttell, who produced considerable distraction both for the girls and for the teachers who boarded at the school. I boarded during the winter months when my family was away in Florida. This was without incident except the historical occasion when my roommate accepted my suggestion of purchasing a quantity of picture wire and in the dead of night, going up to the fourth floor and wiring all the teachers in their rooms. This we did with great stealth and success and the next morning had the joy of all the excitement when the poor teachers were screaming to be let out and no one could fathom what had happened. We were very demure, but for some reason or other, I was suspected and on being asked by the principal, Miss Camp, if I had anything to do with it, I looked at her very courageously and said: "Yes, Miss Camp," which became a notorious statement but for me resulted in being housebound for some time.

During some of those years, Charles Evans Hughes was Governor of New York State and his two daughters, Helen and Catherine, attended the Academy. There were very few automobiles and the Governor did not have one and was provided with a very excellent stable on the grounds with two beautiful horses and an exquisite Victoria upholstered in purple. Each morning the coachman and footman brought the Hughes girls to the Academy in the Victoria and I, among others, used to be on the sidewalk to view the grandeur. The girls were very democratic. Helen was the scholar and recited the Gettysburg Address on Lincoln's Birthday. Catherine was more athletic and followed the practice of using the gymnasium noontimes or recess for playing on the apparatus. I was always there doing the same. On one occasioin, I was using the large jump box; and when I left it for a moment, Catherine proceeded to take over. I walked up to her and made one of my famous remarks: "You might think that because you are the Governor's daughter you can have this box, but you can't because I got here first." There was no offense by Catherine and it became well established that there certainly ensued no discrimination.

While there, the Latin teacher imbued me with the desire and later the determination to go to Wellesley of which she was a graduate. I did, and I enjoyed my academic days there, especially one year of Appreciating Art which she taught. Upon my return, I was asked to teach psychology as an extra-curricular course for a year. I did and enjoyed it.

While I was president of the Academy Alumni Association, we took on the project of the purchase of an athletic field on the south side of New Scotland Avenue, across from the present Albany Academy which was used until it became part of the site of the present Albany Academy for Girls. Much of the money was raised by dances which were held in the Academy Assembly Hall well-lined with chaperones and beginning at 9 p.m. and ending at 12 p.m.

Previous to that, my brother, Kenneth Miner, had attended the Albany Academy down in Academy Park, now taken over by the City Education Department. He told us with great enthusiasm that they had been visited by the famous scientist in the GE named Steinmetz, whose counsel he always remembered, to wit: "Boys, do not ever do nothing—do something, whatever you do."

After Wellesley, I decided to study law and entered the Albany Law School which then occupied an old Presbyterian Church on State Street, later taken over by the Alfred E. Smith State Office Building. It consisted of two rooms, one on the main floor, the second in the basement, which the freshman and juniors occupied, warmed in the winter by a large furnace. There were several girls and we were not maltreated, nor were we enthusiastically received, except for the fact that the boys were all drafted in the war and they urged women to come for the purpose of tuition. The most notable graduate was President William McKinley.

When World War II was over and the boys came back, Harold Alexander became Dean of the school and immediately outlawed all women and for ten years no woman was allowed to matriculate. By this time the school had moved over to its new building, presently located on New Scotland Avenue. Our only feminine retaliation was to refuse to pledge money to the new building until women were allowed to attend, so we really made money. Today there are two hundred women students and one woman trustee.

Politics

As to politics, I was always interested in what was going on, not so much from a political point of view, but as one interested in public affairs. At a very early age, when men would visit my father in the evening, I would ask if I could please sit in a corner and just listen. This I was allowed to do and experienced a childish fascination which grew in concern for what was going on in the political and civic arena. I believe that when I was very small there was a much talked-over debate beween William Jennings Bryan and Samuel Gompers. I also have a vague recollection that I went with either my mother or father to the Senate or Assembly Chamber during the impeachment trial of Senators Conger and Alds, and I believe that they were eventually impeached.

I was born and brought up an ardent Republican and had been instilled with a genuine sense of party loyalty. In those days there was a distinct difference in politics and philosophy; I was taught to cling to the one and stand firmly against the other. My earliest active participation was at the time that the Republicans nominated Taft, and Theodore Roosevelt wanted the nomination after nearly two years in the Presidency. He formed what he characterized as the "Bull Moose Party" and went so far as to run against Taft in the election. It was my freshman year at Wellesley and I stepped off the train onto a campus lively with two camps, to wit: for Taft and for Roosevelt. I joined the Taft camp, worked hard, had a lot of fun which cemented my desire thereafter to become involved. The Roosevelt camp worked hard also with the result that we both had to accept defeat because Woodrow Wilson was elected.

As for my initiation in purely local politics, it was at a time when James R. Watt was the Republican Mayor of Albany and the Republican party had become deeply entrenched under the leadership of William Barnes, editor and publisher of the Albany Evening Journal and the Argus. At that time, there was a trolley strike and poor Mr. Watt decided to show his independence and rode down to City Hall in a trolley operated by so-called "scabs."

All thunder broke loose, Watt was nearly driven out of the city, the Republican party was sorely shaken. To all this was added the matter of alleged illegal distribution of some coal to some of the poor and some illegal acceptance of coal by the politically rich and thereafter deemed by the political enemies as the famous "Coal Scandal."

William S. Hackett, president of the City & County Savings Bank, became Mayor. The Republican party remained lively and so did I, although women did not have the vote. For local color, I worked against Edwin Corning when he ran for Congress and in favor of one Edward Halter, attorney, and Roland B. Sanford, who was elected to one term, I believe, and whose son William Sanford has long been, for more than thirty years, Republican attorney for the town of Colonie. So sincere was my interest that in 1918, one Ada Saxton and I took a trolley to Saratoga to try to get into the Republican State Convention for that year being held in Congress Hall. We arrived and parked ourselves across the street and very shortly had the thrill of seeing Theodore Roosevelt, Charles Evans Hughes and Elihu Root, among others, pass by and enter the convention. The doors were closed and we returned without getting in, but I there resolved that the doors of politics and government should be opened and remain open to women. On this particular date, Roosevelt had just received word of the death of his son Quentin in World War I.

I was not an active suffragette but a strenuous worker; and when we received the vote, I was a delegate to many State conventions held in all of our large cities at different times and three National conventions, two in Philadelphia and one in New York. Of particular interest was the one in which we nominated first, Wendell Willkie and later, Thomas E. Dewey. The story of a delegate to a convention might well be the topic of the memoirs of any delegate, for it was most fascinating and revealing. It was early in the 1920s when Vice President Calvin Coolidge came to Albany and I served on a committee with May Hackett and several others to welcome the Vice President in the Union Station. This experience gave me my first warm personal contact with the national scene.

And so the story goes. We, at that time, had paper ballots and sat up all night counting them. We had no returns broadcast so all gathered on the corner of State and Pearl Streets and viewed the election returns on a huge sheet, each cheering his or her respective candidate. In the country, there were election bonfires for which material was collected all year long and stored, ending up sometimes with the porch furniture which we stole around the neighborhood. My father lost a very excellent driving wagon which did not enhance his pride in my interest in politics.

As for the role of women in those early days, there was a Woman's Republican Club. Mrs. Fred Pryne was chairman, William Barnes presided locally and nationally and we were imbued with great enthusiasm. A State Federation of Republican Women was formed of which Sarah Schuyler Butler was President, but during her tenure the men tried to put us out of existence. But we met wherever we could, one place being in the balcony of the Union Station. To keep our forces intact we finally warded off the doomsday of annihilation and there is still a strong State Women's Federation.

Among the highlights of my political adventures was my personal defeat when I ran for Judge of the Children's Court in 1931 against James Nolan. Completely aware of what was coming, I was a little unprepared on election night to hear the returns from one district in the South End which reported 1763 votes for Nolan and five for Miner, when we had more paid workers than I got votes - something on the political humorous side to remember. When I served as Executive Deputy Secretary of State, my jurisdiction included a number of departments, including the Athletic Commission. So I attended all the title prize fights, sat back of Lowell Thomas in the press box, and saw Joe Louis deliver his fatal punches.

War

When the turmoil in Europe boiled to the breaking point, whether involved or not, the people of the nation were stirred, for in the United States we viewed it as an attack and possibly an annihilation of democracy. While we were not officially in World War I, many of our young men enlisted from Canada and took part in the cause of freedom. One of the consequences was the hemming in of Belgium so that she actually was threatened with starvation. Herbert Hoover rose to the need and dedicated himself to "saving the starving Belgians" and set about to mobilize food.

A small group of citizens in the village of Slingerlands sought to do their part and took over a large field of about ten acres which was on New Scotland Avenue, belonging to William Henry Slingerlands. The group was led by Mrs. Clara Windship. Working for them was an Italian farmer immigrant named Antonio Genovese and a small son, Joe. I was asked to lead the enterprise of turning the ten-acre plot into a cornfield and sending the corn to Hoover. I borrowed a fine team of horses from Mr. Horace Bell and with the help of others, sowed the field to corn, cultivated it and sent it personally to New York for shipment to Hoover for his relief organization in Belgium. We subsequently received a letter of very thrilling acknowledgement and appreciation from Hoover himself.

The shortage of manpower on truck gardens in Colonie became acute and a Women's Land Army was formed by Mrs. Frederick Townsend and Mrs. Charles L.A. Whitney, among others, who took over the North Family Shaker Farm and buildings and mobilized and billeted twenty to thirty girls. The staff to manage, feed and transport them to the truck gardens consisted of Winifred Robb whose father was head of the Electrical Engineering Department of R.P.I., a cook, and myself as agriculturist. I planted about a three-acre plot with seed for all hardy vegetables to feed the household, and at least twice a week drove from my home to be there about 3:30 a.m., while the dew was still on the potatoes, to spray them with powdered arsenic of lead to keep ahead of the potato bugs. I borrowed from the South Family Shaker Farm a horse and cultivator but had plenty of hand hoeing to do myself.

Every morning we loaded the girls in a truck and drove them to the farms where requests had been registered, and picked them up every night and brought them back. It was acknowledged that this was a great service to the farmers.

Another important group which was known as the Victory Girls was organized statewide under the YWCA. The young girls were mobilized and registered to assist in all local war activities and in many and constant services. I was appointed coordinator for the state which called for wide traveling. I only mention this because it was during the first devastating flu epidemic. I had to travel by train and as we approached every station, the train was halted while Red Cross workers would go through the cars distributing masks to each individual before he stepped out. When we did, we had to wend our way to the station in and out between the piles of coffins that crowded the platforms. It was a dismal and sad beginning to each day's work.

Albany was exceedingly sensitive to the war effort and no contingency of mobilized troops ever left the Armory and marched to the Union Station without some citizen escort and sometimes music with the streets lined with appreciative and applauding citizens, many of whom were sad at heart. Albany was a railroad junction, so many troop groups and the Red Cross were women, organized under Henrietta Brett, who met every train, day or night, serving the soldiers.

One of my personal activities was driving a large tractor about twice my height to the driving seat, up State Street from North Pearl and back again, giving a ride to every person who would buy a hundred dollar bond. I had a good response, notably from Mr. Ledyard Cogswell, President of the State Bank, who came out of the bank, bought a $1000 bond and took a ride. It was an exhausting but thrilling experience.

Recreation and Sports

Recreation and sports were lively in Albany in those days with boats on Washington Park lake, wooden swings for the children, beautiful croquet grounds occupied daily by the male senior citizens in hot contest. In winter the park lake was black with skaters and there was sledding on the hills. There was an indoor skating rink on Yates Street just above Lake Avenue and one afternoon a week the Girls' Academy reserved it for practicing ice hockey which I enjoyed tremendously.

There was a race track for harness horses known as Woodlawn which occupied the smooth terrain now known as Academy Road where the Albany Academy for Girls, Temple Beth Emeth and residences now stand.

The Sabbath Day sport was the racing of horses in beautiful sleighs and in the winter, cutters raced down Western Avenue. It was the highlight of the gentlemen's good-natured sport and the sidewalks were lined by a cheering audience.

Transportation, Etc.

There were only trains, trolleys and horses at that time. In the spring the commuter trains from Altamont and Binghamton would have to stop in Kenwood by the Sacred Heart Convent and discharge passengers because of the flooded waters. Rowboats were on Broadway. Trolley fare was five cents. Livery stables spotted the city like garages today. Fire engines were drawn by horses, beautiful to behold but sometimes having hard going on the steep hills. I have seen them struggling to get up and I have seen them sliding down ending up in a fall and mixup at the bottom of a hill while the fire burned. I had my own horse and drove to Albany almost every day, and if visiting, would stable my horse in a livery stable on State Street near Willett across from the apartment house now known as 355 State. The trolleys were braked by hand and once in a while would get out of control on the hills, but there never seemed to be any great calamities. The open trolleys were a delight on hot summer evenings and Sunday afternoons.

Some there are who will remember a number of the old established businesses and stores now gone but not to be forgotten by those who lived in Albany then. There were Coburn's Ice Cream Parlors: Hinman's Bakery selling the famous Hinman's crackers on Broadway, Hobb's Grocery serving the elite of North Albany, located at Clinton Avenue and Ten Broeck Street; Mason's Candies, selling the famous contrabands from Washington Avenue. Hagaman's

Bakery had ten to twelve branch stores throughout the city. When my father was driving a delivery wagon along Broadway one day, he saw Mr. Hagaman peddling pies from a basket on his arm. Mr. Hagaman stopped my father and told him he was tired out and asked if my father knew of a good horse he could get. Father replied: "Yes, I have one and I will send it to you. Try him out and if you like him, keep him and send me the money." Nothing further was said, no money passed and one day my father received one hundred dollars from Mr. Hagaman and there began the famous bakery.

The blizzard of 1888 paralyzed Albany. My father took four of his horses and a big sleigh used in the dairy business and drove over to a large farm on South Lake Avenue. In going through what is now the grounds of the Albany Medical Center Hospital and psychiatric buildings, the four horses sank in the snow and were buried and the men had to shovel them out. They did, however, reach the farmer and loaded the sleigh with cans of milk. But before they could get back to the dairy, the milk was gone in response to women screaming from windows for milk for the children.

In conclusion, let me say in those days Albany was a wonderful, historic, friendly, growing village with wide-awake, energetic, peace-loving citizens whose dream of advancement we are now enjoying.

— Ruth Miner

AN ITALO-AMERICAN'S LIFE IN ALBANY

In 1903 my parents, my brother John, age six, my sister Helen, age five, and myself, age two, immigrated to America from Castelfiorentino, a town located a few miles outside of Florence, Italy. My parents' names were Guiseppe (Joseph) and Rosa Mugnaini. The surname was inadvertently anglicized when my father wrote our name on papers for my sister and brother to give to their school teacher. The Italian script was so different from the English that she read it as Marguin, and in due time that actually became our name.

We arrived in Pompton Lakes, New Jersey, where my uncle, my father's brother, was located and where a job awaited my father in a steel mill called Ludlum Steel and Spring Company. You have heard the expression "another day another dollar." Well, that was a fact, it was what my father was paid, one dollar a day. In this day and age it seems unbelievable that a family of five could possibly live on such an income. But we did and we never felt poor. We were well-fed and clothed and lived in a decent cottage owned by the company which also ran a store where we purchased our groceries. My mother knew how to stretch a dollar; baked all the bread, did all the cooking and of course canned everything from our fine garden. She made all our clothes and could sew beautifully, knit and crochet.

What my parents lacked in formal education they made up for in their wisdom, their great understanding of human nature and their sense of values. I particularly remember my mother telling us that one cannot live alone; we all need friends and in order to have them we must **be** a friend. I expect she was a romantic because she loved to read Italian love stories and listen to the series of stories being broadcast on the radio, such as "Helen Trent" and "John's Other Wife." She came from a family of twelve children. When we used to scrap among ourselves, as children will, she would be shocked. She said they never fought in her family because they loved each other and would not think of such a thing. Well, we loved each other too, but I am afraid we kept right on scrapping.

I shall always cherish the memory of the times when my sister and I would get in bed with my father on Sunday mornings while my mother was downstairs preparing breakfast. He would tell us all about the history of Italy and of Italy's famous men such as Dante, Leonardo Da Vinci, and Michaelangelo. He also sang folk songs and songs from operas for us. We spoke the standard literary Italian at home, as is spoken in Tuscany, except we children spoke English to each other.

My father's reason for immigrating here was to earn enough money to pay off the mortgage on his farm which had been previously owned by his father. After my grandfather's death, my father had gone into debt to buy his two brothers' shares. They were not interested in farming, but farming was what my father loved. His one desire was to return to Italy and live peacefully on his own farm.

In 1907 the steel plant was sold. Some of the employees, including my father, were transferred to Watervliet, New York. By this time another child had been added to our family, my brother, George, born in 1906. The president of the Watervliet plant was none other than Edwin Corning, father of Albany Mayor Erastus Corning, and a former Lieutenant Governor of New York. He was a fine man to work for.

In 1915 my father had achieved his goal and our return to Italy was planned in earnest. However, it was not in the cards for us to go. Confrontations that proved to be forerunners of World War I had begun between Italy and Turkey. Our plans were cancelled because my brother John, just eighteen years of age, would have been immediately inducted into the Italian army if we had returned. My father's dream never materialized. In April 1915 he was accidentally electrocuted by a high voltage wire that was hanging from a pole which was being moved during an expansion operation at the plant. He was just fifty years old.

No other member of my parents' families has immigrated here. However, I had the pleasure of visiting my relatives in Florence, Castelfiorentino, Pisa, Empoli and Certaldo, when my husband and I went to Europe in 1965. It was a real thrill to meet them after hearing so much about them from my parents. We felt a mutual closeness and the time we had together was all too short.

I was fourteen at the time of my father's death and a student at St. Brigid's parochial school, then called Watervliet Academy. In addition to grammar school it also had a high school, all in the same building. Two grades were in each room and we were taught by the good sisters of St. Joseph. Fr. Looney was the pastor and he would personally come in the classroom to teach us Latin. The high school was discontinued in the very early twenties. An annex, a separate building, was eventually built so that now there are two buildings for the grammar school.

St. Brigid's church is located on the corner of Seventh Street and Fourth Avenue, Watervliet. The school, convent, rectory and hall are all close by. My sister, my daughter and I were all married there, several of my grandchildren were baptized there, and four of them attended school there before moving to Westchester County in 1966. Also, my daughter taught kindergarten there before moving away. My parents and older brother John were buried from St. Brigid's.

I have fond memories of the Erie Canal; it ran right smack through the city of Watervliet. We had wonderful times skating on the canal all the way down to North Albany. It was so much fun. There were bridges every three or four blocks which were needed for access to the area "across the canal" as that section is still called. The bridge at First Street and Third Avenue was called Schuyler Bridge, because of the Philip Schuyler home situated there. The area is now called Schuyler Flatts. The section of Watervliet south of the Arsenal (which dates back to Civil War time) is referred to as Port Schuyler. After the Erie Canal was abandoned, the bridges were torn down and the big ditch was filled in.

I also remember when there were no automobiles on the streets. I recall the ragman going along with his horse and wagon shouting "Rags, Rags." There were no supermarkets; groceries were generally delivered to the house, at which time an order for the next delivery was taken. We had no phone. I remember the steamboats that traveled on the Hudson River from Troy to Albany and back to Troy. One of them was called the "Quackenbush." It provided many a happy Sunday afternoon outing. Also I recall the ferryboat that ran from the foot of Sixteenth Street, Watervliet, to Ferry Street in Troy across the river, the fare was two cents each way. It was discontinued around 1914. I remember the trolley cars, especially the open ones in the summer that we liked best; the fare was five cents. Ice cream sodas and the movies were ten cents a loaf of bread ten cents. We could also buy a small ice cream cone for two cents.

I left high school shortly after my father's death and entered Albany Business College, then located on the corner of Columbia and North Pearl Streets. I graduated in 1917 and, at the age of sixteen, went to work at Ludlum Steel Company as a stenographer. In those days nothing was deducted from our pay checks—no taxes, no insurance, no pension, no social security or hospitalization. After working there ten years I left to marry Walter N. Connell, a Watervlietian of Irish descent. He was one of eleven children in a wonderful family. He became the first circulation manager of "The Evangelist," our Albany Diocesan newspaper, which started in 1926 and is still being published. We were married in St. Brigid's church by his brother, the Reverend William B. Connell. Walter died on March 9, 1945 after a long illness. In the meantime I had returned to work at Allegheny Ludlum Steel Corporation. The company had merged with Allegheny Steel of Pennsylvania; hence the change in name.

I worked there fifteen more years and then remarried. Again Fr. Connell performed the ceremony. My second husband, Newton F. Ronan, was a native of Albany. As a boy he lived on the site of the present State Education Building. His grandfather, Newton W. Thompson, had come to Albany in 1862 from Vermont and was a well-known Albany attorney, a law partner of James W. Bentley. Newton Ronan's father died when he was very young, and he was raised by his grandparents because his mother, Julia Thompson Ronan, went to work for the state. She was Chief Warrant Clerk for the State Controller when she retired after forty-five years. She was also a well-known singer with a rich dramatic soprano voice, a soloist with the Musical Arts Club of Troy.

Newton Ronan began working for the State Department of Public Works in 1911 and subsequently became a professional engineer. In 1956 Governor Harriman appointed him Superintendent of Operations and Maintenance for the State Department of Public Works. After the change in administrations, he continued to work as Assistant District Engineer until his retirement in 1962 after fifty-one years of service. He died on Thanksgiving Day 1977 at the age of eighty-five. He was a remarkable person who, I believe, never had an enemy.

I am not alone. My brother and sister are living. I have a daughter and four grandchildren, five step-children and twenty-three step-great-grandchildren with all of whom I continue to have close relationships.

— Lee Ronan

GRANDMA NIELSON—
Nineteenth Century Career Woman

Nowadays when I hear women talking of having a career or of being married and having babies, I can't help but think of Grandma. She was married, bore fourteen children and managed a successful business. She was a remarkable woman. In addition, she was the strongest argument I know for the saying that the good one does lives on, even unto the third and fourth generations. Although I was only six months old when she died, people I scarcely know tell me today, "Any favors we can do for 'Mama Nielson's' family can't be too much."

Actually, Grandma was no mild, even-tempered saint. Any woman who accomplished in a day all that she did, had to have a deal of energy and pep that sometimes overflowed on a quick tongue with no time for wasting on tact. Youngsters coming with muddy feet on her freshly cleaned floor were as apt as not to find themselves swept out, along with the dirt they had brought in, without any "by-your-leaves" — as her grandchildren well remember.

Her story really began back in Denmark where as a girl of nineteen she was slated to marry a member of the lower nobility. Considering him something of a dolt, and having met a fascinating tailor in Copenhagen's leading clothing store, she didn't wait for her parents' consent but decided to marry the man of her choice and to go with him to America to make their fortune.

She used to tell of her last time in her home church where, as she walked decorously down the aisle with her mother, her dashing young man (a description I have always found hard to associate with my jolly, bald and bewhiskered Grandpa) whispered to her a meeting place where they could make their plans. Her mother had frowningly remarked, "That young man is mumbling something with his mouth but he doesn't say anything."

"Oh joy," Grandma thought, her heart pounding with excitement, "How little he has said, but how much it means!"

Having made her decision, Grandma convinced her parents of the seriousness of her desires and was married at home with their blessing. The next day the bride and groom left for the New World.

Once in America, Grandpa started his little tailoring shop and Grandma began having her babies that seemed to come with astonishing regularity until she was almost fifty. In some of her more discouraged moments in later life she would tell her girls who were, themselves, preparing to marry, "Remember, girls. Don't have too many babies. One is heaven; two are fine; three can go; but four, five, six, seven, eight—that's terrible."

However, none of her babies ever lacked for love and affection. My mother, who was twelfth, had her full share of her mother's and father's attention and, in addition, the adoration of the older children. The deep gouges in the baseboard of her living room are mute evidence of the many times carriage wheels were scraped against it as the babies were pushed to and fro, preening while the older children talked and sang to them.

During her early years in America, Grandma was not so content as she became in her middle and later years. In Denmark she had been used to a farily leisurely existence as a young girl - nights at Tivoli or the opera and weekend bicycle excursions to the seashore with her friends. And, much as she loved Grandpa and the children, at times she became discouraged with the plain square home he had built for her and the hard work and unceasing care of the children.

After she had lived in America for somewhat more than five years and had had three of her children, she finally persuaded Grandpa to go back to Denmark. She was eager to sell their property in America, pull up all roots and go "home." But Grandpa would agree only to the trip; he wanted to leave their house in charge of a friend with instructions to take care of it until he should receive word to sell. Finally the great day arrived with Grandma and Grandpa and children all dressed in their best and on the boat, proud to be returning on "second class" when Grandma and Grandpa had come over "steerage."

Just what happened over in Denmark has never been too clear to the rest of the family. Obviously, remembrances of the past are always colored and glorified by the strong physical and emotional exuberance of youth. Also, in five years, friends had scattered or changed and, astonishingly, Grandma found that even she was not the same Marie who had left Denmark. And, probably most important of all, she became convinced that opportunities for developing new businesses were not so good in Denmark as they were in America.

When at last the Statue of Liberty returned to her view, Grandma sighed contentedly and, with her arm in Grandpa's, murmured, "Now, Peter, we **have** come home." As time went on, Grandma found that, though Grandpa *was* an excellent tailor, he was not a good businessman. That was why she became more and more the business head of the family.

The tailor shop was enlarged to make room for Grandpa's assistants, a large millinery section was added over which Grandma presided with the help of the older girls as they reached an age when they could baste and sew, and dry goods and notions were stocked as the demand for them grew. The business flourished under guidance.

From all the surrounding farms their many Danish friends would come to spend a day at "Mama and Papa Nielson's" where they would order the lovely poplin suits for the ladies and plumed hats then in style and, in fact, clothed the whole family right from father's tight-trousered, checkered suit down through the children's winter coats. That always meant an invitation to lunch - a quick setting of the big square table with Grandma's favorite red tablecloth and her blue willow china, putting on the soup tureen for her delicious "bagte boller" soup (beef broth with large pieces of carrots and celery and homemade butter noodles and meatballs floating around) and not forgetting the ever-present coffee cups.

That soup of Grandma's became famous for other reasons, too, for she was never too busy to send one of her youngsters with a pail of it to her neighbors who were sick or having babies. In fact, as Grandma's own family grew, it seemed as though her capacity to mother all her neighbors grew as well until everyone who knew her at all called her "Mama Nielson."

This was also a time of heavy immigration from Denmark and it was not at all uncommon for Grandma to take in young single relatives or friends of relatives and to watch over their physical and moral welfare until they were established in respectable jobs or had married and settled down with another nice young immigrant who had found his way to Grandma's door. Evenings they could be found with the family, crowded around the organ (later the piano) singing and holding hands.

Some of these members of Grandma's extended family circle have said to me, "If it weren't for Mama Nielson, it's hard to say just what I'd be like today. There were lots of temptations for young people away from their families in those days as well as now. But with all the jolly times at her house and with her trust and faith in us, we couldn't let her down."

Grandma's many home charities kept her so occupied that she never had much time or sympathy for foreign missions. That was one point on which she and Grandpa disagreed. They were both active supporters and generous contributors to the little Lutheran church they had helped to build. But, when appeals were made for the foreign mission fields, it was always Grandpa who dug a little deeper in his pockets than Grandma quite approved of. Although, in general, they had no secrets from each other, their respective convictions on this score tended to keep their left hand from knowing what their right hand did.

One time, however, Grandpa's extreme generosity caught up with him. He had contributed heavily, personally, to the pastor's pet mission project but had forgotten to warn him that it was an anonymous gift. Next Sunday in the church bulletin the name of Peter Nielson was prominent at the head of the list of contributors, together with the amount he had given. Of course, it didn't take long after the service for the church members to make congratulatory comments to Grandma and Grandpa, all of which Grandma acknowledged graciously and Grandpa a little sheepishly, wondering what to expect when he arrived home.

"Now, Papa," she said when they were inside their own front door, "I think tomorrow I call Doctor Brown to see what he can do for Tommy." (Tommy was the son of the widow who lived upstairs and whose health Grandma had been worried about.) Grandpa knew he was vulnerable and he cheerfully paid the doctor's bills, thankful to be let off so easily. As for Grandma, she never even mentioned the foreign mission.

As Grandma's many duties crowded in on her, she learned to routinize her chores and to assign duties to her growing family. As in most families, Monday was wash day and Tuesday ironing day. But for Grandma's family, Wednesday was "buying in" day. That was the day when she dressed up in her best black dress with the freshly laundered, white embroidered collar-and-cuff set brought over from Denmark and went by trolley sometimes to Troy, but usually to Albany about twelve miles away. Always, too, she wore her best spick-and-span gloves and had her second-best gloves in her pocketbook, ready to change to, in case she decided to carry some of the small packages home.

One of the older girls (Grandma was able to raise only one boy past babyhood) usually was left in charge of the store and another in charge of the house and the smaller children, while still another had the privilege of accompanying Grandma on the trip. This was always a treat, but also an educational experience, for one needed to learn how to judge the quality of the materials, to determine what novelties might sell and to decide what was really a bargain.

Then, on Thursday and Friday, the goods were priced, with both the code telling how much had been paid for them and the amount they were to sell for, and were put on the shelves for Saturday, the busiest day of the week when the store was kept open until ten o'clock. On Saturday, too, the "big" dinner was cooked, the pot roast and vegetables and pies and cakes, for Sunday was the day of rest, when dinner was warmed over from Saturday's.

On Sunday, church was regularly attended from ten-thirty to twelve, dinner was eaten and then the children were all packed off to Sunday School from one to three. Grandpa was superintendent and the oldest girls were teachers; so that left Grandma her two golden hours of the week, home alone (except for the tiniest babies) and duty-bound to rest. Two hours in the whole week that she could call her own. And yet when the children and Grandpa returned, she would hold out her arms to them and say, "How good it is to have you home again. It's been so lonesome around here for such a long time without you!"

The love that Grandma and Grandpa always had for each other mellowed and deepened as they worked and lived together. Grandma's seriousness of purpose and Grandpa's lightness and jollity gradually merged until they were both the better for their years together.

As he aged, Grandpa became very deaf. He also became somewhat forgetful but, mostly, he just developed his man's habit of never being able to find anything for the simple reason that he expected to see the lost article without moving objects that might restrict his view. All of this tried Grandma's patience and she would scold, "Papa, sometimes I think you can neither hear nor see." Then he would grab her around the waist, pretending he couldn't reach quite all the way, and dance her around and laugh, and all the children would laugh and join in the fun until at last she was out of breath and Grandma's stern face, too, would break into laugh wrinkles and the household would be completely happy and gay again.

For all Grandma's and Grandpa's hard work, they were not able to accumulate a lot of money. Grandma used to say that other women had time to go downtown each day and to stop in the drugstore for a soda. She felt, then, that she was entitled to the "five times five" cents a week (equivalent of their expenditure) for her "nest egg". This sum she carefully put away each week in the local bank, and even Grandpa didn't know exactly how much she had there. Then one day the news came. The president of the bank had mishandled the funds, and there was a run on the bank. Of course, there was no federal insurance on deposits in those days, and most of Grandma's "soda money" was never returned to her.

And then Grandpa's complete trust in human honor led him several times to sign notes for friends in need, only to be disappointed as they defaulted. At one time, in fact, the business was in danger of foreclosure because of a bad note. But Grandpa kept on trusting — he couldn't stand not to.

And so the wealth they left was in precepts and examples of happy, courageous, outgoing living, cached away in the minds and hearts of their children, who, in turn, passed these on to their children. When one of us quotes today, "Pick your roses when you may," or, "This job must be done and that one mustn't be neglected," we smile at each other and say, "Yes, that's what my mother always said that her mother said." And, as we have children, in their bringing up will go, along with all the child development theories we have learned, a great deal of what we consider "instinctive" theories of our own — in truth, Grandma's wisdom come down through the ages.

— Agnes Beck Vedder

REMEMBERING THE TWENTIES

I remember high school days as the "Roaring Twenties" drew to a close, a wacky, wonderful decade of fantastically soaring prosperity paced by the stock market which had no ceiling — it was thought. We sang — "Life is just a bowl of cherries, don't take it serious" while plunking on a ukelele; danced the wild Charleston; rode in car "rumble seats."

We fellows had slicked down hair parted in the middle with louse ladders, as our long sideburns were called. We wore crew neck sweaters and bow ties, raccoon coats, knickers and argyle socks — the louder the pattern the better. The girls' styles featured lowdown waistlines, short skirts with dimpled knees, topped by fancy garters to hold up rolled silk stockings, peeping out from under the hemline.

"There's no tomorrow," another song went.

It was the time of Lucky Lindy, the Lone Eagle; classic ex-Marine boxer Gene Tunney vs. the brawling Manassa Mauler, Jack Dempsey; the immortal

Babe Ruth and the fabulous New York Yankees winning championships with monotonous regularity in Yankee Stadium—"The House That Ruth Built."

During those same days I remember the Hudson River Day Line whose graceful steamers with names as Alexander Hamilton, DeWitt Clinton, Peter Stuyvesant, sailed the Hudson River between Albany and New York City. The boat dock was on Broadway near the D&H Railroad Building and the ticket office, now a gourmet French cuisine restaurant, still stands there. A round trip to Kingston Point was a class week "must" for senior high school groups in the area with a three-piece band providing on-board dancing and sharing a box lunch for a couple provided by that special girl friend. Wonderful, nostalgic days with talk and dreams of the certain bright tomorrow after school days.

I remember the rude awakening after Black Friday in the stock market in 1929 which heralded the Great Depression. Unemployment, breadlines, soup kitchens and apple sellers on every street corner. "Brother, can you spare a dime?" was then the new and doleful theme song. Memories echoing down the corridors of the misty past of an incredible era, an unforgettable experience for all of us who were witnesses to it.

— George F. Venter, Jr.

NO! NOT PAPA!

On a beautiful April morning in 1974, I was washing breakfast dishes and looked through the high window over the sink at the apple tree and noticed touches of red, unopened buds among the new green leaves. It reminded me of another April, 30 years before, when my mother had died and how sad I had been to think she'd missed the miracle of the opening blossoms. Thoughts of her took me back still further, to the sad day when Papa had died and how Mama took some of my hurt away by making me see that death is as natural a part of our existence as the recurrence of Spring.

Sometimes, as a child, when thinking hurt, I'd crawl under my bed and sit with my back against the cool plaster wall. I like the dark. It doesn't ask questions. It hasn't any face. No hands to make you go or stay. I recall the darkest moment of my young life, when I went under my bed to think.

Wasn't it only yesterday when Papa showed Mary and me how to play his guitar? I had had to sit on the floor, because my lap was too small to hold it otherwise.

"Papa, tell us again how you got it?" Mary, who was thirteen, wanted to know. I did too. I was eight.

Papa's smile had made the edges of his blue eyes crinkle. His face was rosy. His dark, red hair curled a little over his ears. His voice was like singing when he just spoke. As a boy he had worked for a man whose big house was filled with musical instruments. Papa whistled as he worked, but the man didn't like whistling. So, one day he said, "Ed, if you'll stop whistling, and learn to play it, you can have any instrument in this room!"

Papa said, "Wow! That's easy." He had chosen a Martin guitar.

And now, from under the bed, I could see the big, wooden guitar case leaning against the wall. It was ugly, black, and awkward-looking, but I knew that there was lovely music inside it. Already I'd learned that covers seldom give away the secrets that are underneath. Even people can look ugly until they smile and then, a kind of light comes out of them.

Mama had tried to tell me that the reason Papa hadn't been in the orchard was because he had died. She asked me if I'd come with her. Didn't I want to see him before he went away? I had stamped my foot and said, "No!"

And then, I'd gone under my bed to try to get away from that awful thought: Papa was going away? I couldn't stay under the bed any longer. I simply had to find Papa. He'd make everthing all good again.

So, I went alone to find him . . . I looked in the orchard first. It was his favorite place. He called it his workshop.

"Lovely all the year," he said, "Pink in spring, white in winter, green in summer, and red-yellow in October!"

Then I'd looked in his den. A tall man was asleep on his cot. He looked like Papa but the rosy cheeks were gray; the warm, freckled hands were pale and cold. Someone else lay there wearing Papa's best suit!

"You're not my father!" I'd screamed. "Where is he?" Then I'd run out of the room and downstairs, right into Mama's arms. We went into the living room. She sat down in the little gray rocker, by the fireplace; she didn't say anything but rocked me close for a long time.

Then she asked me if I remembered how caterpillars made chrysalides. She went through every step. (I never knew that Mama liked caterpillars.) She said that everything that lives will die, and, like the caterpillar, will live again in a different way.

"Like Mary's cecropia?" I wanted to know.

"Yes," she'd answered, "Like that lovely moth. But when people die, . . . there is a difference."

By then I wanted more information. Surely Papa wouldn't become a moth.

"Remember how empty a seed gets when it sprouts?"

I nodded. I remembered Papa showing me how the food went out of the bean seed.

"Well, it's empty because the seed has to die in order to become a plant." Mama said that when people die, God has a special way of changing them. She said that love has a lot to do with it.

"You know that God loves Papa, don't you?"

"Of course. Everybody loves Papa."

But that day there were pink carnations on our door, and flowers all over the house, and the minister came. All our cousins came, but we didn't play games. Then, some men slid a big, long box into a wagon with glass sides. (Papa would have loved the shiny black horses!) and I stayed with Mrs. Ballard while Mama and Mary and Marion went to the cemetery. The house was too quiet. I went back under my bed. All I could think of was Papa's laugh, his songs, and his long arms lifting me to his shoulders, and . . . I just had to cry . . .

We lived in the country. For both my parents, living things were more than birds and beans. They owed their very lives to God because He created them and put part of Himself into them. We children grew up with more than respect for the out-of-doors. There was a kind of awe and wonder about life which made those places where life was, not unlike a church.

Of course we learned of Jesus, his death and resurrection. He became more important to us as we matured. But there was always something holy about all of life, and God was the Almighty Father of us all.

If my little granddaughter ever comes to me when she finds death too hard to understand, and the loss of a loved one too deep a grief to bear, I hope that I may be able to show her that God's love of His children holds them close, even in death, as Mama showed it to me.

— Margaret A. Wheeler

A PIONEER CHILDHOOD: HEALTH, EDUCATION AND WORK

Life on our Minnesota homestead during the first quarter of this century was dedicated to health, education and work. These were our family's prime concerns and our lives depended on them. Our bodies were the temples of our souls and respect for health became a tenet of our religious beliefs. Mama said, "You were born with a healthy body and a good mind; that is your inheritance!" It was hard to know which was more important: good health or a good education. "Get an education!" was the directive, the admonition, the slogan and goal of all our ambitions. Education would open the way for us to escape from our poverty and rural isolation. Food, shelter, clothing, socialization, saving our souls, character-building and work were also essential. We soon learned that the greatest of these was work. Mother challenged us. "Learn to work, so you can work to learn, so you can work to live more abundantly."

In October, 1890, strong-willed sixteen-year-old Mathilda arrived in the United States, all alone: an ambitious, adventurous, romantic, Swedish immigrant determined to find a new life. Father had emigrated from Sweden eight years earlier. They met at the Augustana Lutheran Church in Minneapolis and were married there two days after my mother's eighteenth birthday. Even at that time a woman had to be eighteen or have a parent's consent to marry. A few years later they moved to a log cabin which Papa had built on a 160 acre homestead in the woods 15 miles from Mora and 80 miles north of Minneapolis. Because they arrived on Decoration Day they named their new home "Decoration Valley".

The only medicine I can recall was a bottle of iodine which sat way up on the top shelf of the dish cupboard, out of reach except to grown-ups. I don't remember any new bottles over the years so there couldn't have been a great many bites and cuts. For insect bites we had baking soda, also good for upset stomach and heartburn. Mama had heartburn often, perhaps because of her fourteen pregnancies. One of my sisters and I had bad leg aches, usually at night. I remember Papa, awakened by my crying, going out to the barn for the horse liniment. I wondered if the horses' legs hurt as much as mine. My sister and I had polio that epidemic summer of 1916. I vaguely remember being carried by an older brother, burning hot and unable to move. There was nothing to do but pray and a lot of prayer pulled us through with no residual paralysis and kept the polio from spreading to the rest of the family. Perhaps the leg aches and the need for horse liniment massages were due to that dread disease.

Once my sister and I hid behind a haystack most of a "caster-oil day." We found to our sorrow that castor oil tasted as bad in the afternoon as it did in the morning.

Early one summer morning when I was five there was a great to-do. Mama announced that we would all go to Braham to have our tonsils out. No, not all would go. Only five of the children and Mama could get in the Maxwell with my brother, the owner-driver. All I recall of that operation is lying on the "ironing board" and, as I went under the ether, the sensation of floating over and under, around and around the ironing board. Oh yes, I also remember the soft oatmeal for breakfast afterwards. I didn't like oatmeal for years. The older siblings remember more. The doctor apparently was overwhelmed at the prospect of five tonsillectomies, one right after the other, and had fortified himself generously with strong drink. Whatever the reason, I know that he also took the uvula and part of the soft palate from three of us. On the homeward trip from that memorable outing, Mama and my three-year-old sister were thrown from the car as we turned the corner a half mile from home. Neither was hurt, and the car was later pulled from the ditch, but the accident capped an eventful two days for five tired, dusty, hot, tonsil-less Petersons.

By the next year my tonsils had grown back and my mother took me for repeat surgery. By then my leg aches and "growing pains" in my chest were a matter of family concern. The doctor found some irregularity in the heart beat, but said that I would outgrow it and the growing pains. Sometime in the winter when I was eleven, another doctor ordered me to rest for a month and gave me digitalis drops to quiet the heart's irregular beat. I stayed home, took the medicine, tied a quilt, and kept up with my eighth grade school work.

I have no idea how much the tonsil-doctor charged for the five operations and our overnight stay in his hospital, but I did once ask my father how much the doctor charged when I was born. For me he came twice. The night the Titanic went down they were sure I was coming and called the doctor all the way out from Mora. But, as Papa said, "It was the stirrings in the atmosphere from that tragedy in the Atlantic, not Mildred wanting to be born." Nine days later the doctor came again. "The charge," Papa said, "was a dollar a mile." I have no idea how much of that went to the livery stable for the horse and buggy or if he charged for the return trip at the same rate. If the bill was $30 for each trip, I was an expensive baby. Of course, at that time there was no prenatal or postnatal care. I was the twelfth child and the first to be delivered by a physician. Midwives attended the earlier births. All of us were born at home. Mama always dreaded the thought of going to a hospital. She said she would die if she went to one. Finally at age sixty-three when her youngest was nineteen she went for repair surgery to cure the effects of too many deliveries without postpartum care and died as a result of a surgical accident.

One of my sisters, the ninth child, told me that she had never asked questions about sex and procreation. She had it all figured out. After each baby was born, the doctor or midwife called Papa into the room and that was when he or she supervised the breeding for the next child. Although we children were kept inside when bulls or stallions were brought to service the farm animals, we had enought exposure to the facts of animal life to think we knew all about where babies came from. The babies arrived every two years quite regularly for twenty-six years, so it is easy to understand why a child might think the pregnancies were planned. When the fourteenth child was born I was in school, but my four-year-old sister was at home ready to assist the doctor. She had picked the baby she wanted out of the Sears Roebuck catalog and showed it to him as soon as he arrived. He asked if she would be satisfied with a mama doll instead. Her answer was, "No, I want a real baby. I don't care whether it's a boy or a girl or a Swede." It was a real boy and a Swede.

Smallpox vaccinations became available about 1919. My older brother, Emil, went to town for the vaccine and vaccinated all of us. My mother's was the only one that took. In 1923 all school children in Mora were vaccinated.

In so large a family there were, inevitably, accidents, emergencies, serious illnesses and death. Once a teen-age brother shot a hole in his heel as he went through a fence carrying a loaded shotgun. When my oldest brother was sixteen he had a ruptured appendix; the surgeon gave him no chance to live. He is now eighty-six. In the fall of 1903 the eighteen-month-old seventh child died of diphtheria. Papa made the little coffin and bundled the family into the wooden-wheeled wagon for the long trip over the tote roads to Mora. There he had to dig the grave and bury the baby himself because the townsfolk were so afraid of diphtheria. The six-year-old brother who went along on that sad trip was sick with a high fever; he had diptheria too. One boy had died shortly after birth before the family moved to the farm and a second had died at two months. When Oscar died in 1903 there remained three boys and a girl; between 1904 and 1918, three more boys and four more girls were born. In 1979 there are still nine of us, all over sixty.

Our diet must have been adequate despite our poverty. We had chickens, eggs, milk, vegetables and each fall we butchered our steers and hogs and canned, dried, smoked and salted the meat. Every meal was built around potatoes and peeling potatoes was the first order of business twice a day.

Mama baked many loaves of bread every week. We bought flour and sugar in 100 pound bags and made dish towels from sugar sacks and aprons, petticoats, bloomers and boys' shirts from flour sacks. If we ran out of bread, Mama would make baking powder biscuits or corn bread, and to this day I think of them as mere substitutes for bread.

Sugar was scarce and expensive during World War I, and we rationed it in little glass jars, each labeled with a child's name. There was much sugar lending, borrowing and dealing among us. We had a favorite after-school snack, soda crackers soaked in hot water and topped with heavy cream and sugar. I was teased for saying "The cream settles to the top." I would still say that if everything were not so homogenized. When we were out of oatmeal or cream-of-wheat, Mama would make something unspecial for our breakfast; flour stirred into boiling water which we ate with milk and sugar as though it were "real food."

On the farm we had apples, strawberries, wild grapes, blackberries, gooseberries and raspberries, and there was a cranberry bog not far away. Blueberries were also abundant. Once we and the neighbors had a festival after a day of berry picking. Blueberries in ten-gallon milk cans stood at the corner of the house and everyone ate and ate. I must have eaten too many; I can still leave them alone. Occasionally we had bananas, but I was eight before I saw and tasted my first orange.

Mother inspired us to get an education. She knew that our futures depended on it. I don't know how much schooling she had had in Sweden, but when she came to Minneapolis and started working as a maid, she went to the neighborhood elementary school and registered in the first grade. She wanted to learn to read, write and speak English. She was a "quick learner" and finished the grades in a few months.

For the oldest children on the farm there was a one-room school about a mile away, in session four or five months a year. There were few books; words and pictures were on flip charts. Four of the eight pupils were Petersons. My oldest sister started at four and a half, and in the heavy snows of that winter Papa often had to carry her to school piggyback. She was then the only girl in the family and delighted in playing school. In fact, we all played school more often than any other game. The one-room school was a great institution. Our teachers were young, dedicated, and skillful. There were no age limits so we Petersons all started at four or five, and, when we could, skipped grades. We were anxious to hurry through each school and go on to the next.

In 1909 a Consolidated School was built at nearby Warman, a wide place in the road with a general store and two houses. The school was a two-classroom, two-story frame building with living quarters for the two teachers and a library on the upper floor. In winter sled runners replaced the wheels on the black, covered, school rig in which we were transported to school. When it was very cold we each carried a carpet-covered metal footwarmer. We loved school. The worst punishment we could imagine was to miss a day of school. On March 5, 1918, a raging blizzard piled drifts head high. It was also brother Leonard's tenth birthday and Mama had made a pan of fudge for him to take to school. The three of us bundled up in our several pairs of socks, sweaters, coats, scarves and mittens and carrying the footwarmers, books and candy struggled out to the main road where we waited for the rig. When it arrived, it was empty save for the driver who hadn't expected any pupils in such a storm. He swore, "These g--d-- Petersons, they've got to get an education! No one else would send kids out on a day like this." A mile from home the road became totally impassable and with great difficulty the driver turned the rig around and took us home, cursing all the way. "Petersons! Education! No one else!" That day, indeed, there was no school; we were not counted absent. He was right, though, about the Petersons; no other family in the county was so determined to get an education.

I attended Warman School for three years. In the first grade I learned to read, write script and do simple arithmetic. I still have the certificate showing that I was neither absent nor tardy. My older sisters and brother had spoken only Swedish at home so they learned English in the first grade. We learned to read by reading real literature, no "Dick and Jane" or made-up stories with limited numbers of new words added each year. We read and memorized much poetry. Every Friday afternoon we had programs, and each pupil had to "speak a piece." One of our learning games at home was the poetry contest. We would see which of us could say at least four lines of the largest number of poems.

Several times each year parents, teachers and students had a basket social. Girls and women would prepare box suppers for two, in the fanciest possible packages, and the men and boys would bid on the baskets and eat with the lucky lady. Even the young children participated. The entertainment was furnished by the pupils. I remember reading a long poem entitled "I Can't Get My Courtin' Done." Everyone applauded. I had no idea what "courtin'" was nor that my serious expression as I read the humorous lines was a big part of its success. I was only six.

We, of course, knew nothing of educational psychologists' caution against sibling rivalry nor had we heard about "birth order and descending I Q." Much of our learning took place at home in an atmosphere characterized by both cooperation and competition. Older children taught the younger ones how to read before they went to school. Each day we discussed what we had learned in school as we helped with supper or did the dishes. We were intense rivals for the best report cards, best speller, highest marks in arithmetic. Spelling bees, number games, poetry and Bible verse contests sharpened our wits and enhanced our verbal skills. They also taught us to be argumentative. Every morning some one would ask, "Do you think you'll ever amount to anything?" or "What are you going to be when you grow up and why?"

Although it was all very stimulating it was also possible to develop an inferiority complex in such a constantly aggressive environment. There was no place to hide, no way you could be by yourself and set your own pace. Four of the older children worked their ways through high school. All of us supported ourselves completely after high school. Mama's ambitions for us and her sacrifices and encouragement paid off. Eight of us attended the University of Minnesota and among us we have a total of fifteen earned degrees, including three doctorates, more than any other single family ever got at that large university.

However, Mama had an unfulfilled dream. She loved music and hoped and prayed that some of her children would have musical talent. She must have been lonely in that crowd of tone-deaf musical illiterates. She worked out by the day, carried the mail, sold milk and eggs, scrimped and saved to buy a used piano and pay for music lessons. When the big house burned, the piano was gone, but she bought an organ and hired another teacher. When we moved to town she bought another second-hand piano and all of us took lessons for years without progress. Poor Mama.

Farming was an endless struggle to overcome the elements and eke out a meager living from the unproductive land. We were always very poor. Many hands did not make light work, but necessity made workers of us all. Although the burden of such heavy work as plowing, haying, shoveling snow fell on the older children, even the littlest ones had their chores and learned to milk cows, feed chickens and do housework. The summer I was eleven I had my first paid job doing housework for $1.50 per week on a nearby farm.

Work and learning were never separate. There was always someone who went up and down the rows reading aloud as the others planted and weeded. While milking or doing dishes we recited poetry or had spelling contest. Mama continually recited to us from her store of maxims and homilies to "build our characters" and inspire us in our work. "There is no shame in honest work."

"Never put off 'til tomorrow what you can do today." "It is my will that you should have it, get it the best way you can." "Hard work never hurt anybody." "Your time will come." "Where there's a will, there's a way." "Need has no law." Always there was the expectation that despite our poverty, the skills we learned and the work habits we acquired would enable us to "get an education" and "get ahead in the world."

As I look back at my early childhood, first on the homestead which my immigrant parents had wrested from the virgin land, and then in the small town to which the family moved to escape the harsh farm life and to enable us to attend the town high school, I know that by comparison to most of my peers in Albany, I grew up in quite a different world. In many ways that frontier, pioneer existence must have been similar to rural life in colonial New England, but by now those experiences are recorded only in dusty books and not in the memories of my friends and contemporaries.

— Mildred Peterson Zimmermann

From original by: Sister Mary Charles Lilly

Beaver swimming with a branch to be used for food or building maintenance.

II. HISTORICAL AND OTHER ARTICLES

AN EARLY CONSERVATIONIST

On June 1, 1978, we visited the new museum in the South Mall. The exhibits are splendid! The New York State bird—the bluebird—has a prominent place and can be viewed by many people at one time.

Formerly, the ornithology of the New York State museum was housed in the top of the Education Building. The original ninety paintings of birds by Louis Agassiz Fuertes were also housed there.

The artist had been commissioned by Church and Dwight Company of New York around 1920. Thirty of the songbirds and thirty game birds were reproduced on 2 x 3 inch cards. These were included singly in packages of Arm and Hammer Baking Soda produced by Church and Dwight of New York State. The cards were designed to increase sales of their product and serve to teach love and protection of nature in a period when conservation was receiving little attention. Later the cards were discontinued.

Recently, the company recalled the fifteen of the Fuertes paintings which had never been published on cards. They were the paintings (birds of prey) which appeared in a portfolio featured in the January-February 1977 issue of the "Conservationist" magazine.

Louis Agassiz Fuertes was born in Ithaca, the son of Estevan A. Fuertes, a professor of engineering at Cornell. The father chose the son's name, for the famous Harvard Naturalist, Louis Agassiz. With this inspiring name, Louis A. Fuertes was bound to succeed.

In 1897 at twenty-three, Louis Agassiz Fuertes illustrated the children's book, *Citizen Bird.* While a student at Cornell, he was painting bird pictures for field guides. His illustrations are noted for accuracy since he was an ornithologist and naturalist.

He came to know the most distinguished ornithologists of his day. His uncle, a leader in that field, encouraged young Louis to make it his lifework. At seventeen, he met Abbott H. Thayer, a prominent artist and naturalist, who became his teacher. He was invited by the U. S. Biological Survey to travel as a member of expeditions to Alaska and Florida. In 1902 he went with Frank M. Chapman of the American Museum of Natural History to the Bahamas. This was the first of many such projects with Chapman. Together they logged some 60,000 miles around the world.

When the complete works of John Burroughs were published, the illustrations were the bird paintings of Fuertes. Burroughs and Fuertes would have agreed with Chapman that "birds are nature's highest expression of beauty, joy, and truth."

Throughout his life, Fuertes lived in Ithaca and was associated one way or another with Cornell. He was born February 7, 1875, and died in 1927, a product of the twentieth century, even as you and I.

"Lives of great men all remind us,
we can make our lives sublime,
and departing leave behind us,
footprints on the sands of time."

Ithaca, Cornell, New York State, and the broad world of bird lovers are vastly richer for his inspired and dedicated work.

— Pauline Baker
(From Good Samaritan Nursing Home)

MOMENTS

Some people collect books, some collect beer cans, others, stamps or coins or paintings, but I collect moments. I treasure them as might a collector of gems, though sometimes they flash across my inward eye without any known association. Immaterial and secret, these moments have no monetary value, but are of infinite worth to me.

On the third floor of our red brick house on Schuyler Street, two large bedrooms faced each other, one for the three girls, the other for the three boys in the family. When I was very small, I loved to play in the long, narrow backyard where a walk bordering a round bed of pansies, bleeding hearts, and lilies of the valley led to a grape arbor. At day's end, reluctantly though half asleep, I the youngest went upstairs first, to be followed by my sisters and often our mother, to see that all went well. I still remember a soft kiss imprinted by her on my cheek one night though I was too drowsy to respond. Over the years this moment of affection has symbolized the love that permeated our home, a bulwark in the years ahead.

It was my first dance. I was a high school girl of fifteen and a square white box arrived for me on the eve of the event. I opened it in wonderment. A bouquet of lavender sweet peas tied with a diaphanous silver ribbon was revealed. I have always loved sweet peas.

Not until I was a college senior was I permitted to wear black. The dress I aspired to and finally possessed was velvet with a white satin collar. I wore it when I ushered for a concernt series at Cornell and Pavlova did her celebrated swan dance. This was a moment of ecstasy.

As I walked through the Macmillan Company building on Twelfth Street in New York City, I remember pausing one day and asking myself: "Are you really working for a publishing house?" This moment of realization was a dream fulfilled.

So many moments of delight and poignancy were experienced in the theater, notably seeing John Barrymore in "Redemption," Katherine Cornell in "The Barretts of Wimpole Street," Gertrude Lawrence in "Lady in the Dark," Marlon Brando in "A Street Car Named Desire," Laurence Olivier in the film version of "Hamlet."

Travel moments of wonder and beauty are numerous, outstanding: sensing the mystery of creation at the Grand Canyon; admiring the Golden Gate Bridge; watching the sun rise over Mt. McKinley; flying over the white-capped Andes; visiting the Inca sanctuary, Machu Picchu, and the walled city of Dubrovnik; glimpsing Fujiyama and the Rock of Gibraltar; ascending the broken steps of the Parthenon; actually being in Jerusalem, the Holy Land.

There are sad moments, too, that I cherish for the rich memories awakened. Sitting by the bedside of a beloved sister who was dying of cancer, I saw her wedding ring slip from her emaciated finger. I knew that I would never hear her voice again. This moment recalled a lifetime of companionship and shared experience.

— Florence Boochever

MEMORABLE TOUR OF EASTERN EUROPEAN COUNTRIES

My travel flyer said to "Come Along With Me" and that is what my friends did this summer. Three weeks before departure date, June 29, 1967, we were not even certain of going because of the Middle East Crisis — again! However, Israel within a few days quieted down and we were off for Berlin. We left Kennedy Airport on the ever-efficient Lufthansa Airlines, arrived at Dusseldorf Airport, and via Pan American flew into West Berlin. Tempelhof is a most unusual airport. It is two miles from the city and you come down as though you were landing right on the roof tops! We stayed at the beautiful Berlin Hilton which overlooks the famous Berlin Zoo and were privileged (??) to be awakened by some of the animals! Berlin is a modern, clean and bustling city, with excellent highways, hotels and shops. We started sightseeing with our bus to learn of this divided city. It was quite an experience to finally view Brandenburg Gate, Checkpoint Charlie, and the Wall. What seems to be a tourist attraction to so many means so much to Berliners, and what tales of hardship and heartbreak are told.

In the center of the town is the bombed-out Kaiser Wilhem Church and alongside, the new Memorial Tower. We walked through Tiergarten, destroyed in the war, but today just as beautiful as before. The English garden was given by the English royal family. We marveled at the beauty of Charlottenburg Place with its priceless treasures. Our bus crossed into East Berlin at Checkpoint Charlie where we changed guides and were then given a "pitch" concerning the accomplishments on the east side of the Wall! What we were permitted to see was very new, modern and impressive. We drove down Karl Marx Allee and Unter den Linden and then walked through the beautiful Garden of Remembrance, given by the the Russians. Before leaving, we had a most interesting boat ride on the river and even the water was divided — with boats, sails, campers, swimmers on one side, and watch towers and soldiers on the other side.

In order to leave Berlin for an iron curtain country, it was necessary to drive through East Germany and leave from there by LOT (Polish Airlines) and we jetted into Warsaw, Poland, a beautiful reconstructed city. We were met by Christine, our young and charming guide. At the beginning of our sightseeing, we were shown confiscated German war films of the bombing and burning of Warsaw. It was horrifying! Eighty-five percent of the city was destroyed and there were only 116,000 inhabitants who survived the fire and disease when the town was liberated in 1945. Under the rubble there were 100,000 mines and unexploded shells. However, the people dearly loved their seven hundred-year-old city and decided to rebuild on the same site and to preserve the uniqueness of the older parts. There are now 1,300,000 residents and Warsaw is the pride of Poland. We walked through the "old" market square, saw the ancient fortified gate, and admired the tremendous amount of work accomplished in the last two decades. We visited the Palace on the water (not burned through an error), climbed the steep steps to view the 100,000-seat stadium built upon the bombing rubble, and spent a delightful afternoon walking through the home and gardens at Zelazowa Wola, Chopin's birthplace. In the evening we attended a performance of the ballet in the reconstructed Warsaw Opera House. It is the most beautiful theater I have ever seen, including Lincoln Center! The lighting, crystal chandeliers, pink marble walls, and sweeping carpeted staircases completely walled by mirrors, were magnificient. On the spot where the inmates of the Jewish ghetto rose to revolt, there has been erected an impressive monument made from the very granite which Hitler intended to use for a monument to himself!

Once again it was time to jet away and this we did via Aeroflot, the Russian Airlines. In our opinion, pilots they are not! It was quite a thrill to land at Moscow (Mockba) Airport and to begin our twelve-day stay in this controversial, lovely country. My first impression of the city was of broad avenues, spotlessly clean streets, and the uninterrupted flow of traffic! Nearly all street crossings are via clean, well-lighted tunnels, and one would not think of jaywalking, or of leaving a piece of paper on the ground! Our hotel was on Gorki Street; it was huge, modern, and filled with waste space! All floors have "housemothers," as one of our members called them. The food throughout Russia was excellent, but we felt certain hotels and tourists had the best of everything. The highrise apartment buildings are all over and one has to go far into the country to find the old wooden homes, so picturesque and always with a spot of garden. The people were friendly, interested in us, our clothes, our jewelry, and in America. The young people in particular followed our group every place we went and invariably got up enough nerve to talk—always about America, Presidents Johnson and Kennedy, schools, and money. Contrary to what we had heard, we were free to come and to go. We rode public buses (honor system and fare three cents) and taxied all over the cities. Churches are "non-functioning" and the more beautiful have been restored and are handsome museums. There is no religion.

Natasha was our young, attractive and pleasant guide for our twelve days in Russia, but in each city we picked up a local guide as their people have just never traveled outside; they know only their own locality. We used the

Metro (subway) several times and it is something to see—polished marble, statues, beautiful lighting and spotlessly clean. It is more like walking through a palace. All tracks are extremely deep as there is so much sandy soil, and for bomb protection. They have the longest escalators in the world. We attended a wedding in a "wedding palace" (one every twenty minutes). A woman spoke, a man representative from the State shook hands, and the couple were man and wife! We walked from our parked bus into Red Square ("Red" is old Russian for beautiful) and saw the thousands of people (natives from the provinces) in line to go through Lenin's Mausoleum, open four hours a day, and fifteen thousand people every day of the year file through. The Mausoleum is dark red and black granite. It faces on the Square. Inside one files past an inclined casket with a glass cover and sees the body of Lenin preserved since his death in 1924. At one end of Red Square is St. Basil's Cathedral. The famous G.U.M. Department Store (resembling a huge gray granite state department) is on one side and the wall of the Kremlin and the Lenin Mausoleum are on the other. Along this wall on granite pedestals are statues of famous Russians. One pedestal has no statue. The name at the bottom is Joseph Stalin.

Topping the buildings of the Kremlin are five enormous red stars, most impressive at night. We walked through the gates into the Kremlin (crowded with the "workers" who never before had this privilege.) Here are the three cathedrals, Assumption, Annunciation, Archangel, beautifully gilded and containing priceless artifacts. We were amazed at the size of the Czar Cannon, 40 tons, never fired; and the Czar Bell, 200 tons. We drove to the Lenin Hills and saw the famous Moscow University (thirty-two stories, thirty thousand students); Lenin Stadium and, of course, the largest swimming pool in the world! Everything in Russia seems to be the largest—like the new Russia Hotel with four thousand rooms. Yes, we actually saw it! Natasha "talked" me into taking the group to see the "USSR Exhibition of Economic Achievement" (You'll admit it sounds terrible!) and were we ever glad she did. It was a Russian-style Expo 67, fairgrounds (open all year) with seventy-eight permanent pavilions, beautifully decorated, lovely garden walks, flowers, small lakes, bubbly fountains and fresh gold paint everywhere. At the entrance to the grounds is an exceptionally tall steel shaft to the Cosmonauts. We enjoyed a wonderful evening of ballet at the Bolshoi Theater and another evening at the world famous Moscow Circus.

By Aeroflot, we flew north to Leningrad (formerly St. Petersburg). We stayed at another huge, new, impressive hotel but on the outskirts of the city. We therefore had a good excuse to use the subway again. Incidentally, in

Russia all arrangements are made by Intourist and you are assigned a hotel only on arrival. This city is the most beautiful in Russia, and because of the fiftieth anniversary of the Russian Revolution (November 7), all buildings were being painted. Every structure on the main avenues (prospekts) had to be covered. And who was doing the work? The women! We saw women doing hard labor in the streets of all iron curtain countries. They receive no higher pay and seem not to mind the work. Leningrad has been designated a "Hero City" because of surviving the nine hundred-day siege in World War II. Outstanding was our tour of the world-renowned Hermitage Museum, formerly the Czars' Winter Palace, with its magnificient paintings and priceless treasures. Even the inlaid floors are works of art! There seemed to be more old Dutch masters than in Holland!

Also outstanding was our tour through St. Isaac's Cathedral with its brilliantly gilded dome, third largest in the world. Our guide said it was a monument to the thousands of Russian peasants who labored forty years to build it. That it was originally built as a house of God never entered the picture! One afternoon we went by hydrofoyle on the Gulf of Finland to Petrodvorets, the former summer home of the Czars. The grounds with over one hundred sparkling fountains and water games, and the magnificient golden statues make this place the most beautiful garden I have ever seen. We spent the afternoon just strolling through the grounds and marveling at the beauty and watching the people. I went wild taking movies, but it was worth it! Petrodvorets is truly a showplace, and now another estate the "workers" have the privilege of enjoying. We watched a wonderful local circus in a tent in the fields and enjoyed so much seeing the Russian children there.

We flew to Kiev, the capital of the Soviet Ukraine. Here we were fortunate to see the annual Army Show with excellent singing and dancing. Our group was invited to visit a Pioneer Youth Camp for children of the "good" workers. These camps are all over Russia and the children go for at least two weeks, live in well-kept buildings, have good food, play "instructional" games, and are well indoctrinated with the beginnings of communism! The children presented me as the leader with a bouquet of flowers. We visited the golden domed St. Sophia Cathedral and walked through the underground cells and passageways of Pechersky Monastery. Like all natives, we had a boat ride on the Dnieper River Sunday afternoon, and it was fun.

Time to leave and once more we jetted via Aeroflot. We flew to Bucharest and stayed in the beautiful Nord Hotel. The orchestra here started playing American music every time we entered the dining room. We enjoyed Bucharest, the Rumanian countryside, and the people. We visited an open air restaurant one evening before dinner for a drink but couldn't get out without having a full course meal of meat and potatoes and watching a folk dance. We returned to our hotel for our dinner! On an all-day excursion into the Carpathian Mountains, we visited Sinaia, a lovely mountain resort, and toured through King Carol's home. What a fairyland palace he had! The Village Museum is famous and a photographers's delight with over a hundred authentic reconstructed wooden homes from the provinces of Rumania. They even had a wooden windmill and I am sure the original Ferris wheel! That time came again for the final packing and the early morning departure for home. We flew via Romine Airlines and Lufthansa, stopping at Vienna and Frankfurt. It was a wonderful tour, very enlightening and, I believe, changed our thinking in many ways. Perhaps in some small way we did a little missionary work. I sincerely hope so.

— Dolores G. Fussell

ALBANY

Please believe me when I tell you that Albany was the Birthplace of the Nation. True, Columbus located the Floridas and is credited with finding the New World. The Pilgrims landed at Plymouth. Maybe the Norse and the Irish found Vineland. Albany was the "Cradle of America." Pete Kimball said so. The Committee that was in charge of the Celebration of the Two Hundred and Fiftieth Anniversary of the Granting of the Dongan Charter to Albany agreed with Francis "Pete" Kimball. Pete's book *A Cradle of America,* published in the '30s, establishes his reasons for the title.

Albany was a very early settlement. Before the Articles of Confederation were agreed on in Philadelphia, Benjamin Franklin explained and espoused a Plan of Union — later called the Albany Plan of Union. The Albany Plan of Union would enable the colonies to present their grievances to the King for redress; it was not yet rebellion.

The hands that cradled the Nation also built a big city. Albany is the capital of New York State. Albany is laid out like your hands. Your out-stretched hands, placed side by side with the palms turned up, could represent all of the main streets in Albany. Your fingers will become the streets of Albany leading west from the Hudson River toward the Mohawk River, the Helderbergs, and the Adirondacks.

Long ago the Iroquois came west along the Mohawk River to the Hudson River where they exercised their fishing rights. The Mohawks also converged here. Indian lore told of areas for peaceful meetings of the Indian tribes located at Schodack and Schaghticoke. Here there may have been peace for a while. The clash of the Iroquois and the Algonquins was louder in battle than in peace.

The smell of spice from India, the smell of furs, the smell of trade, all tempted the Europeans who were on the trail of adventure spiked with profit. The French and the Spanish were hunting on trails that brought them to Albany. They turned around when they found the Hudson was a dead end instead of a waterway to the Orient. Hudson's river finally became "The Hudson"; his name was given to the Grande River which had many other names by other people.

Hudson, an Englishman working for Dutch interest, came up the river from the sea looking for a place to establish a trading port. His commission was fulfilled when he anchored the "Half Moon" somewhere near what is now the south end of the SUNY building, formerly the D & H building.

When the trading port was established, the Van Rensselaers and the Schuylers, not Henry Hudson, were the beneficiaries. This was a trading post for the business of dealing with the natives in the area. The Dutch needed beaver skins, furs, and a place to live. The courts of Europe, ever anxious, looked for the furs of North America and the Dutch were in business.

Around the little trading post, these early barterers laid the groundwork for the foundation of Albany. The towers of the Nelson A. Rockefeller Empire State Plaza, the SUNY building, the State Capitol, the State Education Building were all helped into existence by a dozen families who, in that long ago September got their things together and weathered that first winter. These were tenacious people, these early travelers, who had breathed sighs of relief when they got the solid ground under their feet.

There are many doorways to Albany. The footpaths have become Thruways, railways, airways, and waterways. From the east, one crossed the Hudson River on the Parker Dunn Memorial Bridge. From New York City to the south of Albany is an Interchange on the Thomas E. Dewey State Thruway. From the West there is the Thruway and its interchanges. From the North, one arrives on the Northway.

Yes, there are other roads; US9 north and south, US20 east and west, and US4 along the Hudson River to the north. There are more highways with State and County numbers: NY5 along the Mohawk River, NY7 along the Susquenhanna Valley, NY43 to the Helderbergs and the Catskills.

The pathways to and from Albany have given their names to history: *Drums Along the Mohawk, The Advance and Retreat at Saratoga,* the cannons lumbering from Ticonderoga for the defense of Boston, The Hudson River School of Painting, "Rip Van Winkle Asleep in the Catskills," *The Leatheringstocking Tales,* the Millerites waiting for the end of the world and a sanctuary for Shay of Shay's whiskey rebellion in the nearby Nutmeg State of Connecticut.

For many years Albany has been the crossroads of the nation. It is the terminal where boats of the Hudson find a safe berth. The Hudson sloops, the river boats, carried the emigrants up the Hudson on the first leg of their journey west. Men, women and children trekked west on the sandplain trails from Albany to Schenectady, there to find the water level route west. By shanks mare, on wagons, on trains, they went west to open a new country. The Mohawk River is the first water level crossing of the mountain range that starts in Louisiana and ends in Labrador. Next is the St. Lawrence River and its direct connection with the Great Lakes. Our story rests on the Hudson and Mohawk Rivers.

The Mohawk River was an upstream push and carry. It was the way west of Albany to places that became the cities of Syracuse, Rochester, Buffalo, Cleveland, Detroit, and Chicago. In the 1600s how few knew that there was going to be an Ohio, or a Michigan, or an Indiana. The land of opportunity was in the westward movement.

Albany was a mark on the maps of the governments of Europe looking for Colonial adventure. France came from the north along the Valley that was to be called Champlain. Champlain coming south with a war party of Algonquin Indians used gunpowder to rout their enemies, the Iroquois Indians. The choice of these northern Indians as allies lost the Mohawk Valley, the Hudson Valley and the Champlain Valley, but secured the St. Lawrence Valley for France for a time.

The Champlain Valley became the warpath of the nations. Britain's Lord Howe had trouble in the valley. He is reported buried under the steps of St. Peters Church on State Street. It was said that he is the only English Lord buried outside of Westminster Abbey. Whether true or not he was certainly the only British Lord buried under Albany's St. Peters.

General Burgoyne at the head of the army of the crown coming along the same route met defeat at Saratoga. The General and his officer became guests of the Schuylers while waiting for the terms of their surrender. War for the Generals must have been more civilized; war for the foot soliders was much different. Berlin in Rensselaer County became the home of skulking Hessian troops that decided to stay in America. The terms of surrender would have sent them back to their homes along the Baltic-Rensselaer county's Alps. It is interesting that much of the charcoal used in making gunpowder for the Northern armies of our Civil War was produced in Berlin, New York.

General Burgoyne's visit to Albany as Schuyler's guest was not exactly planned that way. He was coming to Albany but he planned on meeting a General St. Leger who, with another army, was coming down the Mohawk River. The people of Albany, Schenectady, and the hinterlands with General Arnold went out to meet St. Leger and said, "No" at Oriskany. Another General, Clinton, was coming up the Hudson to meet the Generals at Albany, but he, too, was delayed and never got here.

This Albany that the generals wanted to see was very important to them. It was the crossroads of the nation. If they could have gotten to Albany these converging armies would have split the colonies. The Birth of the Nation was not achieved without pain, but with victory for the colonists who gave way to joy and killed a fatted calf on the corner of State and Eagle Streets. History records that the citizens of Albany roasted an ox on the hill, that there were tankards of ale, that torch-lights lit the hill in October 1777, and at last the baby and cradle were protected.

Albany is still important because of its location, because it is the capital of New York State, and because of its vitality. When the Dutch got off the Half Moon they built protection against a hostile climate, but more important they planned to eat. Fancy homes gave way to collecting food to fill root cellars. preparing ground for spring planting was more important than planning the curtains for the back bedroom. Go back in your mind and think of Jamestown, Virginia. There, housing took precedence over the providing of food. The Indians and the Mother country would feed them, they thought. But neither came through and the Colonies perished. Albany and the Dutch survived. It was better to live modestly than to die hungry.

The Dutch families that received patents from the Netherlands became obligated to settle land and establish Dutch authority in the New Netherlands. Immigrants who came under the aegis of the Schuylers and the Van Rensselaers were often the same people who had come to Holland to avoid religious persecution. Holland was a haven for persecuted people in Europe, and to her displaced persons the new world looked good and the Hudson Valley became a welcome.

The intestinal wars of Europe echoed in America and the British Crown held authority in Albany. The City Charter of Albany was granted under the authority of the British King by Thomas Dongan. Governor Dongan, a Gaelic-speaking representative of the Crown, was sent to Albany to protect both the Duke's interest in the Colony and Albany's fur trade. Another man, William Penn, with whom Dongan had quarreled at Limerick in Ireland, had founded Pennsylvania. Dongan was a Royalist and Penn a Parliamentarian when they differed in Ireland. The people of Pennsylvania had begun to come up the Susquehanna Valley and were intercepting the furs that should have come to Albany.

Sometimes I think that Albany acts like a City State of old. Politically independent, it goes its own way. It is not big enough to say "Boo" to Manhattan or anyone of its boroughs. Rochester, Syracuse, Buffalo are bigger than Albany and yet we exercise political clout that far exceeds our size. Once I was told that there is more politics per square foot on State Street than on any other street in the nation.

By now you must know that I like Albany. I am an immigrant from Ireland. Albany has been good to all immigrants, the Mohawks, the Iroquois, the Dutch, the English, the Irish, the Germans, and the Italians. According to the census of 1800, there were more than twelve thousand Irish-born persons living in Albany. The next largest group was 6,600 Germans. At that time the total population of the city was 91,000.

A little window into life of Albany in the 1800s allows us to see: twelve hundred shoe makers, eleven hundred carpenters, 424 cigar makers, 441 government officials, 448 teachers. Maybe the relationship between government workers and cigar makers could have some relevance to the number of teachers.

The present population of Albany is about 120,000. All cities have growing pains; Albany is no exception. Except for three or four mansions, there are none of the early homes in existence. The Dutchman's Gable is only seen where an architect has incorporated the old design with the new.

Through the use of Federal, State, and City Funds an effort is being made to reconstruct into livable apartments some of the circa 1800 homes in what are called the Pastures & Arbor Hill. These homes are considered of historic value. It is most commendable that serious efforts are being made in their restoration to usable homes and at the same time they continue to be historic monuments.

The corner of State and Pearls Streets had been for years considered the hub of the city. It was called the Elm Street Corner.

— Patrick Glavin

FIVE FOR FOUR ON FRIDAY
9 a.m. to 2 p.m.

Thoughts remembered by the writer in his attempt to describe the past and present of Albany to blind, adult visitors in a short guided tour, 1979.

If I were a bell and could be part of the carillon in the tower of the Albany City Hall, maybe I could tell you of Albany as the ringing chimes remind us of the men and women who sacrificed so much that we may be free today.

Would I were a wordsmith that could weld words in place like a poet.

If I were a lark singing its heart out in the early, clear morning air, maybe I could convey to you some of the history and the glory and the feeling of Albany.

Bear with me then for I am not a bell or a poet or a lark. Stay with me when I tell you of a great experience I had in taking fellow people from the Albany Public Library on Washington Avenue, Albany, to the State Capitol and the Empire State Mall.

So short a time. So many mistakes, so grand an experience. My eyes for use by four other people. Between my eyes and my brain I will try to say "Welcome" and make yourself at home with the Beaver Clan.

We are not generous with our time. Forty minutes is not enough. Although it is but two and one-half blocks, there is so much to know about those two and one-half blocks. Father Isaac Jogues, William Couture and Rene Goupil were prisoners of the Mohawk Indians here 336 years ago. The Dutch Dominie Joannes Megapolensis of the Reformed Church took up a collection from his neighbors in order to bribe the Mohawk guards, that the Jesuits could escape. Maybe the spirit of Pope John was hovering around, setting the groundwork for the understanding of today.

Further down the street, a building where men and women set in motion the humanity of people in the American Humane Society.

Nearby the Albany Institute of History and Art building, recording and saving the history and life stories of the people who made us the beneficiaries of their lives.

If the Indians, the beavers, the Dutchmen, and the immigrants that have walked this path to a smooth concrete sidewalk could be with us, then we would know and walk softly on the hallowed ground.

Just across the street that is called Washington Avenue, a short distance east of the Albany Institute is the Fort Orange Club. So what! The Fort Orange Club is an important Albany society like many other great clubs throughout the world; but wait, it was out to about here that Alexander Hamilton took his bride, Miss Schuyler, on his honeymoon. Then, there were no jets and the trip from Schuyler's Mansion to where we now stand was right and proper for the Treasurer of the United States of America.

South across Washington Avenue at Swan Street and the State Office Building, thirty-two stories high, is the Alfred E. Smith Memorial Building. Methinks there is more to it than steel, stone, mortar and carvings. The names of the fifty-eight counties in New York State are on it. This was "Smith's Folly"; there would never be enough state employees to use it. Did Governor Smith when he proposed its building believe that the State would grow in rules, regulations and services so as to make it now but an annex to the Nelson A. Rockefeller Empire State Plaza?

The State of New York and Albany have been lucky to have men and women envisioning things to come, that they could not see, but did perceive.

East across Swan Street, and I would like to have you kneel on the grass and touch the flowering tulips. Here between the State Office Building and the Capitol are beds of tulips, soft petals and bending green leaves. Orderly beds—they have bloomed early, before the day we wash State Street during the Tulip Festival.

Overlooking the tulips is a statue of George Washington. The Commonwealth of Virginia gave the Empire State of New York permission to erect their monument by Houdon here. You could know Washington better by feeling his features, gauging his stature and conjuring the problems he overcame. It was my fault, I did not allow enough time; we had a date with Stephen our guide in the Capitol.

I wish we had more time. Each of you, my friends, is going to leave Albany and you will not have felt an artist's conception of "Mother"; it too stands near a tulip bed. You could have felt the flowing lines of a steel structure about six feet tall that the artist's fertile brain offered to honor our mothers. Near the "Mother" monument are trees. These trees are special. These trees are sugar maple trees—the special tree that New York has honored as the State Tree.

The Capitol building—the art of the stone mason. The windows, the gables, the chimneys, the stairways, the doors, it's a commanding place in the center of Albany. Atop Capitol Hill, it's an imposing center where the nerve conduits of State Government become a brain that develop rules and laws, making a complex society harmonious.

Sliding doors and a ramp ease the way into a room of granite pillars, bound together with walls that make rooms. Rooms that have a collection of flags, rooms that have Post Offices, rooms that have whirring reproducing machines, rooms for restaurants, attorneys, pages, Governor, Senators, Assemblymen, and a place for lobbyists. Here there are places for visitors and guides for visitors. Here are rooms for newspaper reporters. Here is the center of New York State Government.

Regularly scheduled tours of the State Capitol are provided without charge to visitors. Our guide is Stephen. Stephen knows of what he talks. Stephen has been trained to tell you about the building, the size, the cost, the time taken to complete and the many changes made while under construction.

Time is a task master. One and one-half hours to see the Senate, the Assembly and the Governor's Red Room. One and one-half hours is not enough. So short a time to trace the efforts of a stone cutter chiseling a face and naming that face. Chiseling a face and giving it no name. An artisan carving a flower on a piece of mahogany. Polishing a slab of marble silky smooth takes time.

Walking on thick carpets says we are now in the Senate. Here we hear clocks that at the end of the sessions are sometimes stopped. The stopped clock gives weary legislators a grasp of time that has gone, in order to legalize pending legislation.

This Capitol is more than stone and brass and conference tables. It is a hive of human activity that must be felt rather than seen. Meet a group of children seeing the Capitol under the direction of a guide, their teachers, and parents. They say that the Capitol is "cool." We felt it was "cool" too, but in a different way. The newsman's job who puts words on paper, so that the citizens may know what the legislator does, the radio reporter who tells the inner thoughts and reactions to others' decisions. The emblem of the State on the rug in front of the Assembly Chambers and on the knobs of the locks that open the doors of government to the public.

Blocks of granite, open hallways, doors that shut you out, doors that open in welcome, printing-press records of laws to be, and laws that are, reams of paper carrying words that say no, words that say yes, and bulletins that invite you to a party. This is the Capitol.

The Capitol is people. Assemblyman Dick Conners is a people. Governor Hugh Carey is a people. We are people. Being with people in the Capitol gives you a sense of existence in the center of where things are happening. Places and things are important, but all must be for the benefit of people. It is good to be with people experiencing new sensations, new ideas, and new opportunities to help others.

The hour and one-half is gone — the Million Dollar staircase — the paintings of former governors — the podium in the Governor's Red Room — the massive fireplaces, an aura of power prevails. Bye, Bye, Capitol and off to the Mall.

The Nelson A. Rockefeller Empire State Mall is great, it's costly, it's new, it's clean, it's big. It's too big to fit in my head, and for my brain to package it in words beyond my power. The tower building is two blocks long. If some giant were to pick it up and sit it on its side on Eagle near State Street it would stretch halfway to Madison Avenue. If that giant did not put it back on its feet after proving his point, there would be a lot of people wondering what happened?

I can see the Mall, but birds seemingly can't. In all the trees between the Capitol and the Cultural Building I have never seen a bird, no sparrows, no pigeons, no blue jays. I would like to invite the birds to come and see our Mall, I would put up with their bad bathroom habits.

Even if the birds don't visit the Mall, this is no reason for you not to become excited about the services provided visitors to the Mall. Skating rinks during the winter, fireworks on the Fourth of July. Outdoor art by the bushelful, wind that blows up from the Hudson and wild geese that steer clear of buildings scraping the sky and sometimes spiking a hesitant cloud.

Before I finish please humor me while I tell you about the man on the steel charger, watching the river from the base of the Office tower. Go in and see him, take down the silk cord that says "Stay out" and feel the legs, the tail, and the nostrils of a powerful horse. Check the boots of a conquistador riding bareback on an iron horse. Discarded steel. Autombile bumpers from junked cars fashioned into art. It's a great way to recycle things that keep us apart.

— *Patrick Glavin*

IN OLD COHOES

I've spent my entire life in Cohoes, and my memories of the Spindle City are legion. When I look at the city today, I find it much changed from my childhood. Industry, commerce, transportation, education and entertainment have changed with the times.

Gone is the New York Central Railroad station, where, on weekdays the platform was crowded with commuters to Schenectady, and on Sundays with pleasure seekers to Dunsbach Ferry.

The Delaware and Hudson freight house has been razed. Here the shoddy from the mills was brought for shipping, as well as finished underwear—the big industry in the Spindle City.

The trolley car, with its personal service, has been replaced by the bus and the private automobile in Cohoes as in other cities. On the trolley cars, the conductors were quite willing to wait for late passengers when they saw them running to catch the trolley. No one was in a hurry in those days.

Gas and electricity meant changes in Cohoes, as everywhere. No more were the carbon lights on the streets, for which we used to wait. When they were changed, we used the discarded carbons to write on the sidewalks. Gas, oil, and electric heat spelled the end of the coal industry for home use.

How well I remember sitting around the parlor stove, with its isinglass doors, through which the bright coals gleamed. It made a child feel so safe and protected, with feet resting on the collar of the stove. The kitchen stove turned out food such as we never again will taste, for it was flavored with home, childhood and love. A reservoir at the back of the stove heated water for household use and acted as a humidifier (although we were unaware of the desirability of this beneficial by-product!).

The automotive age, while a vast improvement in most ways over the horse and buggy, meant the end of leisurely rides, when the horse knew his way about and the driver could devote himself to the enjoyment of his company and of the path he traversed.

It meant the end, too, of the blacksmith shop, the harness shop and the feed store. Payette's Feed Store and Lynan's Harness Shop are only memories.

Industry in Cohoes is much more diversified today than in the old Cohoes. A number of small industries assure the people of continuing employment. Not so in the days when the woolen, cotton and rolling mills provided the means of sustenance for Cohosiers. The Harmony Mills, Brooks, Roots and other smaller mills employed most of the working populace.

Cohoes is known as the Spindle City because of the fact that its main industry for many years was the manufacture of cotton cloth, a process which involved extensive use of "spindles" to contain the cotton thread. The Harmony Mills, begun with the establishment of the Harmony Manufacturing Company in 1837, was the chief manufacturer of this cotton cloth, and its mills were the life blood of the city.

Immigrants from Ireland, Poland and Canada were employed in the Mills. Their lives were arduous for they worked long hours under conditions that by today's standards would be considered intolerable. Not too many years ago, Polish and French were spoken almost exclusively in large sections of the city but today Cohoes is, for all practical purposes, unilingual.

Pay was low and the people knew few amusements. One week during the year the mills shut down for vacation. This was known as "the week the water went out." During this week, excursions were run. Chief among these was the Knights of Columbus outing to Sacandaga Park. A train left the railroad station in the morning and the platform was filled with excursionists. Another train returned in the evening. For many, this was the only outing of the year.

Cohoes was then a busy place. Practically all shopping was done in the city, and on Saturday night, Remsen Street was crowded. (Oddly enough, Remsen Street was always the main street of Cohoes while "Main Street" was one block west of the "main street.")

The Harmony Mills closed in 1933 and liquidated its holdings. The Mill properties, which included tenant houses, were sold. This was a sad day for the city, for not only did it mean losing its main industry, but for some, losing their jobs and homes.

Working six days a week left only one day for recreation. Sunday morning, of course, we went to church. Then, afer a hearty dinner, the afternoon was ours. And how much we crowded into those afternoons! Sometimes it was a boat ride from Troy to Altro Park (midway between Troy and Albany.) The boat left in the early afternoon and returned after dark. An orchestra provided music for dancing. We children leaned over the rail (with our parents holding tight) and ate Cracker Jack. The Cracker Jack then had lots more peanuts and better prizes. (Or was that just part of the glamour of childhood?)

Altro Park was an amusement grove, of which there were several in our area. Rensselaer Park in Lansingburgh, Mohawk Pines at Green Island—called simply "The Pines" by a later generation—Averill Park at Crystal Lake, and The Grove at Dunsbach Ferry—which was the one I went to most often. They were reached by trolley, or, in the case of The Grove, by railroad train. Mohawk

Pines is now the site of the Green Island Ford Plant, selected by Henry Ford while on a camping trip with Harvey Firestone, Thomas Edison, and John Burroughs.

Ferris wheels, hobby horses, and games of chance were featured. Lemonade sold for five cents a glass. We brought lunches, for few were the people who could afford to buy lunch for their families.

One of the attractions at Mohawk Pines was a huge carousel. The figures for the carousel—horses, bears, camels, giraffes—were of solid wood and had been hand-carved in Germany during the nineteenth century by the grandfather of Ed Kolb, the operator. Ed later moved his carousel to Crystal Lake at Averill Park where it stayed for many years. Some time after his death, it was again moved to Halfmoon Beach at Crescent where it is operating today.*

Baseball games were another form of recreation largely attended. The Insular Field on the Island, the Polo Grounds on the Hill, Sunset Park, at the end of Reservoir Street, and the Orchard and Sunrise Athletic Clubs were men's diversions. Ice skating was a popular winter sport. The Erie Canal was a place where we could skate free. Cohoes abounds in history. Its annals produce a wealth of historic lore, much of which is unknown to its citizens. Many years ago, in excavating for the Harmony Mills, the bones of a prehistoric animal, huge in structure, were uncovered. When assembled, it became the Cohoes Mastodon which is now on display in the State Museum at Albany.*

The Van Schaick Mansion, on the west bank of the Hudson River, has been restored and the present owners agreeably permit sightseers to visit the Mansion. The Van Schaick Mansion has a rich history of famous visitors. During the Revolutionary War and afterwards, Generals Kosciusko, Schuyler, Benedict Arnold, Gates, Clinton, Burgoyne and—chief among them—General Washington, stayed at the Mansion.

The Cohoes Falls, in the Mohawk River, has its own particular history. Legend has it that the Falls derived its name from the Indian word "cahoos" which means "a fall." It is said than an Indian traveling down the river, on seeing the Falls ahead, shouted the warning, "cahoos"—and it became Cohoes.

Another legend has to do with the Black Plague—a cholera epidemic. So many people were dying that the authorities, in order not to create a panic, buried at night. It was said that for many years the clump of horses' hooves could be heard in the night, drawing the hearses with the bodies of the victims.

*At the time of this writing. But now is returned to Cohoes.

The small schools are rapidly disappearing from the scene. In fact, three schools which I attended have been completely razed. In those schools the dedicated teachers spent their lives shaping the characters of their pupils while they taught them the three Rs. They preserved discipline without too much trouble. For the recalcitrant pupil, corporal punishment was a matter of course. And rarely did a child who had been disciplined complain at home—that meant more punishments by his parents.

One of the notable changes is its stores. The shopping centers have become the commercial centers. But wouldn't I love to go into one of the stores on Remsen Street where I used to be sent on errands! In those stores, everyone knew everyone else. You could always buy what you wanted—for they had everything. (If they didn't, they would soon get it!).

There were department, shoe, men's and women's clothing stores, millinery shops—we even had a ribbon store, devoted entirely to the sale of ribbons and laces. Pelletier's Music Store sold victrolas and records. We had five-and-ten cent stores—in which nothing cost more than ten cents.

There wasn't much restaurant business in Cohoes in those days. For the most part people ate at home. Saloons (which abounded in Cohoes) gave free lunches. And there were a few lunchrooms—McGill's, Bell's and Vroman's.

The Erie Canal is another memory. It was a calm and peaceful sight to see the boats pulled along by the horses on the bank. One of the diversions for Sunday afternoon was to watch the boats.

As we grew older, Sunday afternoon was the time for a "walk." We walked to Ford's in Waterford, where you could get a dish of ice cream with two flavors for ten cents. We walked to Tully's in Lansingburgh for soda—and the real rugged ones walked to Troy. Our legs must have been sturdier than those of today's children, for we didn't know what "tired" meant.

We had several movie houses in Cohoes—Proctor's, the Majestic, the Bright Spot, the Empire, and the Regent. Tickets were ten cents in the orchestra and five cents in the balcony. I saw the "Birth of a Nation" from the gallery—and I was really scared—I felt like I was in Outer Space.

Oh, those days of yesteryear! There were lots of things about them that needed the changes that have come about. But, in retrospect, they are very dear. Cohoes, my home town! I wouldn't leave it for anywhere else. I walk today with a more measured tread on the streets I once skipped along. But I am happy that they are still the streets of Cohoes.

— Georgiana Cole Halloran

MARTINVILLE

Most Albanians have never heard of Martinville, a small village that once existed on the site of Lincoln Park, formerly Beaver Park. It was swallowed up as the city of Albany expanded. A sewer now running underground, carrying Albany's waste to the river, used to be Beaver Creek which tumbled down Buttermilk Falls, and this is where Martinville was located. The only vestige of its existence remains in the rocky, cliff-like undeveloped section of the park that Albanians drive past on the modern, asphalt-paved road.

Patrick Lannigan of 25 Morton Avenue, remembers the city-encircled village as it was in 1880, the year he came to Albany. He has pictures of it and says it was called Martinville because it was founded by a man named Martin. Perched on either side of the steep banks leading up from Beaver Creek, a cluster of houses had been erected and their occupants lived almost wholly apart from the rapidly expanding city that pressed in on them. Houses were similar to those that line the banks of the Normanskill on the lower side below the Delaware Avenue bridge. My father, John Hunter, lived in Martinville at the time of the famous blizzard of '88.

When the city decided to raze the village and clear it for park development, it first held a Bargain Day. Folks came and bought the homes as they stood and carted them away for $50 apiece. Mr. Lannigan said, "That was some day!"

Martinville achieved considerable fame in its time, not through any intrinsic interest but because of the music and lyrics of one Michael Carey, an Albany newspaperman. He wrote scores of songs, at least one of which, "Learning McFadden to Waltz," circled the globe—a song hit of the '80s. It would make a good heirloom for an owner.

— Thomas Hunter

MR. PIPER'S PROGENY

Have you ever wondered about or questioned the unreasonable success of the Rock sound in comparison to the dismal illogical situation in which contemporary serious music finds itself? The fault, without a doubt, belongs to Robert Browning's legendary fantasy. If you are inclined to say "Humbug," "Nonsense," consider Jules Verne's fantasy that became a truth.

Once upon a time, so Robert Browning wrote, a Pied Piper blew a repetitious tune in Hamelin Town, and hoards of rats, following at a respectful distance, drowned themselves. The Mayor and his board of director were justifiably relieved and immediately voted in favor of forgetting the promised one thousand guilder for the job. According to R. B.'s narrative, the Piper, angered and rightfully so, blew again and this time the children of the town followed the vindictive little fellow through a pass in the mountains and were never seen again.

I read this fascinating narrative poem many years ago and worried and fretted about the kids; I wished R. B. had the foresight of a sequel or two; but therein lies the quality of the writing genius. Let the reader ponder and stir his own mind. And if the chips fall heavy, wonderful! My quizzical nature appears to have stirred up the ultimate in pondering, and I have intuitive evidence that R.B.'s Piper and progeny have danced themselves right out of the book, via the mountain, and are amongst us, living creatures, one and all.

As I see it, Mr. Piper, surveying his noisy possessions, tuned them to sleep for two hundred years in order to meditate on the problem of inheritance. That it took long is quite conceivable for a surreptitious vindictive little man with an almost human-like quality of importance and a bit of greed for good measure.

But on with the story—with one swift movement of the hand, Mr. Piper turned all the youngsters into grownups, taught them the specialized art of promotional tactics, and with proper instructional guidance to match the new age of idiosyncrasies, off they went to promote the Balladeers of the twentieth century.

Thus the first, a hip-swiggling guitar plunker, an unknown from the South, was touched by a furtive promoter's magic ballyhoo, and became the new generation kids' delight. How they screamed and clutched and poured their nickels and dollars, in frenzied foolishness, bought records, charms, etc., and Mr. Hip-swiggler waxed rich and his promoters clucked as the money filled their pockets to overflowing.

After Hip-Swiggler came a group magiced by other promoters and assisted by Amalgamated Publishers. The kids screamed, clutched, and bought records, and the promoters and publishers added new assistants, Discjockeys; and the one group multiplied into many, banging out repetitious tunes and ear-splitting sounds magnified electronically by the Inventors, and the children screamed their screams, danced frenetically and poured their parents money into clinking cash registers.

One day, the Promoters, Publishers, Discjockeys, and Inventors, bored with small events, devised a scheme updating all schemes: an Art Festival would lure the young and oh, how the money would flow! Yes, indeed, so it did.

From all corners of the land they came, fat ones, skinny ones, miserable ones, and they crowded together, made mud of a once green pasture, and with eyes glassy and ears deafened by the persistent bleats of the balladeers, they mesmerized themselves for days. When it was over, a gathering of newspaper people, psychologists, educators, etc., on TV acclaimed the event unique in the annals of festivals.

"The young people were beautiful," they exclaimed, considering the rain-soaked earth and the absence of riots. And the owner of the once green pasture proclaimed the young people beautiful as he pocketed his money. And the Promoters, Inventors, Publishers, and Discjockeys hugged each other with glee.

There you have it, my own conclusive evidence of the after-happening in Hamelin Town, be it approved or no; I have a feeling that R.B.'s Piper progeny are still carrying on, with no end in sight, unless — —.

— Rebecca Richter

A FOUR SEASONS ANTHOLOGY

SPRING EXUBERANCE

Spring is a vibrant, ever young season, nature breathlessly poised to unveil a kaleidoscopic pageantry — a part of the Divine Plan. Spring is exhilirating and exuberant with its warming sun in a fleecy, white-clouded blue sky; the earthy fragrance of softening, pregnant soil; a greening field; the titillating music of a merrily coursing, bank-full brook at long last free of its confining ice shroud; life restoring sap flowing and buds swelling on tree limbs; the singular, fragile beauty of crocus and daffodil courageously flowering, even above the lingering vestiges of winter's white coverlet. Spring is a wondrous miracle — God's promise of life renewed and life eternal. Have faith, and believe in Spring.

SUMMER GENTLENESS

The words of the poet who wrote: "What is so rare as a day in June, for then, if ever, come perfect days," give substance to asserting that summer is the gentle season. It is a time of quiet, early mornings with rainbow-hue sunrises, heralding the hour when the golden chariot of the sun-god begins its fiery ascent into the zenith of the blue-domed sky, to lavish its pulsating heat on the expectantly receptive earth. The cheery, plaintive notes of birds are heard as our feathered friends energetically pursue their food foraging and housekeeping chores, more important now that the next homes are filled with new life. A typical summer day broods lazily unnoticed past the midpoint and into the long, still afternoon which should be fully indulged, ideally in a swaying hammock under a now fully leafed tree. During calm summer nights, the mysterious lights of fireflies are punctuation marks in the darkness and the songs of crickets and katy-dids are ear-soothing rhapsodies, while overhead a mellow moon gleams in a starry sky.

On occasions, after a spate of humid days, summer gentleness is usurped by the fury of a thunderstorm with driving rain, booming thunderclaps and a spectacular, high-in-the-sky pyrotechnics display. Soon, however, the storm abates, the skies clear and the gentle drip-drop of rain from roof eaves lulls us back to summer's sleepy solitude.

Everyone should spend at least one summer day in a secluded forest, away from the raucous, concreted bustling timpani of civilization. Choose a grassy knoll, relax and let the entire being capture the peaceful feeling induced by the sights and sounds of nature;—multicolored butterflies floating by effortlessly on soundless wings, the drone of insects, scurrying noises of small creatures in the underbrush, the beauty and perfume of wild flowers, sun rays filtering through the arching tree canopy and the comforting feeling of warm earth against the body. Overall there is a sense of complete apartness from the everyday world and a nearness to Him who ordained the inexorable rotation of the seasons while decreeing the soul-renewing qualities of summer gentleness.

While summer is upon the land, it is wise to enjoy this phenomenon of nature; for it passes by all too soon, and who of us can assure that it will ever come again.

AUTUMN REFLECTIONS

Autumn is a time of evaluation. The harvesting is accomplished and all nature pauses on the brink of the long winter sleep to come. The days shorten and the sun slants lower on the horizon, reappearing more tardily each morning and seeming reluctant to shed its warmth. Autumn is the season of October's bright blue weather, of placid lakes mirroring the scarlet red and flaming gold bedecked trees, of crisp morning air and night skiers of celestial beauty, with a mellow moon and myriads of sparkling stars. Autumn is the season of reflection in God's Plan—it knows what it is, and is satisfied.

WINTER CONTRASTS

Winter is the season of contrasts. It can be a time for frigid blasts, when the wind demons howl mournfully at the window panes and down the chimneys and swirling snow covers the land. In the great symphony of the seasons, winter has an essential passage. The wild winds and the great blizzards are the strident trumpets, growling trombones and booming drums, sometimes attaining so loud a crescendo in the year's score, that the more subtle passengers are scarcely discernible.

Yet, in the first month, a countryman can stand in a quiet forest glade when a January thaw comes and hear the muted, sweetly gentle voices of the violins, harps and flutes of Spring, nature stirring itself beneath the soft, warm snow blanket under which earth eternally renews itself in sleep.

Winter is the bravissima movement of the Divine Symphony, with aeous-old nuances and he is wise who listens to and enjoys the yearly performance which will continue until time is no more, as God has willed.

—George F. Venter, Jr.

RESCUE FROM THE GRAVEYARD

The little graveyard was beautiful that morning. As a five-year old, I was not interested in the early dates on the gravestones. But I loved the cherub heads with sparrow wings carved on the children's markers. The Peables' family plot contained several headstones and three very tall pines. It was surrounded by a four-foot, white clapboard fence, and the top board lay at right angles, like a flat roof, over those below. There was no gate.

These were my private premises, for I had to climb to get in or out and the fence top was my "tightrope." The carpet was deep moss and a rock in the center of it doubled as platform or pulpit. Here I held church services. I was both soloist and minister. My congregation consisted of deer, mice, rabbits, birds and chipmunks. They were more attentive and less critical than their human counterparts. Maybe this was partly because I furnished corn, nuts, or raisins, and didn't mind if they ate during the services. They seldom left any crumbs.

This morning, having delivered my sermon on how God is with all of us, all the time, I then took a few turns around the fence top. Next, I decided to lie down on my back on the moss and watch the pine plumes against the sky. Pines are very gentle as they sweep and softly sing. I was so comfortable that I fell asleep.

Now I had begun collecting varieties of caterpillars when I was very young. I fed them their favorite kinds of leaves and gave them drops of water from blades of grass. But if there is one creature I've never wanted to caress, it's an army worm! Full-grown, he's about two inches long, striped blue-gray, and ugly.

When I awoke and tried to leave, I discovered the place was surrounded by a continuous line of these caterpillars; head-to-tail, marching around the top of the fence. My fingers touched one individual and he signalled his companions. They raised their front and rear segments in unison, as if to fight me. They resembled a circle of my father's roofing staples, pointing upward.

The crawlers were coming from two directions: down a tree, across the ground, and up a post. Another came from outside the yard, up another side of the same post. At the top, they alternately entered a grand march which had no beginning and no end.

First I swept away a few of them with a stick. But by the time I'd climbed the fence, the line was solid again, and my stick, outside the yard. Repeatedly I removed them but couldn't climb out before they closed their ranks. I began to get panickly. I tried over and over, but I couldn't squeeze between the fence boards. Finally I sat down to plan a way of escape. "God, will you help me?"

Then, miraculously, the cedar waxwings appeared. There is no more immaculately clad bird on earth. He dresses in fawn color with matching crest and narrow black eye-mask. The touch of red "wax" on the wings and yellow on the tail tips gives just the right dash of aristocratic elegance. Not only are they well-tailored, the waxwings have impeccable manners. I felt like saying, "Good morning," with a curtsy.

They are the only birds I know which alight all facing the same way to watch a prospective meal long enough for the whole flock to see before any one of them offers to help himself.

All the birds perched on the north side of the graveyard in trees and on the gravestones. They sighted the caterpillars, waited, and then—as if on signal, with one accord—they dove, each to his own prey. In less time than it took me to gasp, they had cleared the entire east side of the fence top.

Joyfully, I called, "Thank you!" and was over the fence and running for home with an exciting new story to tell my folks.

— Margaret A. Wheeler

Beaver cutting down a tree.

From original by: Sister Mary Charles Lilly

Beaver eating bark from a branch.

From orignal by: Sister Mary Charles Lilly

III. POETRY

THERE IS HOPE

I am one
Who has come up
Out of the fire
Of many desires,
And considerable anguish;
And I have come up answering:
It is not bad
It is not all bad;
I have only been tested.

You will send me down
Into the pitch blackness
Of the despair
Of my humanity,
And I will come up singing
It is not all bad,
There is hope
There is hope.

— Leo Allard

MOMENTS BETWEEN WARS

Oh God, make bright the spark of life again;
Let music, song and laughter e'er be in it,

That this brief candle might the better span
The time between a minute and a minute.

— Leo Allard

HERE IS NO WAR

Here is no war, no blood, no baffling noise,
No beat of muffled drums, no bombs bursting.
Here only are the words of a still peace
The quiet of a voice bursting for song,
The silent strength of one finding release
In words—words probing at the core of wrong;
Words true and deft and swift justice finding,
Spilling no blood and losing never the poise
Of erect prophets meting out the past.
Here is the past, and here are words, the last
Of an era of truth provocation.
Your wars shall be a mute invocation
Of all things dead and gone and forgotten
And my words shall rise strong and salient still,
In ages hence, when the last dead carcass, rotten
With the last remembered war, shall be still.
Here is no war, no noise, no bursting shell;
Only words here—but I have much to tell.

— Leo Allard

CITIES

Cities were shadows with houses between
And we had no light to see;
And people, impressions, too many to mean
Individuality.

— Leo Allard

FIRST SUN

I stood there, rapt as in a dream
And wondered at a crystal beam
Of sun, that through the interlace
Of leaves, alighted on my face.

I wondered as God's health poured down,
At all the tired men in town.
Mused sadly on their death-faced shrouds . . .
There's no nobility in crowds!

I moved my eyes just three degrees
And saw a cloud between the trees,

A snow-white cloud, a vaporous nest
That promised dreams, undreamed-of rest.

I looked up at a woman's face
And saw old lavender and lace.
I wondered at the beauty there
And thought of love and a straight-back chair.

— Leo Allard

TO AN UNSEEN WHIPPOORWILL

Invisible singer of infinite song,
In your green anonymity,
Have you learned the secret of giving unseen?
Need you no thanks, no applause, O serene
Bearer of gifts from infinity?
My heart is clean-swept foir your tune.

— Aina L. Anderson

BELIEVING*

They took away my sight
But God has given me an inner light.

They took away my ears
But God has stilled all my fears.
They took away my speech
But for God I reach and preach.
My soul they could not take away
For that's in God's keeping always.

*Composed as a tribute to all
Helen Kellers.

— *Aina L. Anderson*

THE SCARLET MAPLE LEAF

I'm just a scarlet maple leaf
One of a trillion
That's given shade
In the heat of summer
And now that summer's o'er
The wind has tossed me
Hither and yon;
My color is no longer green
But a brilliant scarlet
And with many others makes a carpet—
Until an admiring lady came along
And picked me up carefully by my stem
Only to crush and bury me between her book.

— *Aina L. Anderson*

EVENING BENEDICTION

All day the snow had swirled so white
I could not leave my gift of bread,
And now at dusk the world was still,
"Surely the birds have gone," I said.
Yet still I took the park path home
And there upon the hawthorn bough

The sparrows waited; then set up
A cry that said, "She's coming now."
And next, both delicate and swift,
A fluttering of brown and gray
Descended to the walk to meet
The crumbs that offered life today.
Here was a blessing I could see;
I took that blessing home with me.

— Aina L. Anderson

WHIPPOORWILL

I heard a bird at close of day
Sing from a summer tree
a tune so sad and doleful
And this was the melody—
"WHIPPOORWILL"

— Aina L. Anderson

TWO OF MANY MOONS

One moon many people
think of first today
is the astronauts' moon
a black and white sphere
bleak dry cold.
This moon
is a madness of measurement
a fully described and limited orb
a dead satellite.

The other moon
is different
at times golden
at times lustrous silver.
It is immeasurable,

for this moon, to some the real moon,
lives in the minds of human beings.
Because of it
artists create
ideas are born.
This moon dwells in the memory
of the human race.
It haunts
the dreams of the world.

— Eleanor Bender

A DEATH ON OUR STREET

I was new to the street
and never found out which one she was.
I came here early one summer
and used to see the three of them together
sitting in the golden sunshine,
pale, white-haired, elderly, frail
but always laughing, laughing and talking.
To me, walking to and from the mailbox,
they looked alike—delicate, old
and precious.
When September's blue light stole over the land
the coolness drove them indoors,
One soon went to her daughter's to live
and during the winter another moved south.
I never saw the third again.
Her family treasured her,
one of them was always with her.
Then in the glowing autumn of the year
I saw all of their cars together at her home
And knew this must mean the end of her life.
I was so new to the street
I did not even know which one she was.

— Eleanor Bender

WHERE WILL THEY GO?

the small wild creatures
when all the meadow's
black top?

And what of birds?
When the last tree's down
to make space for another
development
where will they go?

It's disappearing fast,
our natural world
to which we, too, belong,
on which we must depend.

When everywhere is road, building,
house,
where will they go,
the little wild creatures,
where will they go?

— Eleanor Bender

Small Verse

GOOD MORNING!

Morning is my time of day,
The world and I old-fashioned gay;
Midnight cobwebs swept away,
Ready now for work or play.

ON PICKING FLOWERS

Not every lovely flower I see
Must necessarily be picked by me;
I place some in my mind's eye
Where they stay fresh and never die.

VALUES

I found a four-leaf clover
And threw my luck away.
I carried home my bread and meat
And thought no more that day
Of the rarity I chanced to spy
On the usual thoroughfare.
How strange the values habit forms,
I ponder, now aware.

GRATEFUL

There is a garden up the street
That cheers me up when I am beat:
Tumbling roses, red, pink, white,
Create a truly hueful sight.
Lucky me to have so near
Celestial loveliness appear.

I—USTER

Don't be an I-Uster
Crowing like a rooster:
"I did this and that—
"To church I wore a hat!"
"So what?" the youngsters say:
"Oldsters, it's TODAY!"

FIRST SNOW

The first snow,
Like the first spring flower,
Brings a sense of joy and wonder
At the mystery of the unknown force
That some call Allah, Karma, God.

NIGHTCAPS

Twin dormer windows across the way
Wear snowy nightcaps until day
Melts the white stuff quite away
Causing heady disarray.

MOON LOVE

Good-night, sweet moon;
Above me men have trod.
You soothe my sleep,
Your changing gleam my benison.

THE SEARCH

The small plot in front of the brownstone
is overgrown.
Long suckers stream from the rose bush
Where last year a yellow rose,
A perfect yellow rose bloomed.
I search and search but it isn't there.
My eyes turn to the neglected spot
Every time I pass.

EVANESCENT

I tried to scrub a sunbeam
When I cleaned the other day.
"No, no," it seemed to me to say:
"Evanescently I gleam."

PEOPLE-NEED

House plants do well
When close together set;
Humans, too, excel
When people-need is met.

EACH DAY A GIFT

Only the lucky ones live long;
The good die young, they say.
But I am singing a newfound song:
"It's a gift to live each day."

CHIME CLOCK AT NIGHT

Thank you, clock, for your sweet chime
Telling me what is the time.
You comfort me with friendly ping
When the half and hour ring.

MY MEMORY BOX

My memory box is a lovely place
Filled with moments high.
Riffling through past time and place
Sustains as years go by.

— Florence Boochever

THE WEB OF LOVE

Lovers, like persistent spiders,
Are constantly spinning subtle threads
To bind their loved ones to themselves.

At first one single iridescent strand,
Then two, and three and more;
Until people say, "How strange!
It was not like this before."

— *William Campaigne*

THE MINISTER'S CAT

This is suggested by the game "The Minister's Cat," which is referred to in Dickens' *Christmas Carol*.

Not the ministers' cat, but Aunt June's cat
Is a character known as Fritz.

He claws, he bites, he scratches
And sometimes even spits.

Nevertheless he's a handsome cat,
With soft, luxurious fur.

And the very best thing about him is
That he never chases a her.

This cat of Aunt June's is audacious,
Bumptious and capacious,

A daring, elusive feline
With a gastronomical bloodline.

A haughty, independent jumper
And a kinetic leg-bumper.

He's mischievous, a nuisance and obese
With a peripatetic quiet ease.

A rambunctious, supercilious tail-swisher
Ubiquitous, voracious, warbler snitcher.

Exasperating, yowling, zany—
And these are only a few of many.

— *Stella Carlson*

Child's Hospital

I THINK THE QUIETEST TIME IS

I think the quietest time is in that room
nothing happens
It's just quiet
I think I'll go back to that room.

— Anna Bowman

THINKING OF BEAUTIFUL COLORS

Blue is a word they use
True Blue.
Sky blue, midnight blue
That's dark
Indigo blue
I have a blue telephone
Blue lawn
You know it used to be used for dresses
Blue voile, blue chiffon
Blue scarf that you can wear on your head
Or around your neck.
Blue bedspread, solid blue
Right here in Albany I bought them.

— Lilie Cooper

MY FAVORITE COLOR IS BLUE

My favorite color is blue
I remember at school
My sister and I each
had a blue calico dress
and she had torn hers.
My mother put a patch on it
A little square patch

Blue to match the dress
Behind the group was an American flag
which, of course, was blue, and red
And there was white in it.
As I grew older I still liked blue
And I still do
I like the blue water of the ocean
and the blue of the sky
I have been on the ocean
and flown on an airplane.

— Elizabeth Vroman

I COULD TELL YOU

I could tell you I like colors
My shirt is blue
I could tell you my eyes are blue
And you are a nice girl.

— Abe Figel

THE RED WHITE AND BLUE

I'm thinking of the flag
Red white and blue
Seem like the nicest colors in the world
I love my flag.

Dresses, red dresses
I don't have one, no,
but I'd like to have one.

Now blue is my favorite color
So I have lots of blue things
Dresses, coats, all kinds of clothes.

White is lovely
I think of a wedding

with a beautiful white satin dress
All my friends were there
And I was happy.

— Frances Sackrider

Child's Nursing Home

QUIET

I like to be quiet all the time
I enjoy flowers
I like to get out in the woods and gather violets
And I like to go to church and Sunday School
I like to be quiet wherever I am
I don't like much noise
I enjoy my television
And radio, I love good music
But I don't like it so loud it'd
Drown you out

— Flo Estelle Bryant

LONELY LADY

When I'm sick
I get very quiet
I don't want to talk
I get nervous

Most every time is noisy here;
It's never quiet
It was always quiet.

I had no children
Just my husband and I.

I'm terribly nervous
I worry over every little thing.

— Lena Frebel

I REMEMBER

I remember the sun breaking through
Started to bring in the colors
Particularly beautiful against the blue sky
Then the green mountains with their brilliantly colored
leaves
Red and yellow trees
Leading to the sunset at night.

— Dorothy Hinman

BLUE

Blue is my favorite color
Everybody says I look good in it
It's light and cheerful
Dresses,
My shower, the decorations were blue.

— Mabel

PRIVATE TIMES

Babies sleeping
When the children were playing
They had to be quiet
so they wouldn't wake up
the babies

Quiet when you go to church
So as not to interrupt the minister
and keep your mind on what he's preaching.

Daytime in my daughter's house
when her husband works nights
He's a state trooper and he has to have
his wits about him.
It's a dangerous job.

At night when everybody's asleep
it's quiet
otherwise it's noisy
people hollering.

— *Mabel*

BRIGHT COLORS

I like all bright colors:
the green of the grass
the red of apples, the goldenrod
the white daisy, yellow forsythia
the gold of hair, anybody's golden hair.
I like the blue of the sky.
Did I say the red of apples?
the red of strawberries
the yellow of dandelions.
Did I write the white of snow?
the red of cardinal
Did I write the yellow of forsythia?
I like the color of carrots
and the green and white of a cucumber.

— *Fannie Saxe*

ODE TO MARCH

Today the sun broke through winter's leaden sky
And I fancied I smelled spring ahead
And in the park across the street
I visioned budding leaves on the branches brown and
dead.

Today the mailman brought me news
And even pain did not seem bad
My shut-in life changed from the blues
For I rediscovered a friend I had

— *Ruth Clonick*

TO MY DOCTOR/TO MY FRIEND*

Here's to us the privileged ones
His patients
Who have sat down in the warm sunshine of his care
Whose wounded bones and heart
Have mended and surrendered
To skill given only to the
Very great who dare.

Here's to us the privileged ones
His friends
To those of us who could not walk
Alone he held strong hands to those of us
Who could follow his swift pace
We see and feel a generous cheery understanding heart
Half-boy, all-man whose very presence seemed to heal.

Here's to us the privileged ones
His students
Whose very spark of being what we are
Was kindled on the white hot flame incredibly
And who in turn may pass the spark
As far as far
This then to him may one day be
A kind of immortality.

*Dr. Crawford J. Campbell, Chief of Orthopedics at Albany Medical College, lecturer and visiting surgeon at Albany Medical College; orthopedic surgeon; . . . now semi-retired and lecturer, Harvard Medical School; visiting surgeon, Massachusetts General Hospital in Boston, and Chief of Orthopedic Services . . .

— Ruth Clonick

A GRATEFUL HEART

Dear Lord,
You have blessed me with so many gifts
I cannot keep each one apart;

But if I may have just one more:
Please Lord, give me a grateful heart.

THE DOOR TO HEAVEN

The door of the Kingdom of Heaven
May not be entered with ease;
It's just high enough
For a child to pass through—
Man reaches the goal on his knees.

A MAN'S WORTH

A man is measured by the world
In terms of wealth he has in store.
But how much you are in the eyes of God
So much you are—and no more.

— Timothy F. Cohan

WE REMEMBER PAPA

There are stories and songs and poetry too,
In praise of our Mothers—so dear and true.
But somehow I have always suspected
That Papa has been a bit neglected.
Now that nostaglia has become the rage—
Old movies, old songs, old plays on the stage,
Pot-bellied stoves, and if that's not enough,
Shaving mugs, with flowers and leaves they stuff—
All of these things bring pictures to our mind
Of Papa so stern, but always so kind.
In winter he filled that old stove with coal
Before we awoke for our coffee and roll.
And do you remember that lingering smell—
When he was shaving, you could always tell—
The soap in the mug, the scent of Bay Rum,

Now he was ready for the new day to come.
We had such fun in those years long long past.
And when the circus arrived in town—at last—
Pop was elected to be our escort;
Mom didn't care much for things of that sort.
Family picnics, I can also recall—
Trying to beat Pop in a game of baseball.
When the holidays came, what excitement!
Getting ready for religious enlightenment,
Cleaning and cooking, no time for a rest,
For Papa usually invited a guest.
Everyone busy—Mother, daughter and son—
While to the "Turkish Bath" Papa would run.
When we were ready to sit down and dine,
Papa looked like a King as he poured the wine.
Sometimes if we appeared to be remiss—
A little reluctant to hug and to kiss—
We knew in time of trouble he was there
And we valued his wisdom and tender care.
He understood—he had just the right touch.
We remember Papa. We love you so much.

—Betty Cohen

WHAT IS LOVE?

What is love?
I ask myself . . .
A soft white cloud hiding reality?
A bumblebee buzzing in my ears
To titillate my heart—my senses?
A swirl of moonlight bringing bright new dreams?
An eddying, frothing maelstrom whirling me,
Tossing me, hurling me where I do not know?
Or—is it quietness, safety, contentment, repose?
What is love?
I ask myself
And cannot answer.

—Mrs. Alden H. Doolittle

126

NEW YEAR'S MOTTO

I asked the New Year
To give some motto sweet
Some rule of life
By which to guide my feet
I asked and paused—
It answered soft and low
"God's Will To Know"

"Will knowledge then
Suffice for me?" I cried
And paused again—
But 'ere the question died
The answer came
"Nay, this remember too,
God's Will To Do".

Once more I asked—
"Is this all you've to tell?"
And once again
The answer sweetly fell—
"Yes, this one thing,
'Tis all the rest above—
God's Will To Love".

— *Nicholas F. Dunn*

A TRIBUTE TO THE ESPERANCE FIREMEN

They are ready for action, day and night
To go and help, when there is a fire to fight.
No matter what the season, in rain or snow
When they hear the siren, they're ready to go.

When our Town Hall was threatened with fire throughout
They were right on the ball, and helped put it out.
So when they call on you, for a little gift
Don't you think it's up to us to give them a lift?

They are here to protect your home and mine,
And it costs a bit more than a dollar or dime.
That little extra money and deserved praise
Surely works wonders in these hectic days.

The Ambulance Service is quick, capable and superb
At least, from the recipients, that's what I've heard.
The Women's Auxiliary does a job that's first rate
When they are called upon for coffee and cake.

Their Marching Band—a real treat to hear
On holidays it makes the crowds cheer.
We're mighty proud of our women and men
We say, "Thanks to all' again and again.

— Walter Easton, Sr.

THAT GOLDEN WEDDING DAY

Look over your memory book, the past fifty years.
You will find days of Joy and Laughter, Sorrow and Tears
But you have to admit, that life is worth living,
And God gives us reasons for daily Thanksgiving.
I will always remember that tune, "Here comes the Bride"
As you marched down the aisle, to stand with your Bride at your side,
At the ceremony, on the Bride you place a ring
I wouldn't have missed that ceremony for anything.
I am sure you will want to always remember that day
When relatives and friends came, their respects to pay
And you arranged for the Church Hall, for the wonderful feed
I am sure we all ate, far beyond our need.
Now as you go together, hand in hand, down life's way,
May all your memories grow sweeter, day by day.
Now that you're back home, in Florida, in summer weather, keep on the go
And think of us up here in New York State, in rain, sleet and snow.

— Walter Easton, Sr.

GIVING THANKS

How often do we stop to count
Our many blessings each day,
Which sometimes really amount
To more than we can say?

The gifts of life and love alone
Are so wonderful to hold;
Why should people complain and groan
When all their troubles are told?

God works in many wondrous ways
His plans for us to unfold,
If we could trust Him all the days
When we do nothing but scold.

Once a year we have Thanksgiving
To come together to pray,
And thank the Lord for His giving
Blessings we cannot repay.

— Helen Hynes Germer

SONG OF THE BROOK

Winter's silence of a nearby brook
Is broken by a faint murmuring
Beneath the ice in a sheltered nook
When sun's first warm rays are hovering.

Soon ice grows tired of its winter's hold
On restless water kept still so long,
And fails to stop the movement more bold
Which opens the prelude of spring's song.

As trickling freshets from melting snows
Join forces with the wakening brook,
The tempo of the orchestra grows
With each new page of Nature's old book.

The swelling brook moves on toward the sea
Splashing in ever more vibrant chords
While greeting waterfalls joyfully
In its anthem of praise without words.

— Helen Hynes Germer

MIRACLE OF THE MAPLES

When maple leaves mature each fall
They seem to have some innate skill
Which in response to Nature's call
Brightens scenery of vale and hill.

The topmost leaves are first more bold
To test their chosen color chart
With tints of orange, red or gold
And deck their limbs with works of art.

I wonder how the maples can
Transform green leaves to gayer hues
And bring such ecstacy to man
When autumn foliage is the news.

Do maple leaves anticipate
When end of life for them is near,
And before bowing to their fate
Will have a last fling for the year?

— Helen Hynes Germer

VICTORY GARDEN

They said to plant a garden wide
To beat the cost and food provide
But oh the time that it does take

With spade and trowel, hoe and rake,
To coax along all kinds of seeds
In their race with bugs and weeds.

The odds are great that you will find
More problems than you had in mind.
Too much or too little rain may fall,
Some plants may die—but weeds grow tall.
The bugs and birds can nibble fast
On what should be your best repast.

With aching back and sunburned skin
You finally bring your harvest in.
To count the time that you have spent
Would mean defeat to provident.
But tasting brings a great big smile
And makes it all seem so worthwhile.

— Helen Hynes Germer

TREES
(With apologies to Joyce Kilmer)

I think that I shall never see
A thing so pesky as a tree
A tree whose branches snap and break
Whose fallen leaves I have to rake
A tree that drips with every rain
Whose spreading roots clog up my drain
A tree whose branches climb aloof
And scrape the shingles off my roof
A tree where ants and bugs repose
Whose sticky sap clings to my clothes
The sun's rays foiled by every leaf
Trying to nourish lawns beneath
A tree who may by lightning's wrath
Demolish all that's in its path
Whose decayed branches block the way
To cause discomfort and dismay
Oh trees bring joy to all to see
But only woe to fools like me

— Harry A. Gill

Good Samaritan Nursing Home

NEW DAY

Morning quivers in the thorns;
Birds chirp in the trees
Giving out notes of cheer
To tell all a new day is now.
The cattle in the meadows
Fed a dry grass
You can hear the tinkle of their leader's bell
The sheep too graze on the hillside.
Waiting to be shorn.

— Florence Brandow

THE MAGNIFICENT HURRAH

The 200th Birthday of U.S.A.
A celebration in your mind forever to stay.

It was a colossal and brilliant affair,
People from all walks of life joined in the fanfare.

Regardless of age, farm, city or station,
Millions honored "The Birth of Our Nation."

Scenic ships paid tribute from faraway lands;
There were speeches, parades, and soul-stirring bands.

Tall ships went gliding majestically by;
Fireworks brilliantly spiraled the sky.

And so it was through day and night
Until the dawn tripped coyly into sight.

'Twas a day to remember, both serious and fun,
Where hearts seemed united and beat as one.

A memorable day to tingle your spine;
How thankful to know—that this country is mine!

— Gertrude Kiley

HOME ON THE SEA

The house is on a raft,
Are they going to take
And plant it some place?
First the lumber
Then the pieces
Then the composition
Then they take it away!
I kind of like that!

— Loretta Smith

REALITY

When I read books
I like wild
Chaotic tales
Of rain and
Raging torrent.
Deep-sea books
Of big, bold
Men
With turbulent
Hearts, who
Kill and plunder:
Cruel draconic
Tales.
So odd—
When I like
Nothing more
Than a roaring
Fire,
A deep sofa
With the
Sweet, soft,
Never-ceasing
Sound

Of listless, lapping
Waters:
And friends
Near me,
So quiet
And peaceful —

— Ruth Grossmeyer Greene

MY FRIEND THE GUITAR
(For Leslie Anne Collins)

My guitar is my friend, my friend, the guitar
I sit alone on the steps at home
strumming the strings
as I sing, as I sing
As I chirp with crickets, warble with birds
My guitar is my friend, alleluia amen.

My guitar and I play the school canteen
I pose on the floor inside the far door
strumming steel wires
to the fireplace fire
As I hum my hopes to further my dreams
My guitar is my friend, alleluia amen.

My guitar and I dance off to church
I shout with my brothers, my sisters, others
raising up hands
like fluttering fans
As I shout hosannas in praise to the Lord
My guitar is my friend, alleluia amen.

— Louise D. Gunn

THE GREATEST GIFT

The greatest gift of all is —
the uncounted ticking of time:
the chiming of the hour,
the quarter, the half
and then the whole again.

— Louise Gunn

BEHIND HER WORDS

Bitterness . . .
puckered lips
tasting the fruited lemon flower

Anger . . .
heaving hammer
splintering valentine heart

Fear . . .
adhesive smile
holding back blood tears.

— Louise Gunn

LOVE SONGS NEVER DIE

Love songs never die . . .
they lie, fragrant
in pockets of air
flower-fair

ready, waiting
To be tuned by
invisible winds,
Love songs, waiting
For murmuring word
never meant
to be spoken

Love songs, silent, still,
never dying
ever lying
flower-fair
In pockets of air.

— Louise Gunn

THE SHAKERS, REMEMBERED

When we were children, my sister and I drove out
to see the Shakers in a horse-drawn carriage
The dust from the Niskayuna roads would sift
and settle on our dark blue middy blouses
And on the light blue blossoms of the wayside chicory—
then we were there, visiting the South Family.

A quiet peace inhabited the scrubbed and spacious halls
where Shaker capes and Shaker bonnets hung
Gracefully on wooden pegs and straight stiff chairs were
lined against the walls. It seemed to us
As though the air itself walked softly in this house
where hearts were given up to God and hands
To work, the motto they would quote to us, on end.

Hand and heart, never apart; God and soul make the whole.

The door opened up in slow motion; our Shaker
friends smiled lovingly and greeted us:
The saintly Anna Case, the Eldress (with cheeks
as pink as the wild-wood rose) Frieda;
Ella and her mother, Selina; Mary Dahm
and her sister, Grace. My sister and I loved
Mary and Grace, especially, for they were young.

One time we came to visit and found that
Mary's arm was in a sling . . . from climbing
Up to pick the farthest cherry and plummeting
to earth: unseemly conduct frowned upon
By several elders, so they told us, whispering . . .

Grace was very, very small, and very,
Very sweet; they had fashioned a special chair
for her and tasks that were suited
To her size. She never felt tempted, never, to
climb up and up to the farthest cherry!

Hand and heart, never apart; God and soul make the whole.

The time came as time will, when the Shaker
Road near Albany could boast no more
Of Shaker friends, of bushel baskets filled
with Baldwin apples, of cases of tins full to
The brim with red tomatoes which we would
purchase and carry home for winter.
The time came as time will, when the Shaker
Road near Albany could boast no more
Of Shaker friends, of Shaker hymns,
of Shaker crafts, and Shaker peace and wisdom.
A simple stone marked Eldress Anna's grave
beside the Ann Lee Home where Shaker buildings
Wrapped up the aged and ill in Shaker memories.

But then we followed them and journeyed (by auto
now) over Lebanon Mountain to visit
Sister Mary and Sister Grace among the Shakers there;
we found the pegs along the walls bereft
Of Shaker capes and bonnets; the organ, closed,
did not sing of lively Shaker hymns.
And Sister Mary, still with a lingering mischief
in her eyes, nursed the sick with Shaker
Hands and heart, while Sister Grace, who
still sat upon the lowest chair, was Shaker sweet.
Their Yea and Nay fell softly on our ears and
we noted yet again their loving Shaker ways.

Hand and heart, never apart; God and soul make the whole.

*Footnote: Today in 1979, there is a movement to restore the buildings with the surrounding acreage of the South Family, where our childhood friends lived

. . . And recently my sister and I have made new Shaker friends, among whom are Sister Mildred Baker and Brother Theodore Johnson, who remember the Shakers mentioned in my poem and who travel down from Sabbath Day Lake, Maine, to visit Walter Chura, the proprietor of Simple Gifts who named his bookstore here in Albany after a Shaker hymn. So, once again, my sister and I sing and pray together in Shaker assemblies with Shaker friends.

— Louise D. Gunn

THE VIEW FROM HERE

Made for each other, side by side,
They quietly drink in the sun.
Answering the wind who teased them to play,
They slowly moved, then sank away.
But suddenly emerging from their trance
To an unheard tune they started to dance.
They kicked and swayed and spun around,
Tumblesaulting toward the ground.
Bewitched by the rhythm, they'd flutter and shake,
Entwine as partners, then separate.
They stopped for a moment as dancers do,
Trying to measure the wild tattoo.
Back to the whirlwind, catching the beat,
Once more from beginning with dancing feet.
Into the air, up toward the sun,
Waving like flags, then down they'd come.

My heart jumps to keep in time
With the way they're swinging on the line—
His and Her Blue Jeans, no cares, no where, no when,
They tempt my settled spirit
To soar and fly again.

— Eleanor Huba

HER LAST STAND
Observing my neighbor from the back porch . . .

The old woman emerged from her fortress
Unfurling her battle flags to the wind:
Little plastic bags pinned to the clothesline —
Washed symbols of defiance,
The fluttering remains of her revolt
Against a throw-away world.

— Eleanor Huba

SONG OF SPRING

Nobody grows old by merely living a number of years;
people only grow old by deserting their ideals. Nor is
youth simply a matter of ripe cheeks and supple knees;
youth is a temper of the will, a quality of the imagination,
a vigor of the emotions, and a freshness of the deep springs
of life. Years may wrinkle the skin, but to give up enthusiasm
wrinkles the soul. Whether seventeen or seventy, if there is
in one's heart the love of wonder, the childlike appetite of
what's next, and the courage to play as the rules are written,
that person is young.

Men do not quit playing because they grow old; they grow
old because they quit playing, if I remember right.

Oh for one hour of youthful joy!
Give back my twentieth spring!
I'd rather laugh, a bright-haired boy
Than reign a gray-beard king.
The old man dreams,
Oh, what shall I be at fifty
Should nature keep me alive, If I find
the world so bitter when I am but twenty-five?
To be seventy years young is sometimes far more cheerful
and hopeful than to be forty years old.
Young men soon give and some soon forget affronts;
old age is slow in both.

— Thomas Hunter

WHO CAN TELL?

Who can tell?
Today may be a direful knell
Of yester-year's occurrence—
A day drowned in tears.

Mayhap this fitful cloud,
Like a loosened shroud
Enveloping the rain,
Will tomorrow break, and let the sunshine pour
In ecstacies upon the very bower
Which shadows darken once again.

Who can tell?
Tomorrow may abound with cheer;
And cast the drear of yester-year
To the westward wind.

—Molly Isaccs

SINCERELY YOURS

There was a time when letter writing bound
Old friends and loved ones scattered far and near;
But something's happened to this art once found
To be the means of linking those so dear.
The few the postman drops into my slot
Are one-paged notes—"a line of two to say—"
No one has time to sit and think and not
Rush on to duties crammed into the day.
Good friends will say, "I don't have time to write,
But when the rates are low, I'll place a call."
That's good; we have a brief contact in spite
Of hurrying to keep the toll quite small.
But still I miss the good old days so much,
When folks had time to write and keep in touch.

—Raymond H. Jackson

TWO WINDOWS

Behind a window draped in netted silk
Which lets the patterned light seep in, stood Ignorance.
He pressed his anguished face against the pane:
"Give me more light,
Please teach me how to live;
Pull back the curtains so the light
Bathes my deprivéd self
From head to toe."

The light and warmth soon filled the room
Enveloping the one who asked; he then began
To undergo a change like th'unsightly caterpillar
When the bright-winged butterfly comes forth.
More light! More change!
Until from ignorance
Intelligence emerged.

Behind another window with his back against the pane
Stands Stupidity—defiant, tense, cursing the light
That finds its way between the open velvet drapes:
"Don't bother me! I don't need you!
I'll go my way unorthodox as it may be.
No guidance and no teaching do I need!
In fact, I know as much as you—
I want—and give no help!"

With his left hand he pulls the cord that closes tight
The heavy drapes. How evenly they fall in place!
Each fold and pleat identical with every other one.
The heavy folds sway gently back and forth
For just a spell,
Then cease to move at all;
And for a lifetime hang
Symmetrically in place—
Undisturbed.

—Raymond H. Jackson

A VERY NOSTALGIC LIFE-STYLE

I was a long-wanted kid.
Solution was under the lid
Of what do you thinkum?
Long, I'd remained but a thought
Until my mother had bought
Two bottles of Lydia Pinkham!

On a trolley, one Junesy-day
We rode downtown, you might say—
'Though not quite that graphic.
In 1912 it was rare
For babes to be born down there
At Yonkers Homeopathic.

I spent the night all alone
In their nursery—full blown.
(I got born, all right.)
I could have been awful good,
But what I wanted, was food—
So, I yelled all night.

They took me home to the hill
High above the river, Sawmill,
Here I am—my motto.
Anon, I was taken to Ardsley.
Not by horse and buggy—hardly—
But in a new auto.

For the three or four years, hence,
On Sundays, we rode in suspense—
A little buckboardsley.
North to Dobbs Ferry, then east.
Relatives to visit—at least
Our kinfolk in Ardsley.

Great-grandmother, aged yet spry,
Returned with us, often, to my
House on north Yonkers hill.

She loved to ride in that flivver
Along the old Sawmill River—
Knew each house and rill!

Three cheers for that Model T.
Which gave my doll, Casey, and me
Adventure and scope;
A very nostalgic life-style,
When the world stood still for awhile.
I'll never forget—I hope.

Margaret King Travis of Yonkers—
(my forbears called it der Jonkkers)
I knew who I was.
From my lofty, high, hilltop,
I examined my world, nonstop,
As any child does.

My hilltop was my own kingdom.
I felt luxurious freedom.
Everything, I explored.
I'd tiptoe around, or race
At 38 Tower Place.
I never was bored.

The view from rear porch, upstairs,
Unfolded the world everywhere—
As far as the sea.
The sky was so wide and blue—
Tree and rooftops often with dew—
What more could there be?

"Grandparents" I adopted.
(Or was it they, who pre-adopted
To fill in, for me?)
"Nannah" and "Uncle" Charles Glover
Lived upstairs, and right over
We Travises, three.

I was showered with love and affection,
And set in the right direction
By parents—Mrs. and Mr.

Tea parties with Catskill cousins—
Visitors by the dozens—
A new baby sister.

Cousin Ethel, from Ardsley, came
And walked me, and played endless games
When she wasn't in school.
She'd hold my hand, crossing streets
(Handy things, are hands and feets)
On days, warm or cool.

Greek priests, exercising past,
My hand would friendlily clasp
As they'd pause to chat.
I watched for the lamplighter man
And he'd always wave his hand.
How I did love that!

Our move, over near the sea—
Something new and different for me—
Far away from Yonkers,
A change but not trauma—for
The Glovers moved, too, next door.
New Worlds to conquer!

My Dad's Bakery Business, behooved
In 1916, we moved (to)
Bridgeport, Connecticut.
Our visits to Ardsley declined.
Yet, often I bring to mind—
Memories from my gut.

The harrowing trip in May
Every Decoration Day,
Which we always took.
Auto, ever over-heating.
The pail, in case we were needing
At a handy brook.

Narrow, bumpy, winding road,
My father's patience to goad,
As we chugged along.

We sang to keep our spirits up.
We guessed at the new spring crops,
In the days bygone.

The joyous family gathering.
The food that I was rathering
To fill my empty "slate"!
The narrow, Sawmill River
To gaze upon with shiver
The play with the cats.

The long day would soon be ending.
The departure, with dread, pending.
It seemed such a pity—
That trip back home would predicate
My mother's blinding headache—
Return to the city.

New friends I encountered and won
Indeed, it was lots of fun
At 70 Livingston Place.
We didn't live on a hill
But across from "Spuddy" Bill—
Freckles all over his face!

Beardsley Park, at end of street
Was a place I thought was neat—
To go there to play.
We carried nuts to the squirrels
(My mother and two little girls)
On many a day.

I'd spend hours at Meyer's flat
Where their pictures portrayed that
Cameo on the moon.
Their collection of butterflies
Widely opened my eyes
To insects—cocoons.

"Auntie Nye" was a special friend.
My! There was never an end
To her League of Arts.

With her needle and colored thread
She would fashion a posey bed,
With lines and French knots.

When Raymond went off to the War
He personally asked me for
A personal favor.
Would I, while he was away,
Look in on "Auntie" each day?
(My attention, I gave her.)

We lived on the second floor.
The garret above, you'd adore!
Ideal for my playroom.
But even before it was settled
I became more than just nettled—
I lowered the boom!

I'd searched for days—weeks—a year!
For Casey, my darling, my dear.
She wasn't in attic!
'Though I hunted 'round and 'round,
My doll, Casey, was never found.
Very traumatic!

One day, I saw sitting there—
Huge Roosevelt Teddy Bear—
But HIM, I hated!
I'd not let HIM take Casey's place.
I wanted to see Casey's face!
(Grief and hate, dated.)

I did not learn 'til years later
She'd been discarded by pater!
(Her face was cracking.)
Mother had tried to protest,
But fathers think they know best—
Especially when packing.

The washer-lady, next door,
Whose laughter I did adore
Was named Mary Christmas.

I asked were she Santa's wife.
The biggest thrill of my life
When I thought she was.

Prudence and Marjorie and Dorothy
Were my feminine friends, noteworthy.
We often "played dolls."
We walked with our baby carriages
And talked about "our marriages"—
Like parrots and polls.

Took piano from Elsie Ayres.
Didn't like it much—but there's
"No sense not trying."
I fumbled those damn scales—hours
While my whole world went quite sour.
(I thought I was dying.)

I had a safe place to hide
From things I couldn't abide,
At Nannah's, next door.
She'd play "Melody in F,"
And tunes in 'most any clef—
(That's what music is for.)

Dooryards were prolific with flowers,
Everywhere else, but in ours.
How I longed for a few!
I knew Ten Commandments and such—
Still—how could it matter, much,
To pick one or two?

Brought them home before they died.
My mother was mortified—
Her daughter had stole!
My passion for posies undid me.
My mother reluctantly tied me
To backyard clothes pole.

And as if that wasn't climactic,
To make punishment more emphatic
Nannah was appealed
To open her window wide
And shame me. The while I cried.
(Vowed never again to steal.)

Uncle Charles and Nannah brought books—
Field Guides, showing flowery nooks.
Correctly motivated
From thence—I stuck to wild flowers,
In woods and fields and bowers,
And places uncultivated.

In summer, something most jolly—
Excursions we took by trolley
Crosstown, to Seaside Park.
From beginning to end of line,
That ride was supremely fine.
A wonderful lark!

Laden with baskets of lunch,
Bathing clothes rolled in a bunch,
We'd find a good spot.
To tackle the waves, I would.
To float on the sea, I could
Like a tiny dot.

We'd assemble—the family, all—
To watch the twilight baseball
Near the glistening bay.
We'd blow our whistles and scream
For my father's bakery team—
At Dan Wilsea's triple play!

Margaret T. Lane

LOVE IS

Love is a girl, with stars in her eyes.
Faith is a candle burning.
Hope is an ember out of the ashes.
Charity is a child, picking a bouquet.

— Kay Meehan

UNLESS I CARE

What is this pain
That deeply penetrates my heart?

Why should I care
That men are starving in the streets
And many dying there?
I did not rob them of their bread
And strip their bodies bare.
Why should I care?

Why should I care
That orphaned children weep alone
In anguish and despair?
The bombs that fell on them today—
I did not drop them there.
Why should I care?

What is that light?
A star of hope unto my eyes?

Because I care,
That light may shine for everyone,
No darkness anywhere.
How can there ever be one world
For fellowmen to share—
Unless I care?

— Miles J. Martin

THE ROSE

My lady wears a faint disguise
As down the street she goes
Sapphires shining in her eyes
And in her hand a rose.

Suspended kisses on her lips
Red ribbons in her hair
Harmonic movement as she skips
Mischievous and fair.

Her kiss is for another one
Her smile for all to see
But Heavens! I am all undone —
The rose she gave to me!

—Miles J. Martin

DREAMS

The dreams of age are ever young —
Young as the crocus in the spring,
Young as the bluebird on the wing,
Young as a love song newly sung.

The dreams of youth are very old —
Old as the endless sweep of time,
Old as a never-ending rhyme,
Old as a legend oft retold.

In dreams the strands of life are strung
From youth to age in a web of gold,
For the young are ever growing old
And the old forever young.

—Miles J. Martin

To Jean Robert Foster

OLD TIMES

Oh! For the good old days
When one could day-boat on the Hudson River
Or perhaps hve a joy ride in the family flivver

A ride on the trolley car was a way of commutation
And a shopping trip on Pearl Street was an expectation
A dinner at Keeler's was an enjoyable delight
Followed by a ball game at Hawkins by night.

There were stock company plays at Harmanus Bleecker
And roller-coaster rides for the thrill seeker
The chaperoned dance at the Women's Y
Was a proper place for a gal to meet a guy

Washington Park was a meeting place for friends
With skating by winter, rowboating in summer;
And band concerts enjoyed by all

In the good old days, of first permanent waves
When a girl rolled her stockings and was known as a flapper
A guy smoked a pipe and wore a raccoon coat quite dapper,

For dance, they learned how to do the Charleston,
The Black-Bottom and Big Apple, also in fashion
When talking pictures first came into being
Movie houses were filled, for they were worth seeing

Then came the Speakeasies, and the bathtub gin
But to indulge in such was a social sin
Well the young folks of long ago
Are the seniors now, and we're not so slow

The new Albany intrigues us and we still enjoy good times
But thoughts of the old times and old friends
Do occasionally grieve us

— Agnes M. Neudorf

WHERE TO HAVE LUNCH

Hi! there folks let's eat
It's pay day, who's going to treat
Oh, dutch you say, then where to
Down street, up street, what have you?

Now here's a little suggestion
If it's at Farnum's we'll make an impression
The Ten Eyck will soak us I'm sure
And at Jackson's we'll all look demure

Did you mention the DeWitt?
The bill will give us a fit
If you eat up at the Larkin,
You'll find a good place for parkin'

Who said the Princess Pat?
No, not there I'm sure of that
We want to dine in style
Let's stop at Ed Koonz's for awhile.

When you're hungry without fail
You should try and make the Rail
Or dash over to the Pewter Pitcher
For another time you'll be none the richer

Over to Stittig's the cuisine is fine
You'll want to eat there all the time
Never go to Hosler's if you're in a rush
Everytime you order you are caught up in the crush

Or if you want a thrill
Eat up at the Central Avenue Grill
Maybe you'd like some spinach
It's good up at the Greenwich

You're all too fussy, and hard to suit
Guess today I'll just eat some fruit
And tomorrow I've a hunch
Perhaps we'd better bring our lunch.

I'm broke already, says I
It's the White Tower, for coffee and pie.

— Agnes M. Neudorf

IF YOU LOVE

If you love me, tell me.
Show me that you care.
What good is all that loving
If I am unaware?

Parent, child, lover, friend,
However we relate
Today's the day I need your love.
Please . . . Don't make me wait.

— Rose Panitch

NAMES

Names, names, names, names!
What to call that precious bundle
When it finally arrives,
Straight from heaven
Or from the cabbage patch
Or brought by stork that flies.

After burning midnight oil,
After all that trouble and toil,
Be it for daughter or be it for son,
It's almost sure to please no one.

Best to my mind, give them a number.
The time will fly so swiftly by,
Leave the choice for them to make.
Then no matter what they pick,
T'will not be your mistake.

— Rose Panitch

A STICK OF WOOD, IF TALK I COULD

Friend, now when you look at me
Would you believe I was a tree?
I stood so proud and grand and tall
Yet now there's not much left at all.

My consolation is the thought
Of what my trunk and boughs have wrought.
I cannot feel too sad for long —
Homes and halls and croquet balls,

Toys for joys to girls and boys,
Warmth and comfort by the hearth
To summon forth a happy smile
Be glad, this makes it all worthwhile.

If you would make it up to me,
Just plant a seed from which springs free
That which fills a future need:
A tall and green and stately tree.

— Rose Panitch

THE INVITATION

Hear the quiet, listen to the still,
Sharpen your awareness and let your soul expand.
Tell your eyes to search the heavens,
Let their gaze rest on the land.

Watch the motion of the trees,
The soundless flight of birds.
All this in silence
More eloquent than words.

See the clouds break up and roll away
That covered sleeping stars last night.
Enjoy blue sky revealed
In morning sun's first light.

Detect a perfume in the air
Cast by shrubs and flowers.

The blessed hush will heal your soul
Reprieved from busy hours.

All this treasure
Share with me.
A glimpse of Paradise
And free!

— Rose Panitch

HAPPY BIRTHDAY, AMERICA

You've come a long way, baby,
And on this, your bicentennial year,
All that we can wish for you,
The land we hold so dear

Is renewal of old values
That started your career.
Truth and honor, justice too
To bolster pride we have in you.

You've come through with flying colors
So many crises, big and small,
And now you're facing problems
That seem greatest of them all.

May God, our heavenly Father,
Bless you with his care,
Guide and guard those at the helm
And help us all to share

In finding a solution which
Will bring us in full measure
Peace with honor and security
For posterity to treasure.

— Rose Panitch

Rhymed Thoughts

KNOWING IS HALF THE CURE

Time is an artist
Using weather for ink,
Wind and rain,
And the snow, I think.
His brush an old finger
Long and thin.
Pointing in December,
What a fool I've been.

BREAKFAST PRAYER

O dear God, bless this table.
Bless this food and make us able
To face Your day and catch our bus
Do what You will for all of us.

HAPPY ENDING

We had an Aunt Sadie in Troy,
Who, all her relatives, did annoy.
Then, just near the end
She found a friend,
Who treated her, not as Aunt Sadie,
But just as a lonely old lady.

APOLOGY

One reason why I've little to say,
My mind changes every day.
From week to week
Two things I dread:
". . . But you promised,"
". . . But you said."

AWAKENED

No wonder my understanding
Has so suddenly improved:
I am walking
In my father's shoes.

LAMENT

I never let—
A crumb go to waste,
Nor tear a usable
Scrap in haste.
But money and time,
Such precious things—
I let them go,
On flying wings.

A GOOD IDEA

Never allow
A good idea
To disappear.
You'll be left
With a minute—
But nothing
In it.

— Sara Perlman

AUTUMN

Oh! Oft I've envied others,
Who journeyed o'er the sea
To far and distance countries,
And wished that it could be
My lot to see the wonders
God has made in other lands;
But someone always needed
The care and labor of my hands.
Then, today as I was trying
To make my dwelling neat,
I saw a patch of sunlight
Paint the floor beneath my feet
And from the open window
The leaves cast their shadows through
And dancing in the sunlight
A mystic pattern drew.
And outside the open doorway
Covering field and meadow sod
The glory of early Autumn
Lingering green and goldenrod
Filled the earth with so much beauty
That I feel I must atone
For envious thoughts of travel
Akin to heaven God made my home.

— Persis M. Race

CAPRICIOUS SEPTEMBER

Like a willful mistress of many moods
September comes again.
And flings abroad with lavish hand
Sunshine, shadow, frost and rain.
Red, yellow and brown, the leaves drift down,
And seem to sigh, as they go floating by,
"So soon, September? Oh! much too soon."
Like a crescent of gold, the harvest moon

Hangs low in the evening sky
And lights the glade for the lad and maid
Who arm in arm loiter by.
The tree toads in unison sounding
Like the chimes of muted bells
In the dew-capped grass the crickets chirp
And the end of summer foretell
Then, harvest moon, as your reign is o'er,
And you fade like a dying ember,
We'll bid you both a last farewell,
Harvest moon and capricious September.

— Persis M. Race

LATTER DAYS

Wreath of thorn and wane of leaf,
Honey turned to wormwood gall,
Dry noise of an aging mouth,
Hollow shapes, collapsing, fall
To rivulets of nothingness;
Struggling shadows of old selves,
What is left to haven us?
Turn ravaged eyes unto the hill,
An ancient beauty haunts us still.

HAIKU — SENRYU

Isolation is a fact
Of existence, palpable
As a baked potato, but colder.

TOUCHÉ

The sharp thrust of a word
Has pierced me like a sword

And though I shall not die, its dart
Has critically torn my heart.
Here in this green and gentle glade
Plunges again the gory blade.

— Betty Reed

WINONA WOLF

I had pretended so much
With my thin razor scratches,
Augmenting blood with ketchup,
Fainting in gasless cars and ovens,
Displaying empty poison bottles,
Choking on non-existent bones,
Being bitten by imaginary rats;
So when the real end came
No one would believe me.*

She'd never die of a cold, they said.
Of course she's still alive.

OVERHEARD

I went to the sex talk
And all I can remember
is that parsley is an aphrodisiac.

CAVENDISH

Often I wish . . . I wish . . . I wish
That I'd run into Cavendish,
Cavendish of the speedwell eyes
That scatter sparks of blue surprise;
Cavendish whose every work
Is complimentary though absurd;

Who can be relied on to
Approve of everything I do.
In this bleak world I wish . . . I wish
I'd soon run into Cavendish.

— Betty Reed

THOSE PLACES

I have been in those places
Where the dark dogs of the spirit
Howl hungrily
Tearing the raw meat of dreams
From shrunken bones;
And I have gazed into the blind stares
Of stumbling corpses;
I have seen old fragile people
Marched beneath boiling skies
To exercise in oblivious courtyards;
Wilted girls, once pretty, ironing all day
The lingerie of doctors' wives.

There is nothing to do but rot here,
Nothing but rot,
Says a boy hardly out of his teens;
Alcohol was better, drugs were better,
At least they succored you on false hope.
Here there's no hope at all.

A toothless woman hugs her doll;
Oh baby, my baby, she croons,
Kissing the stuffed thing.

Hush, hush, I cannot hear my voices,
A man cries. They are trying to come through!

— Betty Reed

OLD MR. BLESSING

As I remember,
Age had
Weathered him
Like an
Ancient
Silver boarded
Barn
In a field
Of buttercups;
Wholesome
Clean,
Grown to the
Landscape
And good;
I had stopped
To call —
In conversation
He told me
Of farming days,
Of having lived
Nearly ninety
Years
On this
Same place
"Want to
Show you
Something
Before you go."
He led me
Into the front yard,
Talking
As we went.
"Was only ten
When I
Planted this."

He walked
To a huge
Maple—
And there,
the old man
Leaned tall
To the tree,
And placed
His arms
About it;
His gnarled
Fingers
Could not
Meet
Around the
Equally gnarled
Majestic trunk.
I looked
In awe and,
For a moment,
It seemed
To me
I could not tell
Which was
The old man
And which
The tree.

— *James R. Rhodes*

HARLEQUIN HILLS

Who needs
The flowers
Of summer
When they have
Fall leaves?

The fears
Of winter
Are easily
Overcome
By the
Body-trill
Of our
Mature time—
The wine
So mellow
And the spread
Of yellow
Goldenrod
Upon the hills;
The rewards
Of after-fruiting
And seeds
To the wind—
Are the
Candle-trees
And color-muting
Of harlequin hills
Pinned
Against the blue—
In the season
Of wine
And mellow.

— James R. Rhodes

MYSTERY

I did not
Dream,
Or deem
It of
Consequence,

That life
Should go,
Or arrive
Some place
Hence
In time;
That it
Should be
At all—
Is mystery
Enough
In universe
For my
Theology.

— James R. Rhodes

SUNRISE ON THE MOUNTAIN
(Stowe, Vermont)

The somber darkness of the night,
Moves oh so gently through the hill,
And soundless sounds reverberate,
This then is how it was, and always will—

From cavern depths a shield-like mist
Floats ever upward yet all the while,
The constant mountain holds quite still,
This then is how it was, and always will —

An eerie light reveals the awe
Of His omnipotent perfection,
The sun resumes her spending warmth
With elegant direction,
And soon this glorious wonder
Removes the nightly chill,
This then is how it was, and always will—.

— Rebecca Richter

BUNKER HOLE
(Campus 1962)

In 1772 they stood, together on the top,
Smithy, Plainsman, Farmer, Statesman, Poet,
Butcher, Baker— —
Yes, yes, even Candlestick Maker!
Where? Bunker Hill!
Pre-select group?
Absolute nonsense!

Robert Browning said, "All service ranks the
same with God, etc,"
This so naive faith was strong— —1772

In 1962 the common people dug— —
A hole to shelter their officials,
Taxationists, Legislators, Electronic Statisticians,
Computers, Button-Pushers and, of course, Morticians.
Where? Bunker hole!
Pre-select group?
Most essential!

(The tension of Atomic Bombs in 1960 resulted in a massive construction
underground, at the Campus site Washington Avenue, Albany. This for the protection of government officials.)

— Rebecca Richter

MIRRORED DIALOGUE

I look in the mirror to identify
The me that was some time ago,
The reflective face reveals a sigh,
So changed am I, and it does show.

"Your're old," says the voice,
Indeed not by choice,
I've had no say in the matter,
Your hair, quite gray,

A grandiose array,
Enough! such idle chatter.

Then accept what is, but please no tears,
The placebo voice implores,
Accept what is, and be glad to see
The harvest of your years.

Unfair it seems to contemplate
The passing time I knew,
I'm young inside and still with pride,
What need to sublimate.

There is no age for loving,
And loving knows no age,
Oh mirrored face, with pleasing grace,
Scorn not this bright new stage.

— Rebecca Richter

BIRDS EXIST IN ALBANY

A handsome youth by the name
of Birdie
Met a pretty miss whose name
was Robin
He lived in a cottage on
Quail Street
She lived in a flat on
Lark Street
They courted in a movie on
Eagle Street
Settling down in their nest on
Dove Street.

— Ada Robinson

TO A NURSE

Who wakes patients in the hospital at 5:00 a.m. to wash their faces, when they could sleep until 7:00 a.m.

I know you must do your duty
If you want to be on the beam,
But wake not this sleeping beauty,
Disturb not his pleasant dream.

What though his hands be dirty?
What though unwashed his face?
The weightiest problems are trifles
When you're deep in Morpheus' embrace.

— Harry Rubin

BEGINNINGS

I sat and listened to Sister
while she told the boys what to say
back to Father at mass
She would say it all beautiful in Latin
Agnus Dei qui tollis peccata mundi
and the boys would answer
Bluh bluh bluh under their breath
sort of, wiggling, and grinning at
each other

I knew all the answers but I sat still
my stomach sticking out a little
because of my arms
folded in back of me where they belonged
when I wasn't working

My mind did all the Latin
while I remembered the time the girls
clustered all around Sister
and talked about being nuns
It was a lonely day so

I spoke up and said I'll be a Sister too
a little surprised to hear myself
But Sister Cyrilla looked at me
just at me and said
You'll never make a nun, my dear
and oh she was right that time

My arms tingled
I stuck my stomach out farther to rest them
I thought about Sister giving me a B
in spelling that time
me who could spell anything at all
not because I studied
it was a gift from God, I thought
I cried, I remembered, and
asked Sister why after school

Because you are too proud
she told me
God doesn't like you to be proud
But it's His spelling I thought
more than mine
That time she wasn't right
I said yes Sister

Next day they were practicing again
Agnus Dei tollis peccata mundi
I held on to the desk with both hands
I said
Ora pro nobis
very loud
above the bluh bluh bluh
of the boys

It was very quiet
I put my head down on the desk
in my waiting arms.
Ora pro nobis

— *Alma Skidmore*

MEA CULPA—SOUTHSIDE CHICAGO

One day I took Lou and Joe along
And we went to my church
They didn't have a church—they even went to the public school
So I showed them
The big yellow brick school
The big yellow brick church
Where I sang in the choir
Even the nuns' house where
I went on Saturday for piano lessons
Where the nun answered the door
Without her veil on
(Oh, her head all wrapped in clean white stuff
But no black veil)

Lou said, "Can we go in the church?"
I shook a little but I said,
"Sure we can."
And we did
It took us all three to open the door
We walked all over
Quiet as anything
With holy water just for me
They wanted to go upstairs
So I prayed to myself and we went up
They tiptoed and they hardly breathed
I was scared
Joe stumbled a little over a kneeling bench
But Lou
Oh she leaned forward to the organ
She touched a note
It **played**
My heart fell over
My mind talked to God but my feet ran
All three of us ran, making noise, down the stairs
Outside
Joe giggled and said,
"No one was in there but us."

I said, "Let's go home—"
But I still heard that note
I felt God hearing it . . .
I couldn't get away.

— Alma Skidmore

TRANSPLANT

Out here away from the big city
It's hard to learn the rules
Our school is smaller than the town school
And every day
Walking home down Prairie Avenue
All of us are on one side
And they're on the other
There's more of them
And they're louder
All the way home they yell

Catlickers
Catlickers

We pretend not to notice
We walk together and laugh and talk
We run sometimes
If the weather's nice, and there's enough of us
We get brave too
We look at each other and start in

Puplickers we yell at them
Puplickers
Puplickers

— Alma Skidmore

EYE LEVEL

Tall mountains block my view
This sunless day,

Black against the gray of sky.
Lost horizons taunt me passing by,
Like laughing bubbles vanishing
In space on high . . .
So intent am I
On forging mammoth things,
I miss a yellow daisy
Standing by.

— Elizabeth Snyder

TEMPLE BELLS

Temple bells soulfully break
the somber silence of the
desert evening . . .
Voices of monks harmonize
to the chant of organ music . . .
Now pleading, now exultant,
now jubilant in praise,
now fading humbly into the
glorious majesty and love of God . . .
The bells toll softer and softer,
Finally nestling in the lonely
stillness of the night.

— Elizabeth Snyder

WEAVE OF DREAMS

Frozen in a drop of rain
Are varied shades of blue,
Snowflakes on a windowpane
Are gems of golden hue.

Along a fence where berries grow
In tones of purple, red and green
A butterfly has paused to show
Her colors blending in between.

Of such the weave of dreams is spun,
In this interlude of silver lace,
Captured in a moment's run
In fragment of a misty space.

— Elizabeth M. Snyder

SOLILOQUY IN SHADOWS

If I should walk again the lane we knew,
The hour April and the setting sun
Coating crimson shadows on the crystal dew,
And all the world far, far away, undone . . .
If some Lorelei should whisper our lost song
To lure you back across the restless years,
Would you consider or let time prolong
The wasted hours and the senseless tears?
I've pondered long on April ecstasy,
On Autumn leaves that fade and disappear,
The void that shuns December reverie
Fails to meet the challenge of the coming year:
I shall not dally in the waning light
But, walk on, lonely in the pending night.

— Elizabeth Snyder

MEMORIES AT TULIP TIME

Wild geese and gillyflowers
Yellow tulips in a row
White wigs and silver
buckles
In our town of long ago.
Petticoats from parlor looms
Caps and aprons starchy
white

And hurry to the Pinksterfest
To dine and dance till
night.
Baskets of kuchen, smoky
hams
Good wines of Beverwyck
Made in copper kettles
Over fireplaces of brick.
Mynheer gives a fancy
kerchief
To the woman of his choice
Lettered "Love" then tells
his "company"
"We're engaged, let's all
rejoice:"
When gates are locked,
candles snuffed
The klopperman will ring
his bell
Each hour (we trust he
watches now)
Still calling "All is well!"

— Elizabeth Snyder

ALBANY, CRADLE OF THE UNION, 1754-1954

Their names seem like a
lullaby,
Tuscarora and Cayuga.
We see them tall and
straight and brave
By the waters of the
Hudson;
Joined by Mohawks and
Oneidas,

Senecas and Onondagas;
Come to meet their great
white brothers,
Come to form a lasting
treaty,
Come to form a solid
union . . .
The town is as a tiny
toyland;
Three hundred wooded
houses scattered,
Scrubbed white in clean
Dutch-wifely fashion;
Picket fences framing blossoms
Tulips, pinks and
gillyflowers,
And on the hill a gray
stone fort . . .
We see Red Chiefs numbered
three times fifty
Meet the five and twenty
white men
At the Stadthouse near the
river,
Listening to the pleas for
union,
Listening hard to Doctor
Franklin
Telling them "Unite or
Die!"

Evenings after talks were
ended,
Fathers sit by open fires,
Smoking long white pipes
and smiling,
Thinking of the plans they
made;
Mothers by the cradles
humming

Tuscarora, Onondaga,
Looking past the child
a-rocking
Past the time of doubting,
Past the years of struggle,
To future sons like Mister
Lincoln;
Feeling strength in
brotherhood
And brotherhood is good:

— Elizabeth M. Snyder

ISLE OF ERIN

Lovely is the shale of Connemara
in colors gleaned from lamps of misty hue.

Lilting is the tune of Galway's water
As the moon bends low to kiss her shoals of blue.

Leprechauns still linger near the castles,
From Mallow to Trallee their legends spun.

Longing is the heart at Killone Abbey
Sensing God in chancels molding in the sun.

Lonely blows the breeze at Cliffs of Moher,
O'Brien's Towers pointing up on high.

Leeward floats the currach filled with dreaming
Of Erin, kin to isles above the sky.

— Elizabeth Snyder

LITTLE ONES

Would that I give you the benefit
Of all life's lessons I've had,
Would that I pave your pathway
With a carpet of everything glad . . .

Remove all the stones in the highway,
Paint every skyline so blue,
Keep all the flowers blooming
And birds singing gayly to you.

Would that I take every heartache,
Remove any sign of a tear,
Would that I shoulder each burden
So that you would be happy, my dears.

But perhaps you would not be contented
Or appreciate everything nice,
Unless you had tasted the bitter
And sorted the sweet from the spice.

As the all-knowing God in the distance
Once showed the way for us all,
So you will profit, my darlings,
By sipping a bit of the gall!

— *Elizabeth Snyder*

ENERGY REPORT
(Automotive Division)

I get four miles per gallon
And that should be plenty:
My grandson gets
The other twenty . . .

— *Helen Gorn Sutin*

NO HAPPY MEDIUM

Size twenty casts a longing look
At size sixteen, who yearns
To wear size twelve, who wishes she

Could wear a nine, who burns
To **add** a sliver to her weight
So some day **she** may delve
Into alluring racks of clothers
So tantalizing twelve . .

— Helen Gorn Sutin

PIECE DE RESISTANCE

Magazines and newspapers
Do constantly conspire
To make the things which are not mine
My paramount desire—
Tenaciously, the radio
Inspires beyond a doubt
Possession of the things I once
Lived happily without.
My eyes and ears are subject to
An unremitting stream
Of most convincing argument
(I'm trapped upon the beam)
For every marvel sciences
Contrive to build to please:
From stereos, appliances,
To colorful TVs . . .

Dear copy writers, once I was
Contented with my lot,
Completely, sweetly unaware
Of things I hadn't bought—
Alas, my attitude has changed,
Let up, desist, I plead!
Now everything I do not have
I desperately need!

— Helen Gorn Sutin

THE TRUE STORY OF TOM

Tom was a most unspeakable cat
Old and ugly, ill-mannered and fat
'Twas seldom he groomed his mangy old hide
Nor had he an ounce of felinial pride.

By day he snoozed on a sun-warmed sill
By night he was king of Boylston Hill;
He dined on blue jays and skittering mice
Roving dogs dared not challenge him twice.

In the cowbarn, the old beast reigned supreme
The Master gave Tom daily rations of cream
But the Mistress despised his slovenly ways:
His appearance upset her well-ordered days.

When the dear lady started to cough and sneeze
She blamed the old beast for her allergies
And bade the old man get rid of his cat.
Alas! He knew he must do just that.

The deed was done in the dark of the night
Poor Tom in a sack and tied up tight
And tossed from the wharf to the briny deep.
The old man went home to a troubled sleep.

At dawn as the Mistress was milking her cow,
She jumped as she heard a familiar meow
And fled from the barn with a frightful scream
Leaving Tom to skim the milk of its cream!

The old man smiled and explained to his wife
That cats do most surely have more than one life
But he'd known from the start that Tom would come back
Any cat could escape from a **wet paper** sack.

— Eileen S. Thompson

WHEN I WAS YOUNG

I love to be near the ocean,
I like to watch the ships that sail the sea,

Being once in the Navy myself
Brings it all back to me.
The Navy life is one you can't forget—
It gets into your soul.
I did intend to make it my whole life's goal.

In the evening when the tide comes in and out,
It's a wonderful sight to see!
And it brings back good old memories
Of the days that used to be
When I was young and sailed
The deep blue sea.

— Charles L. Vail
From Highland Retirement Center

PETITION

Give me a river,
Running gently through
Summer sunset, morning dew
At the edge of the meadow.

Give me a tree,
Standing broad and tall
Waving branches, a beckoning call
To quiet times I long to know.

Give me a dream,
When dreams are so few,
And time to dream so precious too.
I need a dream to follow.

Oh God— —
Give me a river, a tree, and a dream.

— Doris Welsh

THE SEVENTIES

I stay away from mirrors.
I don't like what I see.
I'm very glad the OUTside
Is not quite all of me.
When I pass by the mirrors,
I cannot see the wreck
Of flab and upright wrinkles
That dangle on my neck.
The spotted skin that sinks in,
The veins that bulge between
Those knotted bones, my fingers,
Are all too plainly seen.
But INside, I'm not wrinkled.
I laugh. I work. I sing!
I write. I walk in friendship
As young as anything!

— Margaret A. Wheeler

SOMETIMES, LOOK DOWN AT WEEDS

The low spots have their beauty too.
The hidden places we must search
Or we will miss the blue-eyed grass,
The cinquefoil, and the pink fleabane.
On either side the sky bends down
In squared-off blooms of chickory.
The fluted bells of milkweed hang
Adorned with monarch butterflies.
(How fair it is to know again
Those flutter-bys we feared were lost.)
And what would one October be
Without wild aster's amethyst?
The thistle has a rowdy hat
Above its dominating thorns.

Even the burdock's crown-flowers grow
Persistent as is life itself.
We'd never see forget-me-nots
If every minute we looked up.
So, sometimes find what God displays
Even for those who drag their feet,
And those who look down in despair.

— Margaret A. Wheeler

SOME RHYME AND A LITTLE REASON

In fourteen hundred and ninety-two
Columbus sailed the ocean blue,
And look what he's done for me and you.

Without Columbus and his ships three,
There'd be no Statue of Liberty;
And no land of the free and the "Braves",
No escape from tyrants and knaves;
No baseball hero, turned tycoon,
No exploring trips to the moon;
No Indianapolis racing cars,
No contemplated trip to Mars,
And most of all there would not be
Teresian House for you and me.

BIRTHDAY BLESSING

Of all the blessings God bestows,
A loving family ranks high.
As I look round, my feeling grows
How truly blessed indeed am I.

AUTUMN IN PINE BUSH

October woods are brown and gold
With flaming red leaves showing
Fall her beauty now unfolds
And sets our world a-glowing.

— Marion Winburn

ODE TO SPRING

Spring is here; a sweet and gentle breeze
Wafts fragrance from bud-laden trees.
The birds their joyous songs now sing
To welcome back our lovely spring.

That's the way it used to be.
I now look up, what do I see?
Large swirling snowflakes earthbound,
On their way to cover the ground.
The wind is cold, the birds take wing,
What's become of you, O spring?
Why is winter . . . . lingering?

— Marion Winburn

From Teresian House

IV. STORIES

OLD IS BEAUTIFUL

About two years ago I began to think, "It's about time to prepare for a second career." The only thing was that it wasn't exactly my second career. It was more like the fifth! Before I entered the Sisters of Mercy, I finished business college and worked in an office—Career phase I. Then after I completed my novitiate I was sent to St. Peter's Hospital to train to be a registered nurse. This was probably Career phase II. After seventeen years at St Peter's I requested and was granted a change for a year, but the year extended to four. I did catechetical work for four years. This might be called Career phase III. Then at the age of fifty, I started teaching in elementary school—Career No. IV.

Then came the time to turn down another road—the road of retirement. I thought to do this, a time spent in a House of Prayer would help me to take the right turn for the last mile. I requested and was granted the permission to spend a year in a House of Prayer. It was while I was there that I got the idea that I would like to work with the elderly and being one of the group myself, I figured that I could understand some of their problems. The mayor of Cohoes had finished in the nurses' training class with me; and I had heard that a new building, called McDonald Towers, was being erected for the elderly. I wrote to her and was offered a position with the Community Health Services office as a community health aide. Here I was to assist in canvassing a certain area for the purpose of explaining the services available at the Human Resource Center. This was a good "in".

It was doing this that made me see just how wonderful many elderly people are. I was utterly amazed at the number of elderly people, eighty years of age and over, who were still active and alert. One lady eighty-four, was still doing alterations as well as being an assistant to an undertaker. She lived over the undertaker's parlor and would put the lights out at night and do other chores. One woman told me of her cousin, who is a nun. This nun visits the nursing homes and when she sees things that are not in keeping with the proper care of the sick, she contacts influential people requesting them to improve these conditions. Some retired people are doing baby sitting. A report from a sister in Wisconsin showed that one retired sister was a licensed handwriting analyst; another, legally blind, works with the AA and gives talks in various churches; another eighty-year old sister was a ham radio operator; another was working in a Lutheran Nursing Home and a fifth working for the Welfare Department. Of course, I also met some very lonely people. One woman, no matter when we go to see her, would always say, "Ain't it a lonesome day?"

They tell us that it's a myth, that when you grow older, your memory isn't so good. So don't give up. Let us experiment with ourselves. Perhaps we can train minds to concentrate more on the present. There may be many things that will help us preserve and keep our faculties healthy. Someone may come up with some good answers and that someone may be you. Each person is unique in his own right, and not one of us fits into the same mold. One great author claimed that the ages sixty-five to eighty-five were his most intellectual years. We, of course, all have to go at our own pace. The turtle gets where he wants to go as well as the deer. The point is that the turtle still keeps going.

Let us consider attitudes. Do we allow people to brainwash us by certain attitudes? At each stage of life we try to understand the human person. We all love the baby and study the infant. We observe the behavior patterns of the one-year-old, the two-year-old, etc. With the adolescent we try to understand that this phase will also pass. Why can't we also try to understand other phases that passing years bring with them? No matter what our age we must believe that we are important. I may be incapacitated by arthritis or any of the diseases associated with age, but as long as I live I can play my part with the Redeeming Christ. You can announce the good news better than ever. Make the last years the best. Why not?

One writer says, "Life is a gift of love." We can always love. Let us stop saying old age is hell. Each one of us should strive to change the attitude of the younger, ourselves and others toward aging and say OLD IS BEAUTIFUL. We can look at it realistically; our contributions could be a great factor in the present crisis of religious life. We can always use whatever physical, intellectual and emotional energies that we possess. Our retirement time is a real opportunity to feel free to do something we always wanted to do. Everything is up for grabs. As we consider some changes we know that all change involves risk. But what have we got to lose? And if you've never tried, how do you know what you can do? Just think of Grandma Moses. What we would have missed, if she had never tried. We are afraid to launch out into the deep. Much of our training has conditioned us to this.

Ponder the words of Isaiah, "Do not be afraid, for I am with you. Stop being anxious and watchful for I am your God. I give you strength, I bring you help. I uphold you with my glorious right hand." We can make these words our own and all the time we are helping build the kingdom of God with faith, hope, and charity.

The renewal bit has been difficult for many. Some people have always been able to do their own renewal. The missionary priest tells the story of the old Indian who used to walk several miles every Sunday to Mass, and he always carried a banana with him. But he ate it on the way to Mass. The priest questioned him about breaking the fast. The Indian replied, "I thought it would be better for Jesus to lie on the banana than the banana to lie on Jesus."

I find the following quotation from St. Paul very encouraging. "God is not unfair. He will not forget the work you did nor the love you showed for him in the help you gave, and still give your fellow Christians. Our great desire is that each one of you keep up his eagerness to the end, so that the things you hope for will come true. We do not want you to become lazy but to be like those who believe and are patient, and so receive what God has promised."

Failure may be your vocation. We never stop creating ourselves. Our role may change but as long as we are alive, we should be participators. It may be by suffering or praying but we still are responsible for growing and creating to the extent of our physical, mental and emotional well-being. We do this best by working together with Christ. Let us form a life style that will allow us to continue to grow.

I would like to leave you with the thought that you have a right to be here. You have a unique place to fill. There never was, there never can be, there never will be another you.

— Sister Catherine Isabel

GRANDMOTHER TELLS A CHRISTMAS STORY

You wouldn't believe this. That is, unless you're grandparents, you wouldn't.

Yesterday was Christmas Day and this morning, as I remember the events of yesterday, I feel a strong urge to record them so that they will not be forgotten.

Christmas Day started the usual way. I was out of bed at 7:20 a.m., in order to stuff the turkey and have it in the oven by eight o'clock. It seemed so easy to "doctor up" the prepared herb seasoned stuffing mix so that it would taste like our traditional recipe. I hoped Great Grandmother, who would be with us, wouldn't be able to tell the difference. How easy everything is to cook these days. The turkey was already deep basted. That means no more basting every half hour or so. And the turkey lift was some invention! I didn't even need my glasses to read where to put the lift on the bird, because I had done this several times before. However, the red disk, the size of a half dollar, which had fallen off the turkey onto the counter, was new to me. But I thought I knew what to do with it. Someone must have invented this to keep the bird's backbone off the pan. Very good! I placed the disk in the pan and carefully centered the backbone over it.

Half of our family arrived during the midmorning. This year the other half of our family were spending the holidays with "the other side" of their family. Our three-year-old and four-year-old grandchildren were delighted with the gifts Santa Claus had left for them at our house. Our grandson was on his new tricycle before his coat was off. Our granddaughter shyly asked who the doll carriage was for.

We played with the children for the rest of the morning and then came the time for the last minute dinner preparations. This is where Grandpa always helps. He lifted the beautifully browned turkey from the pan and then scooped out the red disk while remarking, "What's this thing?" Well, even I was baffled now. The red disk was out of shape and had a hole in the middle. As I examined it more closely, its identification "hit me!" It was a red poker chip! Then I remembered where it could have come from. Several days before, our grandchildren had been playing with our poker chips. (Well, what do you give kids to play with when you run out of toys?) Someone had picked up the poker chips, put them on top of the refrigerator and then forgot them. On Christmas Eve I put the pan containing the partially thawed turkey on top of the refrigerator to keep it out of reach of our cat. A poker chip must have fallen onto the turkey. (Maybe it's not too late for me to invent a red disk that would keep the turkey backbone off the bottom of a roasting pan!)

Soon it was late afternoon. Our grandchildren were still going strong, but everyone else was worn out. Our granddaughter asked for a towel for her doll. The doll was dripping wet from innumerable bottles of water that had been poured into her mouth and had run out of her eyes and bottom. Only Grandpa had the energy to get the towel. When he came back into the living room, instead of walking through the obstacle course on the floor, he called to our granddaughter to "Catch". With a surge of energy, he threw the towel. It landed four feet beyond the child right into the center of the blazing fire in the fireplace. We were all so stunned that not a sound was uttered as we watched the towel burst into flames. Thus our grandchildren got their first lesson on how accidents happen.

The end of the day was nearly here for two sleepy children. So, everyone joined in to help pick up their toys. Suddenly our daughter-in-law cried out, "Who threw the beads in the wastepaper basket?" Poor Grandpa! He wasn't familiar with pop-beads. Someone had taken apart a pop-beads necklace and left the beads on the floor. Someone else picked up the beads and put them in an empty dish. Grandpa, thinking the dish contained popcorn, had thrown them into the wastepaper basket. We retrieved the beads and Grandpa was forgiven.

Those were the events of our Christmas 1974. May we always cherish their memory.

— Marjorie D. File

THE DRAMA IN REAL LIFE

The drama I am going to write about is not only the drama of my life. It concerns many thousands of citizens of the Soviet Union, who during the Second World War ran out of the country with children, or what was worse, left the children with relatives in the hope that the Red regime wouldn't survive the war and they would have the chance to turn back home. Unfortunately the regime survived and these parents never met the children more. The Soviet Union refused to send the children to their parents abroad. Why did these people run away? I was one of them and I will tell the reason.

Language cannot describe nor imagination paint the misery the people suffer under the Red terror. The people's only guilt is that they were born under this dictatorship. I lived under this regime for three years. I got there when the Red army occupied in 1939 this land where I used to live. It was enough to me to see this hell on the earth. They took everything from me. My house and piece of land were nationalized. I had no right for my own opinion or for belief in God. For all this in return I could only buy a loaf of bread to be able to work for them forty-eight hours a week. If I wanted to buy half a pound of sugar I had to stay two or three hours in turn with other customers before I got to the store. Death, prison, concentration camps, and Siberia were always open for everybody. And believe me, they were not empty. If you didn't applaud strong enough the mentioned names of Stalin or other dignitaries, or didn't show (with empty stomach) enough enthusiasm at work, you disappeared usually at night and never came home. We people educated and grown up in a non-communist world were under special supervision.

Within these three years over 80 percent of us disappeared. Everybody counted his days. They fed us steadily with propaganda. When I compared this propaganda with reality, my stomach was always upset. Then suddenly the Red army under the pressure of German airplanes and tanks disappeared from our territory too. The iron curtain melted. We were free, at least, we thought so. At this time there was a chance to run away. Again three years passed and the Red army was coming back. It was 1944.

At this time we had two small children, a boy Myron, four years old, and Chris, a girl, two years old. Two perfect children, our pride and joy. What would you do in this situation? Wait for another iron curtain and let us and our children live and die in slavery? That would be an inexcusable sin; would you run away? But we could lose the children during the flight. Neither alternative was acceptable; but we had no third choice. After many sleepless nights we decided to run. Even death is better than enslavement. The idea of running gave us a slight hope that at the end we might have the chance to find for our children a better place to live. We asked the children their opinion. Chris said nothing. She only looked at us with her blue-like-a-sky-eyes. Myron, who liked always something new, said to go. He was older, healthy and strong for his age. We knew he might endure. But Chris was another problem. A few months before, because of whooping cough, she almost died. We never would be able to see her so sick once more. Besides there was a question of where to run. And there was only one answer—West, as far as possible. And we had to hurry. The Red army was not far away.

In March 1944 we said with Chris good-bye to her warm room, her small bed and all the dolls she used to play with. We left everything we possessed, locked the house, took the keys, and never came back.

Because we do not have enough room in this article to describe our journey, I will only underscore a few characteristic incidents during our odyssey to find our Eldorado for our two little children. We journeyed partly by horse and wagon and partly by railroad.

We started by horse and wagon. After an hour or so Chris began to cry, "I want home!" she shouted. And she cried so long until tired, she fell asleep. Fighting back tears, we cried with her because we wanted "home" too. The bravest man among us was Myron. As long as he saw the horses running in front of him, he didn't care about home. During all of our journey, his face radiant and eyes smiling, he never complained that he was cold or hungry or that he couldn't walk because his legs hurt him. Looking at his cheerful face, we forgot the troubles that were behind and in front of us. Oh Myron, if you knew how much we owed you! No wonder that Chris always was happy in his company. She called him Minio.

In some places we moved by railroad. But the railroads were extremely overcrowded and in some places were attacked by communist partisans and discontinued running. We were lucky to acquire our own wagon and horses and this solved the problem. We moved days and nights along overcrowded roads. We were almost choked by dust. Our food consisted only of flour cooked with water and salt. We were so tired that we didn't mind being loaded by Germans onto uncovered freight railroad wagons and carried somewhere through Czechoslovakia, Hungary, and Austria. We didn't know that we belonged already to the family of forced laborers. First we had to pass the quarantine camp in Strasshoff not far from Vienna. It was the filthiest place I ever saw in my life. We stayed out there fourteen days. We slept outside because inside millions of bedbugs attacked us. There our little girl Chris caught a serious infectious disease called dysentery. No doctor, no drugs, no diet. She was near death.

By chance we received from our uncle in Vienna an affidavit that he had room and work for us. We were lucky because it was the only chance to keep Chris alive. At the end of quarantine we were placed in a special railroad wagon with a spécial sign written by chalk, "To Vienna." You can't imagine how disappointed and distressed we were when our train didn't even stop in Vienna. We had been carried with other forced laborers west to the German province named Thuringia. Still another camp. There the only food for us was barley soup. It helped probably in recovery of our little girl. After a week we were sent to a barbed wire plant. Seven months we, both parents, worked there. All this time our children played the whole day among the railroad cars steadily loading and unloading, moving up and down. Chris was under Myron's command. Only when there was an air raid did we pick them up and carry them into the ditch. Our main dish was soup of canned peas. We lived in paper barracks. We were every day more weak and sick and at the time when it was impossible to carry the load further came the help from heaven. One day at noon hundreds of American airplanes started to bomb our place. We were in the ditch where we were protected against splinters but not against the bombs. Over a hundred bombs exploded near the ditch. Not one of us believed we could live through this experience.

When after two hours we got out of the ditch we saw a new world around us. Instead of plant buildings were piles of rubble. We were lucky. Not even one bomb dropped into the ditch. We were transferred to another working place. This time it was a dairy. There we had better living conditions with cooking appliances and even with a shower. And what's more, we had milk. Mother didn't work and could take care of the children. But unfortunately we couldn't stay there long. Thuringia became additionally a part of the Russian occupational zone. We had to run again and run fast not to get in Russian hands. The next three weeks of our flight were the worst. No railroads, no buses, and no horses. We had to walk. Chris at this time already four years old, was still too small to walk but too heavy to carry on our backs ten hours a day. The Americans who took care of refugees in their occupational zone could not understand why we didn't change the direction of our walk from west to east and go home. We reached Wiesbaden, the German city on the French border. It was the end of our walking.

Our story wouldn't be complete if we didn't mention one more incident which filled our drama to the brim. While we were in the Displaced Persons camp in Wiesbaden, the camp doctor discovered scarlet fever in our children. Myron was already near recovery, but Chris was sent to the city hospital. When we came to visit her the next day we heard she was crying day and night, calling for her mother. When she did the same the next day, the chief nurse's opinion was that we should not come to her but give her the chance to forget us. Four weeks she didn't see us and all this time she cried and steadily kept looking at the entrance door. Every day we heard her crying already outside the hospital; and in the hospital corridor we saw her through the slightly opened door crying and looking in our direction expecting us someday to come to her. Of course we were crying with her, only she didn't hear us. Four weeks was too much for us. We were sick and heartbroken. We always were ready to open the door and tell her that we didn't abandon her. But we didn't know what was better for her. When she was ready to go home and mother came in to pick her up, Chris reproached her for leaving her alone. She still kept in her hand a ribbon with which her mother had tied her hair together. All the time when the nurse tried to put this ribbon aside Chris didn't want to give it to her. The nurse told us she never had a case like this. The reason for Chris' behavior was probably that all the time she had no chance to play with other children. Her brother was her only playmate. The other reason was that she didn't know the language and couldn't talk to the Germans.

From Mainz Dastel, our last camp, with an affidavit from our sister who was a United States citizen, we came in 1947 to the USA where everything was for us so beautiful only in different ways.

Why did we bring this tale of misery to daylight? First of all we wanted to tell American people why we didn't change our direction from West to East. East meant to go to Siberia, and believe me nobody wanted to go there.

We wanted also to tell our children, Myron and Chris, how much we paid for their liberty and the well-being they enjoy in this country. We hope these memories may improve the quality of their lives.

— Konstantyn Guran

UKRAINE STORIES

Before I start to write this article, I confess under oath that everything that follows is absolutely true. No fantasy. Just real facts.

Once during a discussion with friends about the wisdom of living, I risked a pronunciation that I believe in the predestination of human life. It was too mysterious for them and they did not take it seriously. How did I understand these concepts and by what did I support my beliefs were their questions.

For me it was simple. Everyone has his tour of life designed by some Higher Power. What is this power exactly, I don't know. But there are many other mysterious problems concerning us that the human mind is not able to understand. Can you understand, for instance, eternity or an endless world? At least I don't.

I started to be interested in these mysterious problems when I was nineteen years old and a senior in high school. It happened at this time that a man came to our town who advertised himself in the newspaper able to answer three questions guaranteed to be true for fifteen Austrian kronen.

With fifteen kronen in my pocket, I went to find out how far he cheats the people. According to instruction I picked from a book in his first room my three questions, copied them with their numbers on a piece of paper and put them in the pocket of my coat, looking around the room to see if anyone had spied me. I put three sheets of paper into the other book with plenty of numbers, on pages where the numbers of my questions were. With this second book in my hand I entered the other room. There I met a middle-aged man with a long black beard and a peculiar expression in his eyes. He stretched his hand to me and introduced himself. He looked at the book in my hand and told me to put it on the table. Then he repeated my three questions exactly as I had copied them. From this time I started to treat him more seriously. My three questions were:

1. Is the person I have in mind still alive?
2. If and when will I finish my studies?
3. If and when will I get married?

Before he answered these questions, he looked to the palm of my left hand and said "Before you is a long, long road of life." Then he followed with the answers to my three questions:

1. "The person you think is dead is alive. Soon he will send you a letter and then will come home himself."

2. "You will finish your college education at the right time, not even missing a semester."

3. "You will get married some time very late. Your future wife is still a child. I can't see her face."

It was hard to believe in all these answers. We had a report from an eyewitness that my brother, whom I had in mind, was dead at the front during the first World War.

Continuation of my education was at this time impossible. The students of my nationality were excluded from universities of the country I lived in. And it was hopeless to get a passport for abroad.

The third question and answer was just for fun and I didn't pay much attention to his reply. The episode with these questions and answers had no meaning to me at first. It grew in importance later.

It was a real surprise to me to receive a letter from my brother and see him come home from the war.

After having finished high school, two of us decided to go abroad passing illegally across the Czechoslovakian border. Of course, it was an extremely dangerous experiment. We could be shot or imprisoned. But under some higher pressure I took the risk and was successful. I arrived at Prague just at the right time to register for the first semester at the University in 1920. There I finished college without missing any semester as the old man with the peculiar eyes told me. After four years of help and hospitality from the great nation of Czechoslovakia, I left Prague and went back home in the same illegal way, only this time with a degree in my pocket.

Being home, and having not a bad job, I planned to get married. Twice I was engaged, and sorry to say, both times I broke the engagement. I could not explain the reason. I just felt like this. Not to make a fool of myself, I decided to stay as an old bachelor. Many years later when I was thirty-eight years old, dancing in a ballroom, I met a young twenty-three-year-old girl who I felt was a part of me. That was the girl I was waiting for so many years, I thought. And she really was. She is now my wife.

So much about the three questions and answers. This man with the long beard who answered my questions didn't make even the slightest mistake in reading many years ago a predestined book of my life. A mystery, isn't it?

It seems like the end of my story. But it isn't. He saw the long and distant way of my life. I am now seventy-six years old. The designer of my life, this High Power that I mentioned before, was generous when he predicted for me an old age. But it didn't promise me a rose garden.

— Konstantyn Guran

THE SEVENTH DAY

The years between 1902 and 1917 were good years to be born. We were between wars, and to us who had been born after the Spanish-American War, war was a word of which we never thought. We could plan our future with confidence.

They were years in which families worked and played together. People worked hard—the men spent long hours in factories and mills; the women in the kitchen. They scrubbed laundry on a board and ironed with flat irons in hot kitchens. They prepared heavy hot meals over wood fires. Come fall, they canned fruits and vegetables, made jellies and pickles.

After six days of hard work, when Sunday came they were ready for the day of rest. Mass first, then a hot meal and the afternoon stretched ahead with endless possibilities. Sometimes we went to the cemetery, stopping at the florist's to buy beefsteak plants and geraniums for my grandmother's grave.

Again, we might go to the Grove at Dunsbach Ferry. We took the train at the New York Central Station at the foot of Younglove Avenue and rode a few miles to the ferry. We left the train and walked about a mile to the Grove. Arriving there, we found a nice spot for our picnic lunch; then we strolled around the Grove. We passed booths set up for business, where barkers called out their wares. There was a shooting gallery where the point was to hit a moving duck. Some barkers called out, "Hit the dodger—knock'im out—get a five cent cigar." We looked with envious eyes at the kewpie dolls on a booth.

Another trip was to Mid-City Park or Albany on the boat. Sunday afternoons a band played. I remember their brass buttons and handlebar moustaches. We were all dressed in our Sunday best. We bought Cracker Jack and walked the deck endlessly. In the evening we returned, tired and dirty, dragged along by our parents, who were tired themselves. Arriving in Troy, we were pushed and dragged along by our parents, who were tired themselves. Arriving in Troy, we were pushed and dragged on the trolley car where we promptly fell asleep.

We spent some Sundays at church picnics, watching the boats go down the Erie Canal, or just relaxing on the front porch. Many times we had company, and my mother spent her day slaving in the kitchen while the guests relaxed on the front porch.

This was Sunday, 1902—and how I'd love to relive those days!

—Georgiana Cole Halloram

THE BEST IS YET TO BE

I never thought much about old age, one way or the other, until something I read nudged my metabolism—"To those of us approaching the autumn of our lives the thought that senility will overtake us is not a pleasant one." Approaching autumn? That doesn't mean me, I laughed, but when I scrutinized my reflection in the mirror, the laugh disappeared. And when I spent a sleepless night with that face tormenting me, I began to worry.

As for senility, the article went on to tell me that I was losing more than a billion brain cells every day, and while I felt no actual movement, I was becoming increasingly aware that the rooms up there were getting empty. In addition, the irregular stop and go signals sent by the hangers-on were jumbling my thoughts, making me sound more like an idiot everyday. The picture of myself as a withered old crone, wandering around emptyheaded, suddenly became real—and I made my decision. Maybe I couldn't be young again, but I certainly wasn't going to grow any older.

After a physical warmup period of exercise and hormone creams, I zeroed in on any opening where there was a gathering of young people, and they accepted me with the same warm understanding they extended to other spaced-out members of society. In no time at all, I knew what my legal rights were in case I was arrested; I could tick off the advantages of shacking up using all ten fingers; I adored Hesse, and I wore a sweatshirt proclaiming "Mahler grooves."

My husband thought my approach to aging was utter nonsense. He took the occasion to remind me that if I didn't make it as Miss America the first time around, how could I possibly make it now? That wasn't my goal, but it shows how negative he was. His attitude more than anything placed me in the We Try Harder Group. He was just trying to avoid failure by his lack of spirit, and although we're the same age, I wondered what my life was going to be with this old man.

He seemed to delight in propagandizing old age by spicing his conversations with great truths, such as, "living on borrowed time" and "going down the homestretch". I told him the Council on Aging was looking for slogans, but he just looked at me as though he had given up on my ability to comprehend. Shaking his head sadly, he announced, "You just can't beat Father Time." I knew he was going down the path to an early rocking chair, and I pictured myself, after winning a set of mixed doubles, hurrying home to keep up his spirits with a cheery account of my many exciting activities.

Things I looked upon with euphoric irresponsibility, like planning for retirement, he considered to be milestones to the hereafter. And I really felt it difficult to cope whenever he took the strong box down from the shelf in the closet. It was his habit, periodically, to go through all of his insurance policies, emphasizing with bulging eyes and wagging fingers the double and triple indemnity clauses. He followed this by checking the deed to our huge cemetery plot whose measurements seemed to arouse him more than those of the sexy blonde next door. Then, rivaling the creative thinking of any top travel agent, he offered a running commentary on the comforts and beauty of our final resting place.

After explaining to me in the manner of the grand seigneur that all papers were filed under "D" for Death, he returned them to the box, snapped the lid shut, and with a flair of a man who has just reached the zenith of his career, he proclaimed, "Yes siree, you're going to be a rich widow!" (If I had committed suicide, I'm sure he would take taken it personally.)

By now I was too much into the youth bit to be put off by a nonbeliever. And while I knew I would never be prevented from seeing an X-rated movie, I was sure that I not only looked young but that I had captured the feeling of youth.

I was browsing in the library one day, my eyes roving the titles of the books. I mentally rejected *How to Stay Young the Shuffleboard Way.* That was a trap. But I was a little surprised to find myself actually grabbing the one next to it before someone else did—*Promiscuity for the Married Woman.* There was something I could relate to.

The lady standing next to me remarked that there seemed to be a book on every subject imaginable. She went on to say, "When I was a girl, (she was about thirty), they didn't have such a variety." Confident that she could see how young I was, I paved the way for a compliment by daring to joke, "Then you can imagine what it was like for me before the printing press, ha ha." Looking me over with one fast sweep, she ignored my "ha, ha" and summed up her appraisal with a sympathetic "Y-e-e-s." The next thing I knew she snatched the book on promiscuity from my hand, and rudely disposed of me by throwing a bit of wisdom over her shoulder as she hurried away, "You know what they say about a time to live and a time to die." What does she know, I thought, but underneath my forever young mystique, I knew what she knew—and it hurt.

I needed a lift, some sympathy, some understanding, but I could hardly share my feelings with the Grim Reaper and risk the platitude "There's no fool like an old fool!" Oh, I thought about marijuana, but every time I decided to try it, the picture of myself behind bars was more than I could handle, and I was so shaken there was no way I could light a joint without singeing my nose.

Then, I had another idea. I remembered from past experience that when I got myself together in the morning and out on to the street, the trash men would whistle at me on their early morning pickup—not the old guys up front, but the young ones that hang on the back. It was worth a try.

I glanced up the street, and just as I reached the spot where the truck was parked, the men emptied a big carton into the back. With that, an old dented beer can hit the side of the truck and took off whizzing past my head. The old driver up front looked around and hollered, "Watch it you guys! You almost hit that little old lady." I turned around to offer comfort to this threatened member of the older generation—but I was all alone. I hurried home, avoiding the shame of their apologies, feeling more and more that someone or some-thing was out to get me.

And they were succeeding. That glorious feeling of oneness with youth was fragmenting. I'll never forget the morning it disappeared entirely. I was preparing my oatmeal facial with dying enthusiasm trying to bolster my image, trying to rededicate myself to the cause by talking to myself, "Don't let them discourage you. Hang in there!" And then the telephone rang. It was a friend of mine, impatient to tell me something funny.

"You know last night when your husband picked you up after bowling?"

"Yes," I said, wondering what was coming.

"Well, Millie didn't know he was your husband, and wait 'til you get this—she thought he was your son!" At this point she was laughing so hard her voice was almost unintelligible—but I still got the message.

"I can understand what she meant," she went on, "He doesn't have a single gray hair in his head, and you don't have a single dark one. And although you use all those creams on your face, still—" I interrupted her, muttering something about calling her back.

When I hung up the phone, a sharp arthritic pain stabbed my arm, announcing the arrival of some destructive force as it came in for the cleanup job. My head pounded, little silver things darted about in my eyes, and my whole body sagged as gravity became an instrument of torture. I knew it was over. Lowering my gray head in defeat, I pounded on the table with my gnarled fists and cried out to my unseen enemy, "O.K. so I'm old! Are you satisfied? Old! Old! Old!"

I sobbed convulsively. The reality of the situation was clear to me for the first time. Now I knew what my kids meant when they called me their little freaked-out Mom. All this business about being young was a lot of nonsense. You're as old as you look—and I looked old.

I was ready to cradle my aching body in a rocking-chair and let senility take over, when my husband walked in. He's very big in the father role, and as he put his arms around me, I blurted out my story between sobs. I could hear my voice rising as I forced myself to utter the unutterable words, "and they thought I was your mother!"

The handkerchief which he had taken from his pocket was poised in mid-air, and as I stood there waiting with upturned face, I realized something had absorbed his mind and immobilized his body. And then, like one who was experiencing a sudden breakthrough, he began to smile, and the smile grew wider and wider.

"So they thought I was your son!" I heard the utter delight in his voice as he savored the image. By now he was so pleased with himself his smile had become rolling laughter, and with his handkerchief meant for me he wiped his own cheeks as the happy tears ran down his happy face. As for me, rigor mortis immediately set in. Every nerve, every cord, every muscle in my body tensed. I lowered my arms woodenly from his neck, making sure there was no bodily contact, and stepping back in disbelief, I thought this must be what they mean by mental cruelty. I tried not to speculate beyond that because I knew that going down the homestretch alone could be even worse.

Well, that's my story. As for my husband, the man who was living on borrowed time has applied for an extension on his loan. The more he tries to be with it, the more he seems to be without it. For example, the crew cut he's had since the Big War has been left unattended. The hairdo sticks out all over as it tries to find itself, and the stomach sticks out all over because it already has. If you can visualize Laurel's head with Hardy's body, you've got the picture.

His pattern of behavior has also changed. Guess where I found his survival kit stocked with a fortune in geriatric remedies? Right where he tossed it — in the trash can. I salvaged what I could, and you can well believe me when I say I have the strong box with his insurance papers under my own lock and key.

Like others before him he has turned to the East to rekindle the fire within. When I first heard the weird mutterings behind the closed door, I wondered if our medical insurance covered insanity. He calls it TM, but I call it fantasizing. Anyway, just as I was about to knock, the door swung open. With a powerful thrust he whizzed past me, jogging through the house in jockey shorts and Indian headband, stabbing the air with his fists and shouting at intervals, 'Right on! Far out!''

I stepped back to avoid being crushed by this younger than springtime Methusaleh — but it was too late. Remembering my marriage vows, I feebly managed the peace sign before I slumped to the floor.

How do you tell someone who won't believe you that you can't beat Father Time? You can only grow to look like him.

— Eleanor Huba

A FUNNY THING HAPPENED . . .

Downtown churches in our city have a parking problem, but until a few Sundays ago, I had experienced no serious trouble of any kind. On this particular Sunday, those of my congregation who did not "go down for coffee" had rushed to their cars, happy to have been dismissed ten minutes earlier than usual. My eyes measured the space between a VW and the end of the gateway as I hurried to my car in the upper end of our small parking lot. It would be a close shave, but maybe I could make it. But as others noticeably slowed to look at the space upon reaching the gate, I realized that maybe there was not enough room to drive through.

By this time, twenty or thirty people had walked into the lot, each looking closely at the space, each hoping, no doubt, that his car would squeeze through. A younger man who impressed me as one who knew about such things approached his compact car. "I believe I can make it," he said to no one in particular; but I think he decided against it because most of the others were trapped. He perhaps thought that his driving through the narrow space would encourage others to try to follow. And he knew that few of those older cars belonging to older people could make it. So he too became a member of the captive audience.

There is something about having just participated in a religious service that makes one a little more tolerant, a little more patient, at least for a few minutes. Nobody frowned, nobody used a profane word. There were smiles — directed to people whom we had never taken the time to greet except casually with a nod in passing. Little groups began to form, groups made up of people whose cars were parked nearby.

It is surprising what one can learn about others in a situation like that. For instance, I talked with a man whom I had seen almost every Sunday for the past two years. Nothing more than a nod had passed between us before that day. He is an octogenarian, married to a third wife, having lost two dear ones by death. He retired some years ago from a printing business which he had bought years ago from his father. His health is excellent; he has not seen a doctor for many years. He attributes his good health to the fact that he neither drinks nor smokes. He was born and reared in this area; and since I am considered a newcomer, he became interested in my background and complimented me upon my youthful appearance. This told me that he does not see as well as he once did, or he wanted to say something really nice and encouraging. And more than anything else, he wanted to go to lunch which was being prepared by someone apparently employed to make lunch each day, or at least each Sunday. And he was hungry as was his wife who waited patiently in the parked car. We talked about the type of person who would be thoughtless enough to block the parking lot entrance for twenty minutes.

"Twenty years ago, this kind of thing would not have happened," I said, trying to keep his mind off his lunch. "People just didn't do things like that."

"Young people just don't give a damn now about other people," he said; and I thought the effect of the religious service was beginning to wear off. We did get to know each other; perhaps that never would have happened if we had not been waiting for the thoughtless "youngster" in the red shirt, blue jeans, leather coat, boots, and all that goes with that "young group that doesn't give a damn about people."

Other groups formed, some ladies with bouquets of beautiful flowers, some men who must have exchanged jokes, for I saw them laughing; a dignified couple who sat quietly in their car directly behind the VW—where but for the culprit they could have driven out easily. A few who did not feel friendly stayed to themselves. One woman whom I liked although I do not know her name has a good sense of humor. She and I exchanged glances at times and shook our heads. She never stopped smiling.

Time was passing; the group became unusually quiet. There was some anxiety and patience was wearing thin. I could feel—but not hear—"Damn it, I'm tired of waiting for this youngster."

As the last grains of patience were running out, we heard from the driver of the compact who had chosen to wait with us, "Now we'll get out; here comes the driver." We moved as one toward the gateway. We wanted to see the person who apparently was old enough to drive a car and thoughtless enough to make us forget our recent experience—almost.

What we saw stopped us suddenly. Unlocking the VW was a small, middle-aged woman, clad in spring colors, accompanied by her older sister who had insisted that she "go down for coffee." Realizing what she had done, she became defensive as she hurriedly approached the car. The smiling woman who had shaken her head when we exchanged glances said, "Why would you park there? Didn't you know that no one could get out?" Before she could answer another observer asked, "Why didn't you come out of church first and move your car?" Confused and embarrassed she muttered, "I had nowhere else to park; and what should I have done, taken it into church with me?" And to nobody in particular she said, "Told my sister I shouldn't go down for coffee." The two scrambled into the car. The little VW sputtered nosily, and backed into the street.

Everybody seemed relieved, there were sighs and shrugging shoulders, a move toward parked cars, the usual smell of fumes, and the faint smiles of some who drove past. The exit was orderly.

As I drove home, I could not help thinking about this little woman who had forced a group of people to get to know each other better. My feeling was one of sympathy rather than animosity. What had happened in her home that morning? Had she lain awake half the night listening for a teenager to unlock the door? Had someone dear to her been sick or troubled? Had someone called with a disturbing message? Maybe she herself was sick or lonely and felt the need of worship and fellowship.

Why she parked her car in the entrance I shall never know. But I want to believe she was somewhat troubled and that her experience in the worship service relieved her. If so, I don't mind the twenty-three minutes she took from me.

—Raymond H. Jackson

THE STORY OF MR. HODGE

Mr. Hodge woke up with a sneeze.

It was a beautiful June morning with sunlight sparkling on wet leaves and grass. It had rained during the night and Mr. Hodge had been out in that rain, hence the sneeze. Of course he did not know yet that he was Mr. Hodge; he was just a little yellow kitten lost in the park, still too young to remember much about the day before, or how he happened to be lost. He knew only that he was hungry, damp, chilly, and very stuffy in the head. Also, everything seemed very strange.

The sunlight and dancing leaves seemed good to him, so after a kitten-stretch he began to wander about wishing for warm milk and sneezing now and then. After a while he found some men raking grass. He was not afraid of the rakes, but ran after them and tried to hold them with his tiny paws. The men laughed at him, then chased him off because he got in the way. Anyhow, it wasn't much fun to play when his head felt so stuffy, and he found, when he sat down in a gravel path and began to wash one paw, that his throat was sore.

Then suddenly, right down the back of his neck, Grrrrr, he heard or rather felt a fearful growl. It was a big dog with a black coat, sharply pricked ears, and a huge red mouth! The kitten whirled round, landing on all four feet, his ears laid flat, back arched, and every hair standing on end so that his tail looked almost as big as his body. The dog began to circle round him.

The little cat, very alert, and ready to put up all the fight there was in him, pivoted slowly in the middle of the circle. But he was not afraid.

That was how Pru saw him first, and she loved him immediately.

Dropping her schoolbooks in the path, she snatched up a stick, drove off the dog, picked up the kitten before he fairly realized he was out of danger, and began to smooth his ruffled fur and tell him that he was all safe now and the dog quite gone.

Indeed the dog was quite on the other side of the park by now, chasing squirrels.

Pru saw her scattered books and remembered school. She set down the kitten, picked up the books and started on—but the kitten went along. This would not do at all.

At the other side of the park Pru had to take a bus to Miss Southwood's school several blocks away, where no kittens were welcome.

"Do you know where this kitten belongs?" she asked one of the men with the rakes.

He happened to be the nicest one who had laughed most at the kitten's antics earlier. "Oh, just dropped out of a car yesterday."

Pru looked so distressed that he wanted to say something comforting, so he went on, "Lots of people do that you know, when they don't want kittens." Forgetting, he added, "Mostly they die in a day or so."

Pru looked so much sadder that he made a real effort. "Cute little tyke; he was trying to play with my rake a while back. It'd be nice if you could take him home with you."

"If I only could get him home, maybe my aunts would let me keep him, or they'd get the Humane Society to find a home for him," said Pru. "But I have to go to Miss Southwood's school, and I have to go on a bus, and it's awfully far, and it's getting late, and I'm afraid he's sick, his paws are so hot!"

Here Mr. Hodge sneezed again.

"See," said Pru, "He is sick. Couldn't you look after him for me until half past three?"

She looked so woebegone that the old man felt quite uncomfortable.

"I couldn't do that, you know," he said, "I have to work."

Then suddenly he began to yell and wave his arms, and Pru had just time to jump back and catch up her kitten (for he really was hers by this time) before he ran past her toward the road. She saw a taxi stop and the driver leaned out as the old man ran up to him.

While Pru hesitated wondering what to do, the two men talked for a moment, then both beckoned to her at once.

Pru came forward rather slowly, carrying her kitten.

"Now this is Bill," said her friend, introducing the taxi-man. "He's got kids of his own."

"How do you do, that's very nice," said Pru, wondering what all this had to do with her and her kitten.

"Where do you live?" said the taxi-man.

"Just down that street back there at the end of the park," said Pru pointing.

"Why then," said her friend, smiling all over his face, "Bill can take you home, drop that there cat of yours, and have you to school all in no time."

"Oh," said Pru, delighted, "I can pay the fare with my lunch money."

"Never mind about that," said the taxi-man laughing, and both men yelled, "Geddin!"

And that is how it happened that Pru was back on her own doorstep, not ten minutes after she started for school, clutching her kitten and pushing the doorbell as hard as she could.

"Oh! What happened to you dear?" her aunt cried, startled to see her and the taxi.

Pru thrust the kitten into her hands and said all in one breath, "I found him in the park, a dog was chasing him, he's lost, he's got a cold, and I want to keep him, but if I can't, maybe you can find him a home. I can't stop, he's taking me to school." She waved toward the taxi.

"Bring my change purse," Aunt Em called to Aunt Lou as she ran down the walk after Pru, to "see about the taxi."

Pru's mother and father had died when she was quite little, and her two aunts had brought her up. They were so anxious that she should never feel lonely that perhaps they spoiled her a little.

So when they came back into the house and set the kitten down they just shook their heads and laughed a little. Mr. Hodge sneezed twice. Aunt Lou picked him up and felt his nose and paws. They were hot. While Aunt Em fixed some bread and milk for him, they decided they must keep him, because he had such a cold.

"I do hope we can save him," said Aunt Em. "His markings are really beautiful, and Pru would be heartbroken if anything happened to him after she found him all by herself."

After Mr. Hodge ate his breakfast, Aunt Lou lent him a lap to go to sleep on.

"Do you know," she said, stroking his soft fur, "in Boswells' book, he says that Dr. Johnson had a cat named Hodge, and in the illustration he's yellow."

Mr. Hodge began to sing himself to sleep, thrusting his tiny needle-sharp claws in and out of Aunt Lou's lap and making her wince a little. He had a very loud purr, and every now and then it choked him because of the cold. But he was happy. He had found his home, and he had found his name.

It was late afternoon when Mr. Hodge awakened. A warm breeze was blowing the flowered curtains at the windows of the big old-fashioned kitchen, so that their shadows rippled in the patches of sunlight on the floor. For a while he watched the moving shadows and his eyes grew brighter and brigher.

Then he noticed another cat at the other side of the room, crouched comfortably in front of what Aun Em called the "snack bar" lapping cream.

Mr. Hodge did not move, but he changed. His soft kitten-look was gone. All his muscles grew taught, his eyes wary, his very whiskers looked alert.

Very quietly indeed, he got down from the couch where he had been lying and stole across the floor until he stood directly behind the other cat. He felt quite pleased at getting so near without being heard—then he sneezed!

The other cat seemed to go right up into the air! He landed on all four paws facing Hodgie, his back arched, tail fluffed and ears laid back. He was a big cat, with a shining gray coat, four white feet, a white shirtfront, and long white eyebrows and whiskers. His name was Brandy. He had thought he was alone in the room, and he was dreadfully startled.

Mr. Hodge was not afraid; he sat back on his haunches and admired Brandy, who was quite the finest cat he had ever seen.

After a moment, as Brandy did not try to chase him, he tried to sniff noses, but Brandy growled low in his throat, and then spat. Mr. Hodge admired him even more.

Aunt Em, coming in from the garden, tried to make peace, but Brandy only got more and more angry, and finally ran off upstairs.

"Brandy'll just have to take his own time getting over it; they always do, you know, though sometimes it takes a very long time," said Aunt Lou, who had been watching from the doorway.

"Well, I do hope he doesn't stop eating the way the doctor's cat did when she was jealous," said Aunt Em, who was very proud of Brandy's size.

"But isn't Pru's kitten pretty? The dark stripes in his coat are almost as red as a fox. He'll make quite a cat when he's fed up." (Aunt Em loved feeding people and animals and was a marvelous cook). "Let's get Dick and Doug's kitten for him to play with," she went on.

Dick and Doug Mason lived next door; they were older than Pru and usually couldn't be bothered to play with a girl. However, as a great favor, they were allowing her to look after their kitten while they were away for a vacation. "Boots," as the boys called him, was a little tiger with big eyes and ears and a tail too long for the rest of him.

He and Mr. Hodge got acquainted right away, and when Pru came home from school she found them having a glorious romp, chasing, pouncing and tumbling over one another. She joined in with a spool on a string, and the game kept going until bed-time with brief pauses for supper—and naps when the kittens wore themselves out.

But next morning, Mr. Hodge had more cold. He sat in a miserable little hump, his eyes dull and heavy, his nose and paws hot to touch, and his beautiful yellow fur looking dull and rough.

The aunts managed to give him half an aspirin, and he lapped a little warm milk for Pru, when she held a saucer up for him.

"Look, Aunt Em," she said, "he holds his head on one side when he drinks, and acts as though it hurts him."

"He probably has a sore throat," her aunt told her, "Cats can get practically everything people can, and some extra. We'll take him to the veterinarian right after supper. That's the best we can do, Pru, the office isn't open in the afternoon, so please eat your breakfast, and don't be so unhappy. That aspirin will make Mr. Hodge sleep all day, and the Vet will know how to make him well for you."

Poor Pru, swallowing tears is bad enough, but tears and breakfast at the same time is even harder. But she did manage.

Then she had to leave Mr. Hodge and up came the lump in her throat again.

It was the longest day she could remember, and all the lessons were the dullest and all the games the stupidest; but finally it was time to go home.

When she got there, Mr. Hodge was still sleeping, as her aunt had said he would be. He was stretched on his side, and looked much more comfortable than he had in the morning.

Usually Pru loved to spend the hours between school and supper in the big grassy yard with its gay flower beds and fruit trees at the far end. But tonight nothing seemed pleasant. She wandered into the street and sat on the stoop watching other children play games, too dispirited to join in.

At supper, everyone was rather quiet. Pru could hardly wait to leave.

"But Pru, I made ice cream for dessert," cried Aunt Em, the third time Pru started up from the table.

"The doctor's office will be open at a quarter of seven," said Aunt Lou, "Why don't we go now and have the ice cream when we get back? I'm sure Pru will feel better when the doctor has seen Mr. Hodge."

So Aunt Em went to get the car and to find a bit of blanket to wrap up Mr. Hodge, while Pru helped Aunt Lou with a very hasty "washing-up".

The veterinarian's office seemed full of people and dogs. A lady with a small dog admired Mr. Hodge, and soon Pru was telling the story of how she found him. Everyone was interested and before she knew it, it was time for Pru to take Mr. Hodge into the examining-room.

She carried him in and set him on the shining white table which smelled of antiseptics. Mr. Hodge looked very small, rumpled, and sulky, but he was not afraid.

Aunt Em came over and talked to him and her strong hands held him while the doctor took his temperature, gave him a "shot," and then he said, "Bring him back the day after tomorrow. Meanwhile, give him one of these pills morning and night. He's pretty sick, but I think we'll save him." His voice was very confident, and his hand touched Pru's shoulder very gently.

Pru felt as though she might sail up like a balloon and hit the ceiling—she couldn't remember when she had felt so happy.

She managed to thank the veterinarian and carried out her kitten, walking very carefully and talking nonsense to him.

When they got home, Mr. Hodge drank a little milk and went fast asleep, and the ice cream proved to be the best that was ever frozen.

During the long, bright days of July and August, Mr. Hodge grew stronger and stronger. He was a roamer, but always managed to find his way home to Pru.

"What are we going to do with him while we are away next week?" asked Aunt Lou.

Pru crossed her fingers behind her back and said rather breathlessly, "Couldn't we take Mr. Hodge along? I'm sure the change and being out in the country and everything would be awfully good for him."

"But you don't know how he'd act in the car—well anyhow, you'd have to keep him on a lead every minute he was outdoors. If he ever got away from us up there we'd *never* get him back," said Aunt Em.

On Saturday, when they started out with the back seat of the car piled high with all the things people take on camping trips, there on top of the pile was Mr. Hodge in a new green velvet harness that Pru had made for him.

When the car started he dug his claws into his pile of blankets and hung on tight—but he wasn't afraid.

When he began to get used to riding, he found that he could walk across the blankets and look out of the windows on each side and at the back of the car.

Soon he was having a wonderful time and forgot all about hanging on.

Then Aunt Em had to stop suddenly, and down went Mr. Hodge into the pan of ice which had been brought along to keep his meat cold, and all the blankets and things on top of him.

Pru dived head first over the back of the front seat where she had been riding between her aunts to rescue him. Mr. Hodge was very much startled, and quite indignant, but not in the least frightened.

Pru brought him into the front seat and held him on her lap. Out of the windshield he could see the winding ribbon of road before them, with houses and barns at the sides, more country than he had ever dreamed of, and overhead occasional birds (which made his tail twitch) and the bright colored leaves whirling down from the trees by the roadside. It was so pleasant that he began to sing and then, of course, he forgot and sang himself to sleep so that the next thing he realized he was already in the camp.

It turned out to be a very large room with spaces curtained or screened off for a kitchen and sleeping. There was also a small wood-stove for cooking. Mr. Hodge had never seen one, but when the fire was lighted he just naturally went under it.

Both of the aunts were delighted and said, "He knows where it's warmest! Seems like home to see him there."

Mr. Hodge had never found a house which suited him better. He could go all round it, and in and out of all the rooms without asking to have a door opened.

While the unpacking was being done, he had a very happy afternoon investigating everything, sniffing everything, getting out of sight whenever he was wanted, and very much underfoot whenever he wasn't.

Toward sundown, when everything was settled for the coming week, Pru took him out for a walk. There was a little lawn in front of the camp with a row of glossy pines beyond, but no view of the lake. She was delighted to find that Mr. Hodge had such a good time chasing the end of his lead which she dangled before him as she walked, that he seemed not to notice he was wearing a harness or on a lead. Of course, sometimes he went off after a fallen leaf so suddenly that they both got tangled up, and once he tried to climb a tree with no lower limbs which Pru could not do at all.

After an hour she burst into the camp her eyes sparkling and cheeks glowing from the crisp air, crying that Mr. Hodge was just as easy to lead as a dog.

"I'm sure he isn't, dear," said Aunt Lou, "but I'm glad you managed him so well, and you both look fine again. Mr. Hodge's nose is as pink as your cheeks. Now wash up, supper's all ready."

Mr. Hodge went right over and ate his without washing. But then, he always washed after meals.

Mr. Hodge had a wonderful week. He and Pru had many romps on the sunny lawn in front of the camp, and one day she even took him out on the street. A little way down, they met the "Coon-cat". He was a huge cat with long fluffy fur, striped all over like a raccoon, and a little white on his face and breast.

Pru stopped to talk to him and he rubbed against her legs, arching his back so high that he looked as though he were standing on tip-toe, purring loudly all the while.

His mother (his human mother, that is) came out of the house and explained to Pru that he was a coon-cat from Maine, very smart, and that she and her husband were just crazy about him.

Pru agreed that he was really very beautiful and very friendly.

The coon-cat sat down and grinned up at them both.

All this time Mr. Hodge had been sitting quietly, watching the big cat, not really afraid of him, but just considering how very large he was.

Now he came over very quietly and just touched the tip of the big cat's tail. It twitched. He pushed it gently with his paw. It twitched further. Then he could bear it no longer. He pounced. In a flash, the tail swished away from him and close around its owner.

The coon-cat looked at Mr. Hodge over his shoulder, eyes flashing, mouth half open. But he did not quite spit, and he didn't bother to get up. Mr. Hodge decided that he was no good at playing.

Just then a leaf began to move, and Mr. Hodge went after it and then another and another. Soon he had Pru, who was at the other end of his lead, racing all over the strange lady's lawn—and what do you think—the next thing they knew the coon-cat was playing too, and the strange lady was laughing to see the three of them all chasing her leaves.

The last day at the lake was gray and windy, with great clouds tumbling across the sky. The camp seemed a little sad, so in the afternoon, Aunt Em drove them up the shore a little way, and Pru took Mr. Hodge along "to see the lake."

After a while they stopped, and Pru got out and carried Mr. Hodge down onto a dock. Big gray-green waves, some with white foam on them were rolling up, switching and thudding against the dock. Every now and then spray would wash right over it. Boats tied nearby were dancing. Beyond the harbor stretched a couple of miles of tumbled water with "white-caps" on the waves, and away off on the far side, the trees and houses looked no larger than toys.

For a few seconds, Mr. Hodge stared at all the wild water, and away down inside him he felt something very strange. It grew and grew. His yellow eyes got bigger and bigger, his yellow fur stood on end, and he began to tremble and dug his claws into Pru's shoulder.

For the first time in his life Mr. Hodge was afraid!

He was so afraid that he tried to scramble out of Pru's arms, and she had to run back to the car holding as tight as ever she could.

After they were back inside the car, Pru smoothed his fur and talked to him.

By the time they got back to the camp he had stopped trembling, and when they got inside the camp, he forgot to be afraid.

All the same, he began to feel that if there was so very much water in the world, a cat's own home was the best place to stay, and his own people the best people to stay with.

In the night it turned cold. About four in the morning Mr. Hodge woke up very cold. His foot pads were cold, and his fur felt frosty. He tried getting in bed with Pru, but as soon as he got a little warmer, he realized that he was starving. He tried Aunt Em's bed, but she scolded him in a whisper. Then he tried Aunt Lou, who began to giggle, because she suddenly realized that each of them was too cold to sleep, and was trying to keep quiet so as not to wake the others. Suddenly they were all talking at once about how cold it was, and Aunt Em jumped out of bed, got the stove lighted, and was back under the covers, all, as Mr. Hodge might have said, in the flick of a whisker. After that the three of them took turns getting up to put on more wood, to put on the tea kettle, to make hot coffee and cocoa. When it was Pru's turn to get up she skipped out of the door to look at the thermometer. It said 14. When she told her aunts, they just looked at one another and said, "the car?" and Aunt Em pulled slacks and bathrobe over her nightie and ran out to see if it was frozen. It wasn't, and later they learned that the thermometer had been broken for a long time.

By that time they were all up, so they had breakfast. The day began to feel much warmer. Still the floor was too cold for Mr. Hodge's little toe pads. He'd been born in the spring, and had never had cold feet before. He didn't know what to make of it, he tried holding up one paw then another. Pru saw him, laughed, then got up from the breakfast-table and set a chair for him before the stove and opened the door of its tiny oven.

Mr. Hodge settled himself in a tight little ball and let the heat from the oven ripple over him. After a while he stretched a paw toward the oven.

"Look", said Pru, "he's holding out his paw to warm it, isn't he the smartest cat?"

And do you know he hasn't sneezed since we came here?" And that was true. The week in the country had cured his colds.

— *Lucinda Johnson*

A QUANTITY OF MERCY

It was the unbelievable fragrance that awakened Priscilla Conant. The light delicious scent of the apple blossoms, the heavy musk of violets, a purple sea beneath her bedroom window; the aroma of coffee and pancakes mingled with the smoke and sage of sausages sputtering below in the kitchen—all these things called her to get up.

As she looked outside, the apple trees in the orchard were like a hundred bridal bouquets, delicate and pink against the clear blue of the sky. Everything seemed new and freshly born. Two little lambs snuggled close to their mother in the clover patch. Mittens, the barnyard cat, was exploring with her bright orange kittens. Even Elijah, the sheep dog, took an interest in the puppies he had carelessly sired. He sat on the cellar door looking rather proud of Cindy, his scrawny mate, and their playful offspring. A robin chirped from the syringa bush and the sweet, melodic note of a purple finch sang out from one of the hemlocks. It was that rare and wondrous occasion, a perfect spring morning.

Priscilla leaned out the dormer window and breathed in the freshness of the day. It was a heady feeling to realize that she was mistress of almost everything she surveyed. A yellow school bus was hiccuping down the steep hill by the woodlot.

Thank the Lord that thing won't be stopping here, she thought. She walked across the room to her dresser and guiltily picked up the picture of Judy and Tom.

"Judy is getting to be a stunning girl," she murmured. Priscilla looked in the mirror, searching for her daughter's double. "Each of us has the same wide blue eyes," she decided, "and Judy's hair is strong and brownish-red, just like mine at her age." She looked back at the picture and noted that Judy had inherited her dad's whimsical smile and the Conant cheekbones.

Young Tom, the son, had always been the image of her own father. "It's a blessing he has Big Tom's ways," she said, remembering her husband's calm voice and his consistent kindness.

A door slammed downstairs and she heard Sara, the housekeeper, talking with Carpenter, the farm manager. Priscilla showered quickly and pulled on a pair of faded jeans and an old cotton shirt. As a salute to the uncommon day, she chose her favorite sweater, a light blue angora. She brushed her hair smooth and tied it with a kerchief. She had let her hair grow past her shoulders after Big Tom's death and it bothered her.

"I like your hair long. It's so silky," he had said to her often.

"But it's easier to keep it this way. Neater, too," she had answered over and over as she ran her fingers through the short, tailored bob.

As she raced down the backstairs, she heard Sara say to Carpenter, "Do you want the other cup of coffee now or will you wait for Miz Priscilla?"

Priscilla banged down the latch of the old stair door and bounced into the room. "He'll have his coffee with me," she announced and motioned the little man to join her.

"Mornin'," Carpenter greeted her. "It's a grand day. Did you want me to saddle Jerusha?"

"You're reading my mind. I thought I might ride over to the village and celebrate the arrival of spring."

Sara walked over to the table with the breakfast tray. She stood a moment, unsmiling, exchanging a long look with the younger woman. "I thought you'd be taking off for the home," she said as she filled Priscilla's cup.

Priscilla sighed. "How often do I have to tell you that Mother Conant is not in a home. It's a residence for elderly people, one of the best in New England. She has every comfort you can imagine."

"She don't have the comfort of bein' at home where all her forbears lived. She belongs right here." Sara's face was red and her voice sharp. "She's the one who planted all the violets and tended the apple orchard. By rights, this place is hers."

Carpenter looked uncomfortable. "We had a letter from the old Mrs. yesterday," he said. "She seemed cheerful enough. 'Course she never says much about herself, but was real interested in the farm, especially the orchard. Oh, by the way, Keith had a letter from Judy. I thought she sounded a might homesick."

Carpenter's easy conversation helped Priscilla to get hold of herself. Sara is the thorn of my flesh, she thought. She'll never accept the fact that Big Tom willed the place to me. I should get rid of her, but what would I do without her? She turns out work like a machine and she takes such good care of our old things.

She decided to ignore Sara's harangue and turned to Carpenter with her most pleasant smile. "What did you say about Judy? I was thinking of something else."

"My Keith had a letter from her again yesterday. She seemed a trifle downhearted."

"Really? I've had only good reports from her school. Well, it's the time of year we all look back, I guess. Why do you suppose Sara expected me to visit Mother Conant today?"

"For one thing, it's the old Mrs.' birthday and for another, she always picked the early violets — a big bunch of them — for that marbletop table in the hall. Sara mentioned when I came in this morning that she'd hurried around to get some violets for you to take. Guess it was her idea of a springtime birthday present." He pushed his chair back and stood awkwardly. "Well, Miz Priscilla, if you'll excuse me, I'll be getting back to work. I'll get your mare right around."

Priscilla shook her head. "Never mind. I've changed my plans." She took her coffee into the sitting room, as Mother Conant had always called it, and sat in the bay window.

I'm not going to make that long trip to Dover today, she told herself. That Sara! Why didn't she mention the birthday yesterday? Priscilla smiled suddenly — I know what I'll do. I'll borrow her idea. I'll call the Dover florist and have him deliver a bunch of violets to Mother Conant this afternoon. She walked across the room to the alcove office and placed the order. "That's right," she said to the phone. "Have the card read 'Happy Birthday and Love from Priscilla, Judy, and Tom.'" she hesitated a long second. "Better add, 'Wish we could be there.'"

Big Tom's picture faced her as she opened the ancient rolltop desk, the center of the farm's business. It was the same photograph that had appeared in their college yearbook. She picked it up. The smiling face always reassured her. She sat down in the old swivel chair and reached for the orchard file. Big Tom's copious notes were helping her to keep abreast of her hundred and fifty acres. This morning she found it hard to concentrate and she read the file for the third time before she put it away. She picked up her husband's picture again.

"A year ago you were here," she murmured. For a moment, she was back in the sunny kitchen of the second tenant farm, urging Judy and Tom to hurry with their breakfast. There had been a daily race to get ready in time for the school bus.

Big Tom had always taken breakfast with his mother in the "big house." "No need for you to get up with the chickens," he had told her when they were first married — and she had welcomed the opportunity to stay in bed and have a leisurely morning to herself. At first, she remembered, Mother Conant had often stopped at the kitchen door with a pie or cake or an invitation to lunch.

But Priscilla kept herself too busy to be neighborly. After a while, Mother Conant stayed home and except for holidays and birthdays there were few meetings between mother-in-law and daughter-in-law.

"What's the idea of being so aloof?" Big Tom had said to her with make-believe severity one evening. "I well remember how you used to wangle all those invitations from me for weekends from college. I thought you had a hankering for a country home—and you certainly charmed Mother with your interest in her old quilts and her antique pewter. She looked forward to our living on the farm, you know."

Priscilla had squeezed his hand and smiled brightly. "I was perfectly sincere, darling. I do love your old home and I love your mother, too. But I know myself. I'm a private person. It takes most of my time to keep myself interesting for you."

He had frowned. "What do you mean by that?"

She had slipped her arm through his and laid her head back on his shoulder. "I mean exactly what I said. I've been spending many hours doing our house over and making it into the country cottage we both dreamed of when we first decided to live here. You're crazy about gardens—and those flowers don't grow without help. Then, there's the time I spend reading so I can keep up with my scientific farmer husband and his brilliant ideas."

Big Tom had been the strongest man she had ever known, and it still astounded her to remember that she had always been able to handle him and to keep his love. Of course, she had played her part with discernment. When they went to his mother's that first Christmas, Priscilla had combed the Conant woods for greens and berries and had spent the morning transforming the old farmhouse into a greeting card setting. She had spent weeks hunting the missing pieces of Mother Conant's favorite old Baltimore Pear glass pattern. "And this isn't your best present," she had told that grateful lady who was unwrapping the last goblet. "We're having our first baby next spring—your first grandchild."

Mother Conant had come around the table and kissed her. "My cup runneth over!" she exclaimed. "What a wonderful Christmas present you children have given me!"

Young Tom was born less than two years after Judy. Mother Conant had sent Sara to help Priscilla when the children were little. "Let her do the housework and you'll have more time for your children," she said.

Sara had not been Priscilla's idea of the model housekeeper, but she thanked her mother-in-law and kept her silence. Sara's accomplishments freed her for canters with Big Tom and shopping trips to New York on matinee days. The children loved Sara who had a way of mixing popcorn balls with the most hectic cleaning day and who commanded a store of ghost stories to tell on somber afternoons. As soon as they were old enough, they chased Sara back to Mother Conant's when she returned there after lunch. Again, Priscilla had enjoyed the opportunity to rest and be ready for the evening as Big Tom's confidante after the children went to bed.

Mother Conant, she recalled, had treasured those afternoons with the Carpenter youngsters and her grandchildren. What had Carpenter said that very morning about Judy and Keith? Annoyed, Priscilla stopped daydreaming.

Why did Judy persist in carrying on this silly correspondence with Keith Carpenter? Priscilla had talked with her about it when she came home for Christmas. Judy had said only, "He's always been a real friend to me, Mother. You know that. I like him."

Keith, Priscilla knew, was a good person — and attractive. His lanky height, towering over his father, was commanding. He had an easy humor and a refreshing smile. He played basketball like a champion and he was a serious student. Still, he was the farm manager's son — and a future farmer himself — and no match for Judy. Priscilla was honest enough to admit to herself that she had sent the children away to school to be free of them, but Judy's relationship with Keith had been enough of a nagging threat to accelerate the arrangements for their transfer from the regional school in the village.

For young Tom, an extra year at home might have been a healing ointment. He had taken his father's death so hard. Priscilla had never felt so close to any other human being as she did to Big Tom, but in comparison with the children's open and unbelieving grief when the new tractor pinned him down and beat out his breath, she had experienced only a stony dullness.

Priscilla had often tried to analyze her feelings. Her relationship with her own mother had been as wary and uncertain as Big Tom's alliance with Mother Conant had been open and steady. When she was seventeen, her parents had separated. She had spent most of the time with her father. Actually, his New York apartment had been a place to keep her belongings and to eat and sleep. Her father had been a gallant host when she brought her friends home during college vacations. He suggested the right art galleries and museums; he bought tickets for the best shows; he took the pack to dinner at the Algonquin and Luchow's.

Her mother had kept the saltbox on Cape Cod and during the summer, Priscilla used the cottage for houseparties and entertaining. Her transient young life had lacked peace and warmth. Was that the reason she had been so logical and practical about Big Tom's sudden death? It chilled her to remember that even at the funeral services in the village church, she had sat contemplating sending the children away to boarding school. Within a week, she had moved into the big house, and within a month she had encouraged Mother Conant to join her sister at the residence for retired people in Dover. Even the big house was not large enough for Priscilla and another woman.

Priscilla never completed that recurrent analysis. Memories always sidetracked her. There were all the college classes she had shared with Big Tom. Thomas Conant and Priscilla Cowan had been destined to spend many hours side by side after the alphabetical seating arrangement of their Alma Mater's attendance scheme. They became friends. Big Tom had depended on the notes that her quick pen mastered so easily. Priscilla had relied on his explanations of intricate formulas and his lucid interpretations of involved social theories.

For the first time in her life, she had found someone who valued her as deeply as he respected himself—someone as dependable as he was self-reliant. Everything about their alliance had been steady and memorable. For the average college girl, their romance might have been too smooth and uneventful. But Priscilla had known too much about the transitory way of life; she was ready for the permanence Big Tom's steadiness offered. There had always been a lightheartedness between them, and an active physical attraction. Priscilla thought of those qualities as the lifeline of her marriage and she had worked diligently to keep them alive.

There were times—on a starlit night or a lazy Sunday morning—that she missed her husband terribly, but she had invested her strength so wholeheartedly in the understanding of his business and in making decisions for Carpenter that the pain of separation was eased. She had always known the farm was a going concern, but the realization of the true Conant prosperity had been a surprise. Priscilla knew she had a knack for organizing and planning ahead. And wasn't it the sensible thing to keep busy and sublimate her energy?

I must stop dreaming and get to work, she told herself. My mind is too active. She picked up a letter from the New York hotel that bought their choice apples. The light seemed dim. She realized suddenly that the sunlight had disappeared.

She walked back to the bay window. The sky was darkening and rain-drops were beginning to blur the picture of the farmyard. Priscilla watched Mittens hustle her kittens through the barn door, and she heard Sara call to Elijah. He'll track the floors with mud, she thought. Why didn't she leave him outside?

She started for the kitchen to close the door and was relieved to see that Sara had the big sheep dog on his leash. Sara didn't look up. "Mail's here on the window sill," she announced soberly.

"Oh, thanks." Priscilla picked up the bundle and took it back to the desk. The letter on top was from Tom and his mother tore it open. She was frowning as Sara came into the room.

"Is Little Tom all right? I couldn't help seeing his name on that enve-lope." Sara stood waiting for Priscilla to answer. "I do miss that boy so much, Miz Priscilla." There was no response. "Say, you're not lookin' too well yourself. Is anything wrong?"

Priscilla looked up. She spoke softly, "Nothing's wrong." Her voice rose. "Sara, I wish you'd stop calling my son 'Little Tom.'". She paused and looked hard at the housekeeper. "And please refer to me as Mrs. Conant. I'm the head of the house, not the college girl who used to spend her weekends here."

"What brought all that on?" Sara asked her, squinting her black eyes. "Somethin' must be wrong or you wouldn't be so upset, takin' you feelin's out on me." She whirled around. "Excuse me. I'll be leavin' you alone." She headed back to the kitchen with the air of a champion who had just won another round.

"That woman!" Priscilla could feel her blood tingling. She read Tom's letter again.

Dear Mother,

You've got to help me. I can't stay here at school. As Grandma Conant would say, "It isn't my cup of tea." I know my grades have slipped a lot, but it's because I keep thinking about the farm and you and Sara and the orchard and all. I bet Grandma misses the same things. Please answer this letter today and write to Dr. Thornton. He knows how unhappy I am, and I think he'd return some of the tuition.

If I can get back in time for baseball tryouts, I promise you I'll be on that honor roll again. Please, Mommy.

Your son,

T.

Priscilla walked across the room, sat in the big willow chair by the window, and read Tom's letter for the third time. It was raining hard now and the wind was beginning to whine. She thought, everything was so perfect early this morning. I felt secure. Now, everthing is wrong—even this miserable weather.

She glanced back at the letter. "I haven't heard Tom say 'Please, Mommy' since I stopped calling him Tommy," she mused. For a second her face softened. She shook her head. "He'll just have to learn to adjust." She thought of the times she had been thrust into a new school, or been forced to stay with a grudging relative during Christmas vacation; or, worst of all, had been sent to the summer camp she despised. "I lived through it," she decided. "I'll write to Tom and arrange for him to come home next weekend. We'll have a good talk and I'll make him see it my way."

The telephone was ringing as she went back to the desk. "Peacedale Farm. Mrs. Conant speaking." Priscilla's voice was brisk and businesslike.

"Good morning, Mrs. Conant. This is Marcia Somers, your daughter's counselor at school."

"Oh, good morning, I hope Judy's all right and behaving herself."

"She's fine. She looked pretty as a picture when that young man came for her this morning. I want her to call me as soon as she gets home. We're working together on a folk sing for Founder's Night and I can't find the music. I'm rehearsing the lower form tonight and I need it."

Priscilla gasped. "Mrs. Somers, what do you mean about Judy's coming home? And what young man called for her?"

"Did'nt you know? I hope I haven't spoiled a surprise visit."

"Do you mean that you allow those girls to travel around the country without their parents' written permission?"

"I'm really sorry to distress you, Mrs. Conant. Your Judy is one of the most responsible girls we've ever had. We don't accept students we feel we can't trust. Rules in all schools, public and private, are relaxed these days. Judy said she'd known the boy all her life, so he's probably a friend of your family."

"When did she leave?"

"Several hours ago. Before breakfast, in fact."

"Then they should be here."

"I'm sure they will be there soon, Mrs. Conant. Again, I'm sorry I upset you. You will have Judy call me?"

"Yes, Mrs. Somers. Goodbye."

Priscilla knew that Keith Carpenter must have called for Judy that morning. Did his father know about it? If he did know, why hadn't he told her? Habitually, Carpenter was a forthright and outspoken man. After the confusion of the morning, Priscilla was ready to believe anything. "I'll find out what he has to say," she decided.

She hurried to the hall closet for her raincoat and was just about to open the front door when Keith's car came up the driveway. Judy rushed up the porch stairs. "Mother! Hello! Are you going someplace?"

"Judy, what are doing here?" Priscilla held her daughter at arm's length, searching her face. Keith appeared suddenly and Priscilla turned to him. "Keith Carpenter, why aren't you in school?"

During all his eighteen years, Keith had been used to the younger Mrs. Conant's direct and blunt questioning. He had long ago decided it was just her way. His answer was short; "I just didn't go."

"Why not?"

"Well, for one thing, Judy was homesick—"

"Mother," Judy interrupted, "I wrote and asked Keith to come for me today. It's Grandma's birthday. We're going up there this afternoon and I thought you'd like to ride along. Tom's meeting us there. His basketball team is playing in the town beyond Dover, so it all worked out." Abruptly, she held her mother close and kissed her. "Oh, Mother, it's so good to be home. The place looks beautiful."

"Sun's coming out," Keith offered. "Guess that was a clear-up shower. I'm going to run, Judy. Be back after lunch."

Sara collided with them as they walked into the house. "I thought it was Judy!" she said, wiping her hands on her apron. "You're a sight for sore eyes, girl."

"Sara, I couldn't wait to see you." Judy squealed and lifted her off the floor. "Give me a great big kiss and tell me you've just finished baking a batch of soft molasses cookies. I smell them."

"You haven't changed a bit," Priscilla sighed. "Come on upstairs and we'll talk while I show you the new paper in the bedroom. We'll have lunch in the sitting room, Sara."

Sara headed for the kitchen, knowing that Priscilla was maneuvering a chance to talk with Judy in privacy.

"We'll be back, Sara," Judy called. "You know we're going to see Grandma this afternoon. It's her birthday."

"You can take the violets I picked!" Sara exlaimed. "I'll get them ready."

Priscilla had taken possession of the guest room and Judy surveyed the new flowered paper, the delicate organdy curtains, and the new high poster. "Mother, it's beautiful. This room used to look so—well, neuter. It's really wispy and feminine now."

"Glad you like it. Judy, sit down. I want to talk with you."

"Yes, Mother. What's wrong? You're so tense and stand-offish."

"Judy, don't you think it's more than a little irregular for you to come home like this without writing to me, or calling?"

"I wanted to surprise you. Besides, I didn't know for sure that Keith could come for me." Judy looked up. "You weren't even taken unawares, Mother. You seemed to expect us."

"Mrs. Somers called. When we go downstairs, you're to call her about some music." Priscilla got back to her subject. "Judy, you might have asked *me* to go for you. We could have stopped in Dover on the way home. To tell the truth, I had forgotten about your grandmother's birthday. I have so many things to take care of these days."

Judy had walked over to the dressing table and she leaned over to look more closely at a picture there of her parents.

"Mother, I know how hard it must be for you without Daddy. He loved you so much. But honestly, I think you made it hard for yourself when you moved so fast to make changes. Grandma would have been a big help in making decisions about the farm. Daddy always went to her when he was stuck. Tom and I didn't want to go away to school. You railroaded us. Tom's miserable. I'm worried about him, Mother. That's the time kids start taking drugs and get into all kinds of trouble."

Priscilla stood speechless for a minute. "Have you anything more to say, Judy? Let's get it out in the open."

Judy hesitated. "Yes, Mother, there's more. I'll finish this year at school and graduate, but I'm not going away to college."

"What do you plan to do?" Judy took a long breath. "Keith and I are going to get married."

"Married?" Priscilla shrieked. "You can't be serious. You're children. It's time enough to think of marriage when you're in college, meeting some interesting men."

"Mother, I'm going to marry Keith." Judy's voice was very firm and very steady. "We've loved each other for a long time—almost forever."

"And just where do you propose to live? And what will you use for money? Judy, this is all nonsense. You're not looking ahead."

"Yes, we've been looking ahead, Mother. Keith and I plan to go to the Community College in the village. I can study music there, and he'll take an agriculture course. We'll be free in the summer so he can work the farm—weekends, too." She hesitated. "Mother, we'd like to live in our old house—it's empty. Daddy always said Peacedale Farm was a family commune. It belongs to all of us."

"You certainly have everything organized," Priscilla said slowly. "If you'd only discussed this with me at Christmas . . ."

From the foot of the stairs, Sara called, "Lunch is ready. Shall I dish it up?"

"Yes, we'll be right down," Priscilla answered. "You go ahead," she told Judy. "I want to slip on a dress."

Alone in her room, she walked over to the dormer window and took a long look at the farmyard. Just that morning, it had been an idyllic scene. Everything in her world had been the way she had planned. Now, a few hours later, her world was in chaos.

"I suppose next year this time, they'll all be back," she reasoned. "Tom will be racing for that school bus every morning; Sara will be playing straight man to Mother Conant; Judy will be Mrs. Carpenter when she could be Mrs. Somebody."

She walked back to the dressing table and picked up a comb. A shaft of bright sunlight played against her husband's picture. She remembered Judy's words, "He loved you so much."

Yes, he did love me, she sighed. She reached for the picture. Suddenly, she was trembling and her face was wet. "Oh, Tom," she murmured, "I loved you, too. You are the only person in my whole life I have really loved."

She thought of what Judy had been saying—"Daddy always said the place belonged to all of us." It wasn't going to be easy, but she would find a way. For the first time since Big Tom's death, she felt close to him. She sensed a warmth, the old lighthearted peacefulness they had shared so many years.

"Mother," Judy called. "Come down. The salad looks delicious, and Sara's made biscuits."

—Mary Kosegarten

THE LITTLE BALSAM

It was cold—cold and dazzling white. The whole world glistened in the winter sunlight like the vast pleasure dome of Xanadu. The shimmering snowscape was punctuated here and there by a few lonely sycamores, their spindly branches tipped with clumps of snow like fur mittens. Casting weird futuristic shadows on the white hillside, they looked like grotesque skeletons reaching skyward for a covering for their bony nakedness. Two rows of fence posts capped with tall busbys, made, it seemed, from the skins of polar bears, stood like a double file of honor guards between which we trudged, Erik and I, panting up the hill toward home—my home. Our breath spouted forth in vaporous jets like puffs of smoke from the Indian peace pipe that Grandfather used to tell about after his third or fourth mug of hard cider.

That was a long time ago—more than half a century. But I recall it now as clearly as if—well, as if it were happening here and now, to you and me. It was Christmas Eve near the end of the Age of Simplicity, and before the invention of global warfare robbed the entire world of its innocence, once and for all. It was a Christmas to remember. Would you like me to tell you about it? Would you like to experience it yourself?

Then sit back and clasp someone's hand tightly in your own. Close your eyes and listen to the muffled notes of the village church bell swelling and fading as the gusty wind carries its Christmas message across the broad valley of the years. Are you listening? Are you prepared for a true Christmas story? For I swear to you by all that Christmas means to boys and girls and to their grandfathers everywhere that my story is true. This is how it happened.

I was coming home for Christmas after my first extended absence from my boyhood home in a remote rural community in Ohio, which had been my pleasantly circumscribed world for nineteen years. Suddenly, there it stood in all of its sturdy dignity inherited from its Pennsylvania Dutch ancestry, the rusty brick walls casting luminous purple shadows on the sculptured mounds of drifted snow. In the open space in front of the parlor window stood the majestic horse chestnut tree of which my father was so proud, the only one in all the county—for all I knew, the only one in the world—robed in a thick ermine mantle, like a huge, fat king in Alice's wonderland. On the other side of the now invisible walk leading to the front door, cowered the old mulberry tree, an aging and humble page in this Graustarkian court, creaking arthritically in the wind. The woodpile was stacked with great sticks of taffy for Paul Bunyan's Christmas stocking. From the huge brick chimney ribbons of aromatic purple smoke drifted on the vacillating wind like Indian smoke signals telling all the world that it was Christmas. It was an original Currier and Ives, the scene that greeted Erik and me as we trudged breathless and fittingly hungry up the deeply drifted lane.

Erik was my new friend. We were living together in the grimy, smoke-enveloped river town dominated by the soot-blackened, cacophonous steel mill, which was manned by hordes of denim-garbed immigrants from every country in Europe. Erik had gone there from his home in Minnesota, where his family held extensive interests in the iron mines, in order to learn the business of steelmaking from ore to finished product. To that end, he was working in the mill as a roller's helper on the night shift.

I had ventured into this industrial and, to me, foreign environment to teach the three Rs and such related arts as elocution and basketball to a heterogeneous assortment of vigorous young animals of diverse origins— second-generation Americans. It was a task for which my one year at normal school and a rather bucolic term of teaching in a one-room country school had scarcely prepared me.

Erik was a young Viking, six feet-five, blond, suave, and very handsome. My statistics were the inverse of his, barely five feet-six. I was neither dark nor fair, rather mousey, I guess, and certainly nobody's idea of a dashing cavalier. But we had many things in common—a love of music cultivated, but only partially satisfied, by an old tone-limited Edison phonograph, and an avid taste for theater meagerly nourished by the Steubenville Stock Company: *Tess of the D'Urbervilles, Wuthering Heights, David Harum.* We also shared a love for books. Erik went in for the heavy stuff: *War and Peace, Anna Karenina, The*

Brothers Karamazov; while I leaned toward lighter fiction—the emotion-packed romances of Marie Corelli and the moralistic novels of Hall Caine. For recreation there were tennis outdoors and checkers indoors. I could beat the white ducks off Erik on the court, and he regularly made a fool of me at the checkerboard. Whatever we did, we were happy doing it together. Although we managed to get into as much mischief as we dared, or as opportunity allowed, we never engaged in anything really spectacular, such as setting fire to haystacks or stealing a lady's unmentionables off the backyard clothes line—to say nothing of exploring the cardinal sins that Hall Caine described so devastatingly, along with the inevitable punishment "to the third and fourth generations". Hall Caine literally scared the devil out of me.

All of this is by way of telling you how Erik and I came to be plowing through the drifts to my Ohio farm home on Christmas Eve. Minnesota was too far away for him to make the trip over the three-day holiday which a fortunate concurrence on the calendar allowed him. I had, therefore, invited him to spend Christmas on the farm with my family. Consequently, after two hours on the stuffy, jostling narrow-gauge railroad that wound its tortuous way among the hills, another hour in an open bobsled drawn by a team of steaming bay Percherons, followed by this half-mile trek through snow drifts up to our knees, here we were—home.

We entered the house by way of the large screened side porch, where we always ate in summer, thence through the back door into the kitchen. The imposing front door, little used at any time, was boarded over with a rough storm door against the blasts of winter.

Our kitchen was the most comfort-radiating room that I have ever been in. The central feature was a large, square, cast-iron range that did double duty around the clock as cook stove and heating plant. Generously stoked with wood—or coal, when it was available—this black monster radiated a bone-warming welcome that no words of mine can describe. Its ebony coat was kept clean and shiny by frequent applications of Rising Sun stove polish. Often half concealed by a canopy of mittens, stockings, and long flannel drawers hung up to dry, surmounted always by those ubiquitous twins, the steaming tea-kettle and the bubbling coffee pot, its capacious oven emitting the tantalizing odors of baking bread, the kitchen stove was the pulsating heart of the house.

Along one wall of the room was a structure that we called the "sink," a long pine counter top containing a submerged wooden box lined with zinc. Into this receptacle a stammering, coughing trickle of water could be injected by the cast-iron lift pump whose lead esophagous terminated in the cistern just outside the kitchen window. The cistern was supplied with rain water via a down spout from the eave troughs. The waste outlet from this strictly functional system was always a mystery to me. I think it must have led straight through to China. For drinking water there was the long-handled, Ichabod Crane pump that stood like an emaciated cigar-store Indian on the porch just outside the kitchen door, and drew the coldest, purest of ambrosia from the stone-lined well below.

The round kitchen table, flanked by six sturdy oak chairs including an over-size one for Father, stood by the west window which looked out over the orchard with its aging population of Baldwins, Winesaps, Grimes' Goldens, and the homely, but delicious, Northern Russets. If you pressed your face tight against the window pane without concern for the plastic distortion of your nose, you could just see the old mulberry tree out of the corner of your eye. I once nearly foretold an untimely conclusion to this tale by a precipitous descent from that tree while trying to compete with the robins for a fair share of the luscious fruit. Come to think of it, that mulberry tree was dearer to my heart than any tree on the farm, except one—the little balsam that is the central feature of my story.

But I must defer a little longer while I introduce you to my family, who were assembled in this cozy family room to greet us. First, there was Mother. Mother cannot be described—only loved, as she was by all who knew her, whether it be the frightened, pregnant young wife of the hired hand, seeking comfort and reassurance, or the itinerant peddler with his case of thinly gold-washed trinkets, sponging a good meal—he cheerfully cheated everyone except Mother—or just anybody who needed the warm, consoling touch of a woman who faced life fearlessly and lived in peace with man and God. Erik fell in love with her on sight, and she, of course, promptly adopted him as another son. She must have been in her early forties at the time, without a thread of gray in her chestnut hair and with just the faintest of crow's feet to accentuate the incipient laughter in her eyes. She hugged us both and gave us each a fresh doughnut from the skillet sputtering and sizzling on the stove.

Father should have been a gentleman farmer, if only the lords of finance had so decreed. He loved the broad meadows with their clean, well-kept fence rows. He had little love for flowers and an exaggerated abhorrence of weeds, but he was not always able to distinguish between them. For instance, he could not tolerate a single spray of that gay wild flower, the ox-eye daisy, in the meadows; he spoke of it as if it were loaded with lethal doses of arsenic and opium. He would walk clear across the farm to pull up one intruding root of wild carrot, a beautiful and prolific plant, which you probably know by the lovely name of Queen Anne's Lace. He was proud of the "park," as he called the woodlands on the other side of the creek and kept it as immaculately manicured as the German forest that we had read about in *Hansel and Gretel.* Most of all, he loved "the knolls," a pair of symmetrically rounded hills that rose in graceful slopes just across the road from the house. Indeed they were beautiful, and now with their pristine covering of snow, they seemed like the white breasts of Mother Earth herself.

Father was a somewhat reserved and dignified person—proper, but not at all religious. In spite of being descendant from a long line of Quaker ancestors, he had little truck with the church and posed—with some trepidation I think—as an atheist. Mother, who was a devoted Methodist, though not of the holy-roller, psalm-singing ilk, held her peace, and with calm dignity, led her two sons down the aisle of the village church every Sunday.

When Erik and I stomped into the kitchen that Christmas Eve, shaking the snow from our mackintoshes like a pair of Alaskan huskies, Father was seated at his harness bench by the window mending a bridle. He stabbed his awl into the bench and rose to greet us with a hearty handshake. He seemed a little subdued, but was obviously pleased to see me.

My brother Ray was a year younger than I. He had been a victim of infantile paralysis when a baby and as a result walked with a slight limp. Also his right arm and hand were affected, which doubtless accounted for his being left-handed. Perhaps as compensation for his physical handicaps, he had a buoyant spirit and an outgoing personality. He and Erik hit it off at once and were soon engaged in a game of checkers, at which Ray made a better showing than I had ever done.

This was the family circle into which I introduced Erik and within which he was to spend his first Christmas away from home. I was determined to make it as happy and enjoyable for him as I could. It was to be the most festive and fun-packed holiday of our carefree lives.

But there was something wrong. I had noticed some uneasiness in Father's manner when he greeted me, and I sensed a hidden soberness back of Mother's welcoming smile. It was intangible, but it affected me with a strange apprehension, as a dark cloud appearing unexpectedly in the azure sky casts a somber shadow that creeps ominously over the bright landscape.

It came out when we sat down to a supper of oyster stew and home-cured ham, just as the sun was plunging into the snow banks in the west and the full moon was beginning his mysterious ascent from infinity in the east. After my third bowl of stew, I asked Ray about the Christmas tree: Where had they found it? Was it as tall and well formed as the spruce that we had last year? The response was disconcerting. Ray stammered and shifted in his chair as Father cleared his throat and coughed in embarrassment. Then Mother spoke quietly, "We aren't having a tree this year."

The shock of this announcement was too paralyzing for immediate speech. It was as if she had said, "The President has vetoed Christmas." As the ham and fried potatoes turned to tasteless rubber on my plate, I tried to assimilate the sickening news. No Christmas tree? How could such a calamity befall an American family in this era of comfortable orthodoxy under the paternal benevolence of President Woodrow Wilson? We had always had a tree in the parlor at Christmas, the only time that sacrosanct chamber was used all winter long. When no evergreen could be found—they were scarce in that corner of the state—the ubiquitous sycamore was made to substitute, an unlikely role which it filled with modest grace and beauty. But no tree at all?

After supper Mother took me aside and explained what they had heretofore carefully kept from me, that family finances were at a precariously low ebb. What with the failure of the corn crop and the loss, from an unknown disease, of over half of the carload of white-face Herefords that Father had imported from Kansas City, money was scarce and spirits were low. Certainly there would be a few modest presents and, of course, the customary Christmas dinner, for Mother's larder was far from bare, and the smoke-house was still redolent with the pungent odor of hams, shoulders, and "side meat." Moreover, the chicken yard was well populated with speckled Plymouth Rocks and glossy fat Rhode Island Reds. But evergreens were hard to come by, and the task of procuring one, or even a lowly sycamore, was just too much for my dispirited family.

Clearly something had to be done, and I determined to do it. Not just to keep up a revered tradition, but to lift the spirits of my dejected family and to make this Christmas one never to be forgotten for its true and eternal meaning.

There was on our farm one solitary evergreen, a small but beautifully formed balsam. It stood alone in a triangle of land that had been severed from the corner of our quarter-section by the road, which had been laid out by some drunken surveyor in time long past. Instead of trying to have the road properly relocated, Father decided to make this green triangle into a picnic spot, for there was a spring of clear, cold water bubbling away in the northeast corner. The little balsam stood in the center of this plot, which was called by the somewhat over-pretentious name of Balsam Park. Sometimes on a Sunday afternoon we would spread a table cloth on the shady side of the tree and, sitting on the thick grassy cushion, feast on fried chicken, deviled eggs, and biscuits thickly covered with blackberry jam. For a beverage, there was always lemonade made with water from the spring and for dessert, home-made ice cream and marble cake. This family picnic spot was a very special place in our world, and the little balsam was its guardian spirit. We, Ray and I, had been warned never to injure this tree under threat of direst consequences. Through all of our boyhood years, the little balsam had endured and flourished under our benevolent protection.

But this was a crisis. The time had come for the little balsam to make the supreme sacrifice in a just and righteous cause. As a symbol of Christmas jubilation throughout the Christian world, it is the destiny of the evergreen family to provide gracious guests in the homes of human beings to delight the children and to revive poignant memories in their elders. It is a duty that dare not be ignored. And so I resolved to cut down the little balsam.

First, however, I must somehow obtain suitable trimmings for his shiny green coat. Tradition demands that the Yule tree be gaily decked with ornaments appropriate to the gala occasion. Of course, Mother had an assortment of decorations — colored balls, paper bells, and strands of tinsel — stored away from other Christmases; but I could not ask her for them, for I dared not confess to the crime that I was about to commit.

The village store was always open until eight o'clock on Christmas Eve for the benefit of stragglers who found themselves embarrassed either from procrastination or forgetfulness. I took Erik and Ray into my confidence, and we went into an executive session over ways and means. To begin with, we set a limit of one dollar for all expenditures, an amount that constituted the sum of our pooled resources. Then, while Father was immersed in the current issue of "The Modern Woodman" and Mother was disjointing the several chickens for tomorrow's feast, the three of us set forth through the drifts for the village half a mile away. We had no need for the customary lanterns, for the full moon cast its cold radiation over the land, revealing the road, lined with its white-capped sentinels, as a muted, mauve ribbon descending to the bridge across the frozen creek and then ascending to the village beyond. In the illusive moonlight we could see the ghostly sycamores waving inanely to us and tracing eerie, moon-made shadows on the ground. We could hear their sorrowful sighing and whispering in the wind, like the keening of witches over their gruesome caldron. It was just as well that there were three of us.

In the village, all was still and dark, save where the lucent glow from the windows made amber beacons along the one shadowy, deserted street and traced flickering, geometric patterns on the snow. The lighted windows of the village store marked our destination. Have you ever entered a country store on a winter night to be enveloped in an exotic atmosphere of pungent odors — smoked sausage, aged cheese, soap, linament, gum boots, tobacco, horehound candy, and an indescribable assortment of spices? You can travel the world over, from Cape Town to Murmansk, from Tokyo to Tashkent to Chicago, and not find anything to equal it as a tonic for tired blood or a distressed spirit.

We did not dawdle long over our purchases, for there was much to be done before our furtive task could be consummated. A dollar would buy considerably more then than it does today, but nevertheless, it didn't take long to spend it. Two pounds of ribbon candy, a pound of popcorn, some red and green crepe paper, a spool of Aunt Lydia's thread, a dozen candy canes, some chocolate Santa Clauses, half a dozen bright tin trinkets, and three sticks of liquorice for us to chew on the walk home.

I don't think Erik had ever been inside a country store before. It was only by persistent urging and the promise of a return visit after Christmas that we finally persuaded him to forsake this congenial atmosphere for the cold, antiseptic air outside. It was past nine o'clock when we got back home, after hurriedly repassing the spectral denizens of the night. Father and Mother had gone to bed, a circumstance that conformed ideally with our nefarious scheme. I went to the woodshed and got an axe and my homemade wooden sled with strap-iron bands on the runners, and we set out across the white and indigo fields.

The little balsam seemed more untouchable than ever, standing there with his white cloak shining in the moonlight and looking like a patron saint presiding over some Nordic altar. With beating heart and troubled conscience I led the assault. When we had shaken the snow off the branches, the little balsam looked hopelessly vulnerable standing among the drifts without his cloak.

Erick volunteered to do the cutting since he was the stronger and doubtless the handier with an axe. But I refused. The guilt was mine, the blame must be wholly mine. It didn't take long. A few blows with the axe and the little balsam lay, a martyred saint, on a moonlit tomb. Suddenly it grew colder. The livid moon seemed to summon forth a frigid, avenging wind, while fixing us with a merciless, accusing stare that chilled us to the bone with fright and misgiving. Hurriedly we placed the little balsam on the sled and made for the warmth and security of home.

Once inside the house, our confidence returned. We planted the tree firmly in a bucket of sand that was kept handy for sanding the front walk when accumulated ice made traversing it hazardous. We stationed the tree in a corner of the parlor farthest from the fireplace in which tomorrow morning's fire of apple wood was laid with kindling all ready to be ignited. Treading like cats in our stocking feet, we were careful not to awaken the sleepers overhead.

When the tree was in place, we set about preparing the decorations. Ray took over the corn-popping duty, muffling the sound as best he could be placing a pillow on the lid of the skillet. Soon there was a heaping dishpan full of exploded white kernels. Then we all set to work stringing the popcorn in long strands, using Mother's darning needles and Aunt Lydia's thread, which was extra strong and well adapted to the purpose. When the beaded chains were draped in snowy festoons on the green tree, the effect was quite impressive. We tried dying some of the polished horse chestnuts with cake coloring, but the results were disappointing, so we settled for wrapping them in red crepe paper. With their flared skirts they looked like a royal corps de ballet swarming over a green hillside. The chocolate Santa Clauses made fine partners for the ballet dancers. The ribbon candy was an inspiration; the gaily striped curlicues made wonderful ornaments. And the candy canes added just the right Yuletide flourish. Finally, the bright red-and-yellow trinkets were strategically disposed over the handsomely decked tree. My, how festive it looked!

We spent quite a little time with paste and scissors making chains of alternate red and green loops of crepe paper. We hung these colored chains as festoons on the doors and windows and over the mantlepiece. When all was complete, we stood back and admired our handiwork. The effect was really stupendous. The little balsam looked quite magnificent in his holiday attire and appeared happily resigned to his new role.

By now it was long past midnight. After placing our unpretentious, but gaily wrapped, gifts under the tree, we tiptoed up the carpeted stair and plunged into the enfolding warmth and comfort of the feather beds.

Christmas morning! Does anyone ever become wholly immune to the magic of this Christian holiday? On this Christmas morning it was colder than ever, with the snow blowing in opalescent sheets and creeping through the crevices around the windows like an army of white ants. Only the excitement of mingled anticipation and apprehension could have induced me to leave the snug depths of my feather mattress. By this time Father must have seen and recognized the little balsam. What would he say? What would he do? I recalled with belated qualms his severe injunctions about "dire consequences." By now I was filled with remorse and misgiving. The elation of the night before had completely washed away, leaving me trembling more with fright than with cold as I dressed, shivering in the unheated bedroom. My fellow culprits must have felt the same, for no one ventured downstairs until we were all ready to face the music together.

The apple-wood fire was blazing and crackling on the andirons as we entered the parlor in faintly disguised terror. And there was Father standing with his back to the fire, arms folded across his chest, like Wellington before the battle of Waterloo. "Merry Christmas, boys," he said with a smile and a suppressed chuckle. Words cannot describe the wave of relief that swept over me, liberating the suspended animation of my heart and halting the trembling in my finger tips. Just then Mother came in bearing a tray of mugs full of steaming cocoa and a plate of fresh doughnuts. "What a lovely tree," she said. Only then did I dare to look across the room at our tree. I saw at once that something had been added. Perched like butterflies on the outstretched branches of the little balsam were five crisp, new one-dollar bills. "Where did they come from?" I cried. "How did they get there?" Mother glanced at Father with a look on her face seen only on the faces of mothers at Christmas time, and she said, "Santa Claus made it after all."

And so the bleak depression of Christmas Eve was transformed into the overwhelming joy of Christmas Day. Gone were the shadows back of Mother's eyes and the quaver of uncertainty in Father's voice. The spirit of Christmas enveloped us all in Yuletide gaiety and the pure delight of mutual faith and family togetherness. It was a miracle! And the little balsam had done it. This small woodland saint had moved from his snow-white altar under the sapphire sky to our fireside bringing his miraculous spirit with him and bestowing his divine blessing upon us all.

You may open your eyes now. My story is nearly finished, but not quite. Bear with me a little longer. I will refrain from regaling you with the events of that wonderful Christmas Day—the opening of the presents, the breakfast of pancakes and country sausages, the trip to the barn to care for the stock in their sheltered stalls, the cracking of butternuts and shellbark hickory nuts around the aromatic fire, or the crowning event of the day, Mother's incomparable dinner of fried chicken, mashed potatoes, yams, cinnamon apples, hot biscuits, assorted jellies, jams, and relishes, and a dozen "side dishes" that I cannot now identify—the whole topped off with a quarter of hot mince pie.

It was not a Christmas of *things,* such as I see piled in profligate profusion under electrically spangled Christmas trees today. But it remains the most memorable Christmas in any of our lives. And the central figure, the presiding spirit of that Christmas celebration was the miraculous little balsam.

My vacation passed all too quickly with no intimation that this would be my last Christmas in the home of my boyhood. Erik had to leave the day after Christmas to return to his job in the steel mill, but I remained until after the village church bell had proclaimed the birth of a new, and hopefully brighter, year. As was our custom, the Christmas tree was dismantled on New Year's Day and relegated to the brush heap back of the barn.

On the night before my departure, in the shadowy, evanescent hours between midnight and dawn, I was startled into an indeterminate consciousness by the sudden realization of something missing—something *lost*. The axe! In our haste to leave the scene of vandalism on that moonlit Christmas Eve, we had left it, forgotten, where we had cut the tree. It must be there yet.

Sometime—still in the twilight zone between reality and fantasy—I tramped alone across the undulating fields, alternately white and purple like a rolling sea under a fickle sun. I walked in a land of fantasy, where vision is unhampered by mundane restraints, and where human perception transcends the literal experience by which we interpret our cosmic world.

When I surmounted the gentle rise of the knoll that sheltered our picnic place, I saw something that stopped me dead in my tracks. There in the center of its triangular domain stood the little balsam, green and perky in a lacy dusting of fresh snow left by the light snowfall of the night before. I couldn't believe my own eyes! I went up to the little tree and felt of the branches and shook the slender trunk. It was alive and unharmed! A gust of wind made a soft whisper in the branches as if the little balsam were trying to tell me something. And he was. He whispered a secret that I shall share with you.

But the axe. Although I searched the area thoroughly, it was nowhere to be found. There were our overlapping footprints in the snow, and there were the tracks of the sled like a pair of narrow ribbons flung carelessly over the hillside and leading unmistakably to the house but no axe. Strangely shaken, yet more strangely reassured by a mysterious inner glow, I retraced my thoughtful way. When I reached the garden gate, I went directly to the woodshed to see if the axe was there, possibly found by Father and returned to its proper place. The axe was not there.

Then I understood the whispered secret of the little balsam, a saintly message that I will now share with you: *No one ever loses his life by giving it to a righteous cause.*

—Miles J. Martin

THE STRANGER

It was a still, hot day in July and the village street was almost deserted. The sole passage through the country hamlet was merely a dusty segment of the turnpike where it flattened off for a quarter of a mile after descending abruptly from the ridge and before starting down the long, winding hill past the graveyard to the iron bridge across the creek. The unpaved thoroughfare was bordered on each side by gravel sidewalks, broken here and there by short stretches of brick or stone. Along the east side of the street, the shades were drawn in the west-facing windows against the enervating rays of the afternoon sun.

All of the porches were vacant, save one. In his creaky wicker rocker, old Captain Jones, the last survivor of the Summerville chapter of the Grand Army of the Republic, dozed with his ancient panama pulled down over his eyes, like the awnings on Clyde Crowley's feed store just down the street. The Captain's calico tabby cat lay curled in contented somnolence on his lap. The only audible sounds were the incessant, high-pitched rasping of the locusts and the desultory rattle of Willie Myers' lawnmower in the little green adjacent to the Methodist church.

In front of Jim Wharton's general store, which also housed the post office, Clyde Crowley and old Sheriff Brown sat on the wooden bench that had once been a pew in the recently demolished Quaker Meeting House. They were awaiting the arrival of the "hack" which daily brought the mail in a brown canvas bag from Jonesville, a town on the B & O railroad some seven miles to the north. The term "hack" was a hangover from the past, for it was only within the last two or three years that George Wilson's Ford touring car had replaced the two-seated, horse-drawn vehicle that had conveyed mail, supplies, and personnel for as long as anyone could remember.

Jim Wharton came out through the screen door of the post office just as the hack drew up beside the wooden hitching rack, which still marked the boundary between the street and the short stretch of brick sidewalk in front of the store. George turned off the ignition, and the car coughed asthmatically and shook itself like a horse with the heaves before settling down with a final hiss and a spurt of steam from the brass radiator.

A bare-headed, shirt-sleeved passenger descended from the seat beside the driver, taking his coat, straw hat, and a worn valise from the back seat. He was probably in his mid-forties, but with his thinning, iron-gray hair and deeply incised wrinkles, he gave the impression of being much older. His voice was deep and resonant as he inquired where he might obtain board and lodging for the night. The sheriff pointed to the Brown Hotel across the street and a little farther down. The stranger thanked him civilly and started down the street carrying his valise and walking with a peculiar gait, as if he had an artificial leg. Sheriff Brown observed a look of dark melancholy in his deep-set gray eyes and an infinite weariness in his manner. There was some speculation among the four bystanders as to who the stranger might be, but even George Wilson could provide no information, for his passenger had been uncommunicative on the ride over. He was just a stranger looking for a night's lodging.

The visitor was not seen again until evening. As the great bronze disk of the setting sun was slipping behind the western hills, villagers savoring a respite from the heat of the day in their rockers and porch swings, observed a middle-aged man in a worn alpaca suit walking with an odd limp down the village street. He spoke to no one, but walked with his head lowered as if in solemn meditation.

At the end of the street where the gravel sidewalk gave way to untended turf, the stranger turned aside and, unlatching the iron gate, passed into the little graveyard, which lay like a green blanket draped over the gently sloping hillside. A country graveyard is a peaceful place, and the Summerville cemetery on its cool, sequestered eminence high above the green valley traversed by its meandering creek was a benign resting place for those whose worldly accounts were now entered in the Book of Time.

The stranger walked slowly along the clipped paths between the rows of gravestones, stopping frequently to read the inscriptions and to muse over the memories they must have called up. At length, in the farthest corner of the graveyard, he seemed to find what he was seeking. A little removed from the rest of the graves, under an ancient hawthorn tree, stood a square column of rough granite with a small, polished rectangle bearing a brief inscription. The stranger stood for a long time with bowed head, one hand on the gravestone. Then he began to pace slowly to and fro beside the grave under the hawthorn tree, as twilight deepened into darkness. It must have been far into the night before he returned to the hotel, for no one saw him come back.

Mrs. Brown reported the next day that she could hear him muttering and pacing about in his room until nearly daylight.

* * * * * * *

On a wild and stormy April night in the final decade of the old century, a covered buggy, shrouded with canvas side curtains against the driving rain and drawn by a lean, black horse, wound slowly along the lonely valley road. It was midnight, and in the enveloping blackness, the driver could barely distinguish the outlines of the horse as it plodded, resentful, along the muddy road. A chill wind swept down the valley in vicious gusts and drove the rain full into the face of the lone occupant of the buggy lunging in and out of the streaming ruts. Thunder rolled in ominous waves down the ravines tributary to the narrow valley, while fitful flashes of lightning momentarily revealed the madly swaying trees and the swollen, tumultous creek rising ever closer to the now almost impassable road.

Louis Douval was an angry and determined young man of twenty-five bent on an errand of desperation. He loved Elizabeth Barton with a passion characteristic of his Latin temperament, but he was frustrated and bitter. He had been violently driven from the Barton farm by Beth's irate father and her two elder brothers with the dire threat never to come near Beth again if he valued his life.

Douval was a relative newcomer to the township, having been sent out from the city as a surveyor by the coal company that was endeavoring to acquire mining rights throughout the county. He was slight of build, but deceptively strong and agile, an excellent horseman, and a strong swimmer. He had jetblack hair, flashing eyes, and a bold, devil-may-care manner. In his cordovan boots, dark green shirt and belted trousers, the young surveyor cut a dashing figure as he strode over the hills with his transit. It was rumored that Douval had been a gambler working the Ohio River towns before taking up the more steady occupation of surveying. His vague reputation as a Lothario made him an object of consuming interest and curiosity among the local females although he had not cast an eye on any of them — until he met Elizabeth Barton.

The Barton family lived on a remote farm deep in the hills that bordered the valley on the west. Beth had just turned seventeen. She was a handsome, fully developed girl with eyes the color of gentians and long braids of blond hair that she wore coiled upon her head like a coronet. She was the only female in the family, her mother having died of typhoid fever when Beth was but ten years old. Since then she had been the woman of the household, preparing the meals, washing and mending the men's clothes, tending the vegetable garden, raising the chickens, caring for the lambs, calves, and pigs, and often helping in the fields.

Aaron Barton and his two unmarried sons, Nathaniel and Peter, were unlettered farmers, fanatically religious, and uncompromisingly bigoted. They felt it their bounden duty to shield Beth from the perils of carnal sin. Their protective concern for her moral welfare was not the sole motivation for shielding Beth from the attentions of male admirers, for with her marriage, they stood to lose the comfort and care that only a woman can bring to a home. Under the complete domination of her tyrannical father and her overbearing older brothers, Beth was little more than a drudge in the Barton household.

The attempts of the Barton men to insulate Beth from male attraction were not wholly successful. One day, when the men came in early from the fields, they found Beth and Louis in a passionate embrace in the shady seclusion of the grape arbor. Aaron's fury knew no bounds. In a tempest of self-righteous wrath, he ordered Beth to her room while, with a cruel blow, he sent Louis sprawling in the muck of the farmyard and ordered him to leave the farm and not come back. Towering over Beth as she lay sobbing on her bed, he warned her never to see that "hell-bound gambler and lecherous rake" again. In his narrow, bigoted mind, the fact that Louis was a "foreigner" and, worst of all, a Catholic, was enough to mark him as the blackest of scoundrels. Aaron Barton determined then to sever, once and for all, any communication between Beth and her lover.

But passionate young love is not easily defeated, even by the overwhelming forces of bigotry and brutality. The lovers found opportunity for precarious meeting when Beth made her weekly visits to her grandmother and a maiden aunt who lived together in an old farmhouse on a rocky forty-acre tract that Aaron owned a mile or so further back into the hills. It was Beth's regular duty to take them a basket of provender from the farm—a dozen eggs, a jar of butter, a bucket of fresh milk, and two chickens killed and dressed by her that very morning. Her path was a short cut that led across the open meadows and through a dense thicket of hazel and hawthorn, which crowned the brow of the hill. It was here that the lovers met for one rhapsodic hour each week, and where they planned the elopement that would free Beth from her bondage and unite them in lifelong happiness.

Thus it came about that the solitary rig was making its storm-racked way along the deserted valley road in the dead of night, threatened by falling trees and the rising flood waters of the swollen stream. When the battered conveyance drew up at the foot of the lane leading to the Barton farmhouse, a bedraggled figure in a man's mackintosh crawled out from under the wooden platform built to hold the milk cans that were collected daily by a wagon from the Jonesville creamery. Louis jumped down and helped the girl into the buggy, placing the shabby satchel that contained her meager wardrobe under the seat.

As Louis turned his rig around in the muddy road, the horse gave a disconsolate whinny, as if in protest of his enforced participation in this ill-favored safari. At once the farm dogs broke into a wild chorus of barking, and soon lights appeared in the upstairs windows of the house. Fearing that Beth's absence might be discovered and that they would be pursued, Louis lashed the horse into a wild run as Beth clung to him weeping and trembling with fear. The frantic dash down the deeply rutted road through the increased fury of the storm was a nightmare of danger and desperation. On every hand trees and branches were crashing in the tempestuous wind, and the torrential rain loosened great boulders which came thundering into the road with the force of an avalanche.

When the careening rig approached the bridge by which Louis had crossed the creek only half an hour before, the horse suddenly slid to a halt and refused to advance a single step. A quick reconnoiter revealed the reason. The bridge was gone, and the stream was pouring over the banks. Frightened and frustrated, the runaways decided that the only course left to them was to retrace their way to the crossroad a mile back, which led in a roundabout way to the Jonesville pike, after crossing the creek by another bridge two miles upstream. If they could make it to the turnpike, they might yet be able to get to Jonesville in time for the early morning train to the city. Upon leaving the state, they would be safe from any attempt by Aaron Barton to enlist the force of the law in bringing his errant daughter back to parental authority.

As Louis was leading the terrified horse in a precarious turnabout at the very edge of the cascading stream, a bolt of lightning struck an oak tree only a few yards away, splitting it down the center with a deafening report. The severed tree fell with a dreadful crash directly across the road, completely thwarting any chance of retracing their way with the horse and buggy. Trapped by the forces of nature, there was nothing left for them to do but to abandon the rig and continue on foot.

Hastily tying the frantic horse to a branch of the fallen tree, they set out through the storm. After half an hour of slogging wearily through the mud, carrying their luggage, and bending low against the force of the wind, they came to a crossroad that led to the other bridge. Praying that the bridge would not be washed away, they trudged along the slimy road with as much haste as their misery and fatigue would permit. They were within a few yards of the bridge when the ominous thud of galloping horses told them that their escape had failed. Before they could seek concealment in the bushes beside the road, their pursuers were upon them—three infuriated men on their rearing, snorting mounts.

Leaping from their horses, the brothers tore the exhausted lovers apart. As Peter held his sister in an iron grip, Aaron beat Louis mercilessly with a huge horsewhip. When Louis was near collapse, Aaron and Nate dragged the beaten young man to the bridge, ordering him to cross it and never come back. With Beth's anguished cries ringing in his ears, Louis crept out upon the swaying bridge not more than a foot above the raging torrent. He had gone but a few feet when a tree born upon the seething waters crashed into the wooden bridge, causing it to break in two and crash into the flood, carrying Louis with it.

At this final disaster, Beth fainted dead away. Peter quickly mounted his horse and Nate lifted the unconscious girl into his brother's arms. At a gruff order from Aaron, the party hastily left the scene. The storm had passed its peak and its fury was abated as the Barton men returned to the farm, bearing the defeated and disgraced girl with them.

The next morning, workers investigating the damage caused by the storm, found a man washed up on the bank of the creek, along with the timbers of the bridge to which he had evidently clung. As they hurried to the wreckage, they heard a feeble groan, indicating that the man was alive. When they endeavored to free him from the tangle of joists, beams, and other flotsam, they discovered that his right leg was badly crushed and that both arms were broken. He was delirious and could provide no clue as to how he came to be there.

Sheriff Brown, when called to the scene, identified the derelict as the young surveyor, Louis Douval. Because his injuries were so grave, an ambulance was summoned from Jonesville, and he was taken to the county hospital, where his leg was amputated. Weakened by prolonged exposure and with his vitality sapped by multiple injuries, the unfortunate young man hung precariously between life and death for many weeks. Although it was midsummer before he was sufficiently recovered to be discharged from the hospital, no one in Summerville ever learned the true story of the disaster.

The discovery of the abandoned rig only intensified a mystery that was never solved. The livery stable owner confirmed the identity of the driver, but the trail stopped at the fallen oak tree. Douval was not known to be courting any young lady in the neighborhood, and certainly the Barton farm was the last place to be thought of as the scene of romance. The tragedy remained one of the many stark secrets buried in that lonely valley. Louis Douval simply disappeared never to be heard from again.

Beth's child was born on a blustery night in November. Attended only by her inept maiden aunt and a slatternly midwife summoned from "The Settlement", an immigrant colony down the creek, the unhappy girl endured her sorry travail as best she could. When the time came, her screams drowned out the imprecations of her father and his pious ranting about the inevitable punishment for sin.

The baby was a girl, as fair and sturdy as Beth herself had been. But Beth was fated never to see her little daughter. Before daylight broke on that bleak November morning, she had yielded her life in the pain of dishonored childbirth and the agony of a broken heart. Thus it was that the ill-starred elopement led to the solitary grave under the old hawthorn tree.

* * * * * * *

After a troubled and sleepless night, the stranger again made his halting way in the bright morning sunlight to the little graveyard on the hill. As he approached the corner with its hawthorn tree, he looked up to discover that he was not alone. Seated on the grass beside the grave, now strewn with daisies, wild roses, and brown-eyed susans, was a fair-haired girl of seventeen or eighteen. With her face buried in her hands, she was weeping bitterly and moaning aloud to herself. Not wishing to intrude upon the grief of another, the stranger turned to leave, but as he did so, the girl looked up and regarded him with a pair of brimming, gentian eyes such as he had seen but once before in his life.

Wondering at a grief that could endure so long in one so young, he said in a low voice, "Forgive my intrusion, Miss." And then, hesitatingly, "Is this the grave of someone dear to you?" "Yes," the girl replied, "my mother." But that is not why I'm weeping. I never knew my mother. She died when I was born."

The stranger seemed distraught himself as he asked, "Why then are you so sad, my dear?" He was not prepared for the desperation in her cry, "Because I have no father. I never had one. I am a bastard!" Shocked and trembling, the stranger sat down beside the girl and took her hand. "Can you tell me about yourself?" he asked gently.

The girl seemed to sense a comradeship with the stranger. She told her story simply and without further tears. Her name, she said, was Louise, and she had been raised by an aunt who was now quite elderly and had little understanding of the feelings of a young girl. She was in love with a young man from a respected, well-to-do family, but her illegitimacy was an insurmountable barrier to their marriage.

"But why do you say that you are illegitimate?" the stranger queried with averted gaze. "Because", she said, "my father deserted my mother before I was born. She then gave him the story of her birth as it had been told to her. In this account, her father was portrayed as a graceless scoundrel who had seduced her mother and left her to endure her shame alone.

Suddenly she startled the stranger by asking, "Did you know my mother? Do you know who my father was?" To these piercing questions, the stranger made evasive reply, saying that he remembered her mother as a beautiful girl, but that he could tell her nothing about her father. He then bade her goodbye with a lingering handclasp that was almost a caress, and limped painfully out of the cemetery. Later in the morning he was seen boarding the hack for Jonesville.

A few days thereafter, Sheriff Brown received an official communication from the county courthouse and a letter that caused him to make a trip to the Barton farm, where he delivered a packet to Louise. In it there was a brief note which read, "Dear Louise, Put your troubled heart at ease. You are not illegitimate. Your father and mother were secretly married by the Justice of the Peace in Woodsfield. They met in the valley and drove to Woodsfield one day when your grandfather and your uncles were attending an auction near Jonesville. The evidence is enclosed herewith. With sincerest wishes for your happiness." It was signed simply, "A Sympathetic Stranger."

In the packet were the facsimile of an authorized marriage certificate signed by the Justice of the Peace and a faded snapshot of a smiling, handsome young couple in the costumes of a generation ago. On the back of the photograph was the inscription, "Beth and Louis Douval—March 15, 1895."

—Miles J. Martin

JIMMY

Dextar Hills is not only an unusually attractive suburban area, it is also unusually exclusive. Whatever beauty God failed to supply initially, ample money has more than generously provided and it is noteworthy that dogs from Dextar Hills will bark only at Blue Ribbon from their own or equally affluent neighborhoods.

Built on facing sides of gentle slopes, each of Dextar Hills' less than two hundred homes overlooks one of three converging valleys. At the center lies a relatively small but vodka-clear lake. The effect could be said to be rather intoxicating. In the early morning hours, when the sun becomes a spotlight to flood the stage of the earth and minute insects leave slightly rippling trails as they scurry across the water to hide from its penetrating glare, the lake serves as a mirror to reflect the loveliness of nature which surrounds it. The only interruption to its primeval shoreline is the rambling granite and redwood recreation center of the Dextar Hills Golf and Country Club, available only to members and their well-screened guests.

Byways, which in their twisting and turning more closely resemble tentacles than roads, lead to the gracefully curving blacktopped drives of expansive, luxuriously landscaped private estates. There, nestled among arborvitae, juniper and yew, but dwarfed by towering pines, stand the picturesque villas of Dextar Hills.

Five miles away, on the other side of the city, is Sherwood Hills, in its own way still attractive, but no longer in any way exclusive. Money needed to enhance its beauty is used for more important projects, and it is equally noteworthy that the few dogs living in Sherwood Hills will bark at anybody or anything and frequently do.

Formerly the glamorous estate of a prominent local multimillionaire and self-styled playboy, Sherwood Hills is presently administered by a small band of hardworking nuns. They operate it as a home for orphaned children. Dominated by a huge sandstone and brick mansion almost completely enveloped by conical spruce and Austrian pine, the property gradually falls away to a badly polluted river whose glory has long since flowed out to sea. Scattered like racing boats among the many box-type hedges, and stretching from the water's edge to the main building are the boat house, swimming pool, stables, tennis courts, hothouses, barns, garage and servants quarters, all kept in reasonable repair. The nuns even achieve moderate success in maintaining the extensive formal gardens immediately adjoining the rear of the mansion.

Though visible in the single glance of a swooping crow in flight, Dextar Hills and Sherwood Hills are miles apart in more things than distance.

The residents of Dextar Hills represent some of America's oldest families. Many of those families predate the Revolution and all of them at least predate the Civil War. They are extremely proud of their heritage.

Although following very productive lives, a few of Dextar Hills' men have already retired and are now wallowing with their wives in the luxury of leisure, most are still successfully active in engineering, law, medicine, technology or commerce. Some of the women realize satisfaction in careers of their own, but most enjoy the life of a social lioness with the standard daytime activities of tennis, swimming, golf and gossip over bridge. Their nighttime activities include cocktails with gossip, dinner with gossip, dancing with gossip and then home to bed too tired to give their husbands anything worthwhile to gossip about. Most of the children are registered in good prep schools or better colleges, but when at home, gallop gleefully down privately owned bridle paths on privately owned horses or smoothly sail their own sailfish over the area's privately owned lake. Of course, the Golf and Country Club offers the usual pre-teen, teenage and teen-plus dances and parties. All in Dextar Hills, men, women and children are a tightly knit, self-sufficient community.

The residents of Sherwood Hills represent none of America's oldest families. For the most part, they spring from immigrants who flooded the United States at the turn of the century, having originated from Ireland, Italy, Germany and France. A few Asians and Africans are blended in. With the exception of the nuns, the residents of Sherwood Hills aren't old enough to understand the meaning of "heritage" and really don't care.

Having lived lives filled with love and caring, most of the nuns should have long since retired. Instead, a serious shortage of replacements leaves them wallowing in the worries of running a home for two hundred needy youngsters. They forever struggle with just enough money to fall slightly short of that which is required. They are buoyed only by their faith in God's promise to provide for his little ones and by the inspiration of a few novices in the community who begin work with the first hopeful chirping of a robin in the morning and fall exhausted into their beds with the last tired hoot of an owl at night.

The staff also boasts three lovable elderly gentlemen, reclaimed from Demon Rum, who without Sherwood Hills would be completely friendless and alone. They get on wonderfully well with the children and honestly attempt to do all the maintenance work at the home, but their limitations have forced sadly overworked nuns to tackle carpentry, plumbing and electrical work. Those of the children who are old enough attend school on the grounds. In their free time they share tricycles which they rambunctiously race down paths on the property. They also fight furiously over the lone rubber raft in the once ornate swimming pool. Of course the home offers the usual birthday, Hallowe'en and Christmas parties . . . with real ice cream and cookies . . . when some outside benefactor is generous. All in Sherwood Hills, men, women and children, are a tightly knit, completely dependent community.

Among the better known and best liked couples at Dextar Hills is Armand and Babette Barclay who with their three girls and one boy occupy an imposing Swiss villa at the southern end of the area. The Barclay family is extremely active in all phases of Dextar Hills life and a definite moving force in the community. Other residents often wonder what would ever have happened to local social activities without the Barclays. They almost found out: The Barclay family very nearly never came into being. After five years of marriage, and listening to all kinds of advice, both solicited and unsolicitied, Armand and Babette had been childless.

Armand, a successful attorney, could have well afforded to support a family. Babette, equally successfully as a speech therapist with retarded children whom she loved, was well qualified to mother that family. Unfortunately, God did not see fit to bless their fondest hope.

At the completion of numerous visits to gentlemen of the medical profession and faithfully following procedures prescribed by them . . . with negative results, Armand and Babette resorted to old wive's rituals guaranteed to produce positive results . . . and experienced no greater luck. They were understandably discouraged, but through it all placed deep faith in the power of prayer. Finally they decided that God's not blessing them with a family of their own, in spite of their perfect physical capabilities, was God's way of asking them to care for one of His less fortunate little ones. Their decision to obey the will of God led them to Sherwood Hills.

At that time among the better known and best liked youngsters at Sherwood Hills was six-year-old Jimmy Church, so named because of his origin.

Late one very cold December night Jimmy Horan, the sexton at Saint John's Roman Catholic Cathedral, was making his rounds preparatory to locking up. As he walked down the dimly lighted center aisle, he thought he saw a shoe box resting on the cushioned seat of the rear left pew. Jimmy was pleased to have his investigation prove his eyesight to be still quite good. It was a shoe box.

When Jimmy picked up the box and opened it, a smile spread quickly across his face. The proud father of a little girl himself, he gazed tenderly at what he believed to be a child's doll covered only by a piece of torn blanket. His tenderness slowly turned to amazement and then suddenly to fright, as the doll squirmed and opened its tiny mouth. Poor Jimmy was in a quandary and his hands shook as he held the box. Mumbling a prayer to our Blessed Lady, he carefully carried his precious cargo across the street to the rectory and thankfully delivered it in safety to the rector, the Right Reverend Monsignor Edward J. Flynn.

Monsignor Flynn quickly notified the proper authorities and immediately rushed the infant to Saint Mary's Hospital where it was determined that the baby was a boy and only a few hours old. It was also apparent that the baby had·been delivered by the mother herself or by the mother with the assistance of someone equally as inexperienced. The baby's left foot was badly damaged and would result in his being crippled for life.

To honor the man who discovered him and to commemorate the place of his discovery, Monsignor Flynn baptized the boy Jimmy Church and as such he was bundled off to Sherwood Hills.

The initial reaction of the nuns to poor little Jimmy Church with his serious deformity was one of great pity and sympathy. Each of them wanted to take him in her arms and mother him as her very own. Sister Mary Margaret, in charge of the nursery and a real martinet, wouldn't hear of it. She commanded that no one was to spoil Jimmy Church, but then proceeded to do that very thing herself.

Sister Mary Margaret, under normal conditions, would not permit her infant charges to enjoy the comfort of pacifiers. She felt dependence on crutches in any form, unless absolutely necessary, was not the proper way for children to embark on the odyssey of life. However, Jimmy managed accidentally to get a pacifier in each of his puffy little hands and Sister Mary Margaret allowed him to keep them. She defended her action by saying Jimmy was an exceptional child who needed the security the pacifiers afforded. The truth was it broke her heart to hear him cry so pitifully when she tried to take them away from him. Jimmy soon dreamed up a good use for each of his acquisitions. He put one in his mouth, as most normal babies do, and the other he wedged between his tiny pug nose and his curled upper lip. Iron-willed Sister Mary Margaret thought he was so cute.

Sister Cherree Ann also thought Jimmy was so cute, until his second birthday. On that supposedly happy occasion, she joined him on the floor of the playroom to help build a castle of wooden blocks. The two of them had a grand time. Unfortunately, Sister momentarily looked away and Jimmy playfully let her have it over the head with one of the biggest blocks he could find. Jimmy went back to his room immediately and Sister Cherree, later repenting her desire to commit mayhem, hurried off to confession the very next Saturday.

Sister Marie, a buxom young lady who taught kindergarten in the morning and assisted in the kitchen in the afternoon, vibrated with mirth when she heard the story. A psychology major while in college, Sister thought it wonderful that Jimmy was learning to express his true feelings. Every time she received a visitor, Sister enthusiastically recounted the incident, while laughing hilariously. Sister's hilarity had the power brakes applied and skidded to an abrupt stop one morning as she bent far over to retrieve a toy in the classroom sandbox. Wonderful Jimmy Church stealthily attacked from the rear and sank his sharp baby teeth deep into Sister Marie's fanny. Sister, with good reason, also found her way to the confessional.

Actually Jimmy was never a malicious child. He merely sought attention and, like most children, did some things without fully realizing the possible consequences. When he did realize he had done something wrong, he would be quite upset and resort to tears. It was then that all the granite hearts surrounding him proved to be nothing but velvety soft ice cream in the sun and melted into sympathy and love.

On a day beautifully flooded with sunshine in celebration of a mid-January thaw, Sister Theresa dressed five-year-old Jimmy Church in a spanking clean snow suit and put him out to play with some of the other children. Between stitches on a child's skirt she was mending, Sister kept tabs on all of them. Her view was unobstructed as she sat in a picture window overlooking a snow-whitened lawn. Most of the children were off on her left, rolling huge snow balls, as they attempted to bring to life Mr. and Mrs. Snow. The snow would not cooperate and slowly turned to water as the children worked with it.

Jimmy, carrying a small American flag, had enlisted Bobby and Paul, two of his buddies, to follow him in a spirited parade behind a low hedge. As Sister watched the march up, down and around, she could see all three of them from their hips up. In spite of his bad foot, Jimmy stepped out like a Major General and the others followed with ready enthusiasm.

Looking up from her work from time to time, Sister Theresa got the impression that either the hedge was rapidly growing or the children were rapidly shrinking. She now thought she could only see them from the stomach up. A few minutes later, as they moved back and forth, she was sure she could only see them from the chest up. But . . . no . . . she must be imagining it. Not too long after that, when she could see only their heads bobbing along the line of the hedge, she knew it was not her imagination that was playing her tricks. The marchers were actually disappearing.

Sister Theresa dashed out the side door and raced down to the hedge only to stare in amazement. The miniature Major General and his tiny troops, completely covered from head to foot with thick brown mud, were slowly deepening a path in a huge puddle of melting snow and thawing dirt.

"Jimmy Church", screamed Sister Theresa, "what in heaven's name are you doing?"

"Havin' a pawade," answered Jimmy, as he and his army froze at attention.

"Well, you . . . all of you . . . have a parade right inside the house this very minute!" The three of them ran for the house as quick as they could, but only Bobby and Paul made it. Sister caught Jimmy by the arm and spun him around. "Jimmy Church, I'm ashamed of you and you should be ashamed of yourself! Just look at your clean snow suit!"

Jimmy looked up at Sister and his big eyes filled with tears. "Sisser," he pleaded, "Please don' whump me!"

Sister Theresa didn't whump him. Her heart swelled as she reached down and picked him up. That night she not only washed three muddied snow suits, she also washed one muddied habit.

Jimmy Church was a normal child. He liked candy, but he disliked spinach. He wanted to be like all the other kids, but smothered his sliced bananas in catsup. His most distinguishing characteristic, however, was his enormous capacity for love. He batted out affection like a pro and waited patiently for it to hit the far wall and bounce back. He rapidly developed strong attachments.

It was the policy at Sherwood Hills to place all adoptable children with good families as soon as possible. Many were taken from the home when only two and a half or three months old, while others weren't adopted until they were two and a half or three years old. Unfortunately, some were never to know the security and love of family life. Although Sister Theresa who headed placements recommended and showed them as often as she dared, there were some few children who for one reason or another appeared less than perfect and whom no one seemed to want. Jimmy Church with his badly crippled foot was one of these.

It is impossible to know exactly when Jimmy Church first became conscious of the disappearance of those around him with whom he had played and shared. It is not even possible to know when realization awakened in him a knowledge of where they were going. It is only certain that, as each day passed, Jimmy became more and more aware that buddies for whom he had nurtured great friendship were going away to experience the love and affection for which he longed so very much. Children in his age group who finally became adoptable and were accepted by prospective parents spoke with great excitement of their new daddies and mommies. Many nights Jimmy lay awake in his bed, wishing for a daddy and mommy of his very own.

Somehow Jimmy sensed that Sister Theresa and the office in which she worked had something to do with these new mommies and daddies. He began frequent pilgrimages down the long hallway to visit Sister and although his expedition rarely involved more than the sticking of his head through the doorway to say "Hi," he was consistent three and four times each day.

Once Armand and Babette Barclay had decided to enter a new phase of life by adopting their first child, they were a couple transformed. Everything around them seemed more vital, more alive. The morning sun was more golden, the grass of their lawns more green and even sales taxes more tolerable.

Miss Priscilla Prudence, the spectacled case worker at Catholic Charities, was understanding and cooperative but warned them they would "just have to be patient." As she laughingly put it, "Adoptancy takes as long as pregnancy . . . nine months," and she was right! Although Armand and Babette busied themselves as much as possible with paper work, interviews and both necessary and unnecessary preparations, the nine months moved along at a pace equal to that of the fast racing speed of a snail with only one lung.

The prospective parents reasoned that having their own baby would have dictated their acceptance of a child of either sex but adoption gave them a clear-cut choice. They both wanted a daughter so badly they could almost feel her in their arms. They not only planned for their dark-haired little girl, they provided for her as well by redecorating and refurnishing one of their larger upstairs rooms completely in pink. What's more, they assembled a sizable wardrobe for her and almost totally filled a separate closet with her toys. Although they entertained no intentions of planning her life, they enjoyed visualizing her progress from childhood through college, career, and marriage.

The day for Armand and Babette to see a little girl who was available to them had arrived. Each reassured the other that they were perfectly calm and in control. However, Babette was in the car and straining to go before she realized that a slip and blouse were hardly the attire in which to visit Sherwood Hills for the first time. She dashed back upstairs to pull on her skirt. Armand, who never got a traffic ticket in his life, not even for overtime parking, got two in a row, one for going too fast and one for failing to maintain a minimum speed.

Arm in arm, as they exchanged jitters of expectancy through the contact, the excited couple joyfully made their way to Sister Theresa's office. When they had almost reached it, Jimmy Church came around the corner at the opposite end of the hallway. He stopped momentarily, looked at the Barclays and then broke into a big smile. The Barclays also stopped, looked at Jimmy and smiled back. When they did, Jimmy, moving just as fast as his crippled left foot would allow him, ran toward them. Instinctively Armand reached down and scooped Jimmy up in his arms. Jimmy responded by wrapping his arms around Armand's neck and hugging him tight. "Are you my Daddy?" Jimmy asked.

Tears quickly started down Armand's cheeks, as he looked to Babette to see eyes also filled to overflowing. Babette slowly but definitely nodded her head. Armand's grip around Jimmy tightened like a vise, as he clearly said, "You bet I am."

The people of Dextar Hills didn't quite know how to react to this adopted child. However, they had great admiration for Armand and Babette and so agreed to at least be reasonable. After meeting Jimmy, the entire community fell in love with him and immediately welcomed him as an important part of it.

Yes, Dextar Hills is not only an unusually attractive suburban area, it is also unusually exclusive, though not quite as exclusive as it once was. Jimmy has broken the barrier. Dextar Hills has welcomed its first white resident.

— *Charles Leo Miller*

LOVE STORY

Ned entered the sunny kitchen on a beautiful May morning. With the characteristic gesture of thirty years he tapped Bertha on the shoulder saying, "Let's take a little ride."

In the Model A Ford they drove slowly toward Lake Ontario savoring the warm fresh breeze, the clean foilage, the blue sky with small scattered clouds. Around a curve they saw a dilapidated farmhouse with a spectacular old lilac bush in full bloom.

Spontaneously Bertha exclaimed, "I wish we had such a bush under the kitchen window."

Ned drove another mile before turning back to the house.

An hour later Bertha heard a commotion in the backyard. Investigating, she found four men and a truck. The men were busily digging a great hole. Bertha looked at Ned for explanation. His eyes twinkled as he said, "Your wish is coming true."

An enormous hole was finished before the workers tackled the difficult job of uprooting the old lilac which Ned had bought that morning. Under Ned's supervision the bush was set gently into the truck; blankets protected the roots from sun and wind on the short trip to the house.

The roots were spread, covered with friable soil to half the depth of the hole, watered thoroughly, the soil around the bush leveled, watered again. Not a bloom withered.

— Alice Pirnie

NATURAL GAS FOR COOKING

Grandmother slit the envelope with the New York State Governor's flower insignia. With excitement she read, "I have been informed that you use natural gas for cooking. At your convenience, may I inspect the exciting development?"

Grandmother invited the governor and his official party for a midday dinner. The governor accepted with alacrity. Upon entering the Victorian farmhouse the governor asked if he could see the cook stove immediately.

Grandmother led him to the thirty-foot square kitchen. He had no eyes for the two bay windows or the table set for fourteen. The big black stove was the attraction. It looked like the iron stove every housewife used in 1890. The difference appeared when Grandmother lifted the griddle. A two-foot flame came from an iron pipe, heating the pots on top of the stove. Turning a gasket, Grandmother extinguished the flame. Holding a lighted wooden match to the pipe, she relighted the gas.

The governor gasped—such a simple laborsaver, no wood to cut or carry, no time spent replenishing the supply in the firebox, no emptying of ashes, no continued source of heat in warm weather.

Removing his coat he seated himself in the Boston rocker. "Please give me the whole story." Shoving the pots to the back of the stove Grandmother readily related the facts: "One of the farmhands told us that he had found an area in an adjacent field where nothing grew—not even the toughest weeds. 'There is a peculiar odor there', he said."

After family inspections, there were speculations. How long had the condition been undetected? What was the unfamiliar odor? Why was the water slightly greasy?

The mystery was discussed in the presence of a relative recently returned from Oklahoma oil fields. Bill, as an explorer and developer, had knowledge of most facets of the industry. Approaching the depression in the field he cried out, "That odor is natural gas. No doubt. Let me try capping it. Perhaps we can find use for it. In Oklahoma it is used for cooking fuel."

The well was capped successfully; the gas was piped into the kitchen stove where it has been used for fifty years.

— Alice Pirnie

FIDELIO

He was called Fidelio by his captors, a group of marine biologists, whose assignment it was to study in detail the common dolphin. They caught him with a net among a large body of dolphins somewhere off the coast of the Atlantic, heading out to sea.

Fidelio was lifted very gently on to a boat and transported in a plastic-lined box kept full of water. He was subsequently transferred to a 20-foot circular pen with a wide wooden platform to which a 100-foot deep net was secured and anchored.

A newsman accompanied scientists on this trip to write a story about dolphins. "I understand that dolphins have many human-like characteristics; you could say," he told the scientists, "I'm doing a human-interest story."

After having measured, weighed, and examined the dolphin, a scientist exclaimed, "We have a fine specimen. He's a young bachelor."

"How could you tell so much about him with only a brief look?"

"Simple, his sex is apparent. Look under the belly."

"Oh."

"Fidelio isn't fully mature yet," the scientist said. "He's just under five feet and weighs about ninety pounds."

"What else can you tell me about this fish?" asked the newman.

"He isn't a fish," the scientist retorted. Fidelo is an aquatic, air-breathing mammal."

"I'm sorry, I should have read all these things."

"Did you know that this species is one of the fastest of all dolphins? They're powerful swimmers, having been clocked at 25 knots. When there's a ship in sight these dolphins pursue and then race ahead of it, leaping out of the water at great heights, playfully and joyfully."

"Aren't these dolphins the ones we see performing in the marine shows?" asked the newsman.

"No, that's the bottle-nosed dolphin which has a short beak in contrast to the long-snouted Fidelio. But that's not the only difference."

"What's that?"

"Bottle-nosed dolphins settle well into captivity. They remain alert, inquisitive and playful, and they feel secure enough to even breed and care for their young. They're fine subjects for study."

"What about Fidelio's species, the common dolphin?" queried the newsman.

"Oh, that's another story. Poor subjects. They slowly and fatally languish in long captivity."

Then why study Fidelio?"

"Perhaps at age four he has not yet reached a state of inconsolability, though I don't think it makes any difference. His feeling of design is probably inborn. But we shall see under these circumstances."

252

The scientist excused himself and returned to the others who were already engaged in the first test, leaving the reporter to observe for himself.

The scientists, anticipating the inevitable downward slide, carefully watched for the first signs that Fidelio was about to cross the threshhold into the nether world. They hoped when the time came to snatch him back before he reached the irreversible state of torpidity.

They proceeded. Electrodes attached to Fidelio's brain were activated and sound waves were recorded. And as experiments were completed, they rewarded him by feeding him lots of herring and sardines and slapping him playfully, but gently fortifying him with a little extra solicitude.

The tests went on for days. Changes were beginning to occur. At first they were barely perceptible. "The abyss," as they reported in their diary of the tests," has not yet been reached. We probably have a few good days ahead. But Fidelio's speed, agility and resiliency suffered slightly. He was not the same as the day before. His eyes, to a close observer, were a little duller, and his skin, black on top and white on the belly which is usually shiny, was a little duller.

The scientists were not yet ready to release Fidelio. They wanted to try one more series of experiments. They would fasten a fish to an electronically controlled device and plunge it down one hundred feet, the full length of the net, and return it to the surface at a speed approximately that of the dolphin. He would be expected to follow the bait, and as it went faster Fidelio would increase his own speed, mindful that air is essential for this breathing mammal.

The signal was set, and the fish fastened to the mechanism was ready. A buzzer sounded and Fidelio saw the fish submerge. An instant later he dove after it. The bait as planned was kept just out of Fidelio's reach. But the dolphin, not totally prepared for the test, abandoned the chase and returned to the surface for air. The scientists assumed that for the first time around he was caught off guard, and his response was not due to slower reactions or failing psyche. But at the next dive, if it was a repeat of the first, they would take another look.

As with the first test they attached a herring to the mechanism knowing how much dolphins like it, and repeated the test. Only now Fidelio was prepared. He knew what was expected of him, and his eyes were riveted on the fish. He plunged down in full pursuit of the herring. The scientists controlled its speed down, again putting it beyond Fidelio's reach but on the way up they let him catch it.

The scientists repeated the same tests on a number of occasions, and after a while the dolphin exhibited some of the signs of slowing down. He was not interested in the fish. He seemed to go through the motions and he pursued it halfheartedly, and then it happened. One day, Fidelio followed the bait down when he was jolted by seeing a hole in the net, not big enough to let him pass through, but a start. A hope. He surfaced with a forceful splatter, a surprise to the scientists who understood the waning power the dolphin was beginning to show. Would they be puzzled by this change and investigate? Could they possibly attribute his sudden exhilaration to the hole, investigate, and make the necessary repairs to the net? Would they go right to the source, or rather think there was some sudden and inexplicable change? Dolphins are highly intelligent, and Fidelio tried to restrain his elation, to keep it private. He must shield the hole.

Another signal was raised and the dolphin went after the fish-lure, only this time he kept a good distance behind it, partly to put the scientists off and more importantly to snip the hole. And then, in a burst of speed, he caught the fish and surfaced. He had a good day.

The scientists were puzzled. In their diary they wrote: "Until recently, Fidelio showed the usual signs of lethargy, common to his species in captivity. But today there was a perplexing change. His eyes looked brighter, he seemed more alert, and his color was more vivid, almost the way it was when we first caught him. It's baffling. It doesn't fit the text. Maybe it's the last spark before flickering out. Of course, let the record show that Fidelio would be thrown back before that happens."

Fidelio found it difficult to suppress his inner exultation. With every pass at the hole in the net he bit a little more into it and finally it was big enough for him to slip out. Freedom was at last within his grasp. But he could not escape yet. He had to weigh planning for an escape against leaving immediately; he chose waiting for the right moment. The risks seemed great and these were anxious moments.

The scientists, observing Fidelio's muted excitement and a quickening of his heartbeat on the instruments, wrote again in the diary: "Fidelio seems agitated. I don't know what provoked the change. Could this be the sign that something is going to happen, the final climactic event before the end? Or maybe not. Who knows what factors are present to defy the predetermined course of events. Perhaps age, length of captivity, degree of positive re-inforcement, strong will to live are offsetting factors. Our colleagues would take a dim view of such unsound, emotional and shaky views about a member of this species. We might add that we feel a great deal of affection for Fidelio, and we hope he pulls through."

The next dive was to be a rehearsal of every detail of the escape. Fidelio would have to consider speed, duration of the dive, and the distance traveled. He would have to swim close to or at the bottom of the sea until the last agonizing moment when he had to surface for air.

This mammal could stay under for as long as six minutes. But most dives last less than one minute, usually for a few seconds. A miscalculation of this critical instant and the dolphin would drown, although this mishap rarely occurs unless in a desperate effort to escape he swims too close to the bottom, and at the last second fails to make it in time.

Fidelio was psyched up for this moment. He was fused into a mass of steel-like muscles and tendons, holding back a propulsive thrust of great force waiting to be sprung. The signal was raised, the fish-lure was ready, and Fidelio swam around the fish in nervous anticipation. And in an instant the fish-lure plunged downward, as it had done so many times before. Fidelio dove after it with great velocity and followed it until he reached the hole and in a frantic burst of speed made it to freedom. In his effort to get as far away from the pen and his captors as possible, he did not stop for his moment of elation. And when Fidelio finally surfaced, which for him must have seemed like an eternity, he was a good distance away, too far for easy recapture by the surprised and dismayed scientists. The final entry in the diary read: "Fidelio is gone. Frustrating. All we had left to do was to evaluate his characteristics measured against those of others of his species."

In retrospect,we now understood his deep and desperate yearning to be free. The hole in the net must have revived his spirit and given him the pathway to hope. Adios, Fidelio, good luck. You'll need it. As the reporter put it, "Now I have a real human interest story to write about."

Fidelio paused. It was his first opportunity to slow down, look around, and take his bearings. In his headlong dash to freedom he did not consider the consequences of being alone and lost. Sooner or later he thought that his own group of dolphins would find him and he would be happily reunited with them, once again taking his place among the order of young bachelors.

Fidelio had no concept of time, space, and distance. He lost touch with a sense of reality since his captivity over a week ago, and he thought his group must be nearby. Fidelio called to them. He signaled with grunts, creaks, yelps and whistles. Over and over again. No answer. He continued calling to them for some time. Still no response. Where were they? No doubt miles away heading north or south for a run of herring or sardines. What did being lost mean to the young, inexperienced dolphin, plucked from his group long before his education was complete? Fidelio comes from the highly intelligent genus delphinus. His brain is large, and the convolutions deep and he has a sizable storage capacity to absorb much that has gone on before. And had he remained with his dolphin family a little longer he probably would have learned to navigate by the position of the sun, moon and particular clusters of stars and constellations, instead of seeing a mass of meaningless bits and pieces of heaven that could tell him nothing. He was like a compass needle gyrating aimlessly.

One adventure was ended, but another was about to begin. What Fidelio was not aware of was that he was easy prey for a pack of sharks who could attack him savagely or a killer whale, the Dolphin's most feared enemy, who could strike suddenly and swallow him whole. A chilling prospect.

Fidelio's senses were intact, especially hearing which was very acute, and it was his only defense. He listened intently and at first there was no sound or at least any distant sound that he could instantly recognize. But it was a matter of time before he did hear faint noises from some distance away. As the sounds grew louder and more distinct, and with an absorbing intensity, he knew instinctively it was not a predator. He was soon able to tell that they were the sounds of dolphins, even before a visual sighting. When they finally came into view they excitedly made whistling, clapping, and yelping noises, but not one sound penetrated Fidelio's psyche.

They were of a different species with faint grayish stripes and an ill-defined beak. Although both species feed together, they eventually go their separate ways, and on this occasion they were indifferent to his plight and brushed past him. Soon the striped dolphins were out of sight and their sounds grew barely audible, until he could no longer hear them. Again he was alone.

The encounter with these striped dolphins gave them a deeper longing than ever to be in the midst of his own grouping with familiar and meaningful cadences of his language. Soon the name "Fidelio" became a fading memory, a receding reminder of his brief, dark past. He had a name given to him by his mother when he was very young, in need of instant recognition and maternal protection against predators and occasionally an attacking male of his species.

He was completely engrossed in his old identity. First, hestitatingly and then with firm assurance he uttered his name, "Long whistle, three grunts, a click." He repeated his name many times, expressing it slowly and lovingly, giving way to a more imploring sound, then a high pitched sound that seemed like crying. Finally hunger distracted him, and he became silent while he looked around for fish. To his great surprise Fidelio found himself in the midst of a very large school of herring. He ate all the fish he could, and when satisfied he had a good feeling about the abundance of herring and a vague sense of expectancy that he would not be alone very long.

Fidelio was right. A group of other dolphins swam by, fed themselves, and left without a gesture acknowledging his presence. Many other dolphins came by, even his own species, but not his particular group, to enjoy this bounty. Suddenly, there was wild commotion among the dolphins. They yelped and whistled loudly and frantically. It was a danger signal, a language which all dolphins understood, including Fidelio who swam furiously toward the other dolphins.

They caught the sound of approaching predators as far away as two miles, and they assumed a tight defensive block. The source of agitation was a pack of blue sharks swimming toward them.

Often these large sharks lead a ferocious attack against a small band of dolphins. But this time a dozen sharks came face to face with about two hundred disciplined dolphins ready to do battle.

These ordinarily gentle creatures were transformed into a swift-moving, hard-hitting force set against the scourge of the seas. With a sudden, lightning thrust, the dolphins rammed into them chasing them away.

With the episode over, the dolphins whistled their relief, and they gradually fanned out to assume their normal pattern. Fidelio, aware that the crisis was over, broke out of formation and swam away.

He resumed listening intently for a sound peculiarly his own. His mind was sifting through the sounds of the sea still teeming with herring. In time other delphinids were criss-crossing the seemingly endless supply of fish. The procession went on and on. But the link of Fidelio's past and present was still missing. He felt despair once, and it was about to overtake him when nearby a group of dolphins was yelping in the precise language, the right pitch and cadence to which Fidelio could respond. He barely moved, concentrating on the first faint sounds made by the dolphins. As they approached, their yelping became clearer until he finally saw them — his own familiar grouping. And what happened next was an expression of joy, a feeling of elation. He leaped high out of the water, doing a spontaneous somersault. Many other dolphins joined him in a frolicsome spirit and in a noisy greeting they yelped, wailed, whistled, clicked, bleated and squeaked. He was back at last, and he knew instinctively where he belonged in the "pecking order" among other young bachelors.

Fidelio imagined questions the dolphins could ask him about his whereabouts. He was thinking of ways of telling them of captivity, captors, despair, escape, and adventures afterwards. He was aware that their experiences were limited to a passing ship or fishermen hauling in a big catch; but not of the trauma of being caught and prodded and pricked by them.

The dolphins did not ask any questions, nor did they show the least bit of curiosity about his absence. They were happy he was back, and that feeling too was brief. A moment's digression, and then back to feeding. Fidelio's experiences, etched into the furrows of his brain, put him a cut above the others. He was a delphinus delphis raised to the second power, marked by special insights into a little more of the world than dolphins normally get at sea.

— Arthur D. Rosenberg

HOME AWAY FROM HOME

Sometimes I think now that we were just too stupid to be properly afraid. For three weeks we lived in Frankfurt in a rather grand room in a residential hotel, three houses from the corner of the block. We were insulated by the propriety of our block. Now and then late at night I would be awakened by loud cries, sometimes joyous and drunken, sometimes furious or disturbed. Or there would be roaring, revved-up motorcylces going by, and farewell shouts, and sometimes singing. We were immune. Except for the one time we stopped in the forbidden territory instead of going straight home.

Beyond our block with its quiet houses and well-kept yards were three long blocks of organized sin, I guess you'd call it, if you believed in sin. Between us and the railroad station, where we went almost every day, was this gauntlet of shops, of businesses, of buildings harboring, I was sure, all the wicked things I knew about, and some I hadn't dreamed of. But they had nothing to do with me.

By day, everything was hidden. Discreet curtains covered display windows, shops were nearly empty if they were open, or were frankly closed. A few men with briefcases hurried in and out of the buildings. A few housewives, obviously from other neighborhoods, walked impersonally through the deserted streets. An industrial fur fair in town lent a bit of action. Once I saw a young man pushing a wire frame loaded with mink pelts along. He was too bored to care that the bottom shelf of furs was dragging all its tails along the dirty sidewalk. I had the hysterical thought that in France the sidewalk wouldn't have been dirty. I was trying to decide whether a French cart-pusher would have let those tails drag, but was saved from deciding when the German worker turned the corner.

We would make our way to the plaza in front of the immense, rococo railroad station. I could never fully appreciate the flowers and fountains, and I think now there were some statues too, because I was trying to get myself safely across six or seven streetcar tracks and into the station. Then by the time we had found the right train track for Heidelberg or Würzburg or Bad Homburg, I forgot all about Frankfurt's vice district.

I had to, in the healthy effort of every day to keep my place in line and to avoid being out-maneuvered, out-pushed or out-talked by the traveling public. After ending up on the end of several lines and having to be rescued by my more athletic husband, I had accepted the challenge and was now, I felt, cheerfully improving. My German is at best more understood than uttered, but I had learned to draw myself up haughtily, (not an easy thing to do when one is short and overweight), to assume an attitude of assured authority and rectitude, which was helped by white hair piled high on my head, and to utter, in a tone of contemptuous assumption of surrender, the magic word "Bitte!"

It worked, to my repeated amazement. Strong men fell back from in front of me. Arms already thrust over my shoulder to show a ticket were withdrawn. Little old ladies did not step on me anymore, or stab me with their umbrellas. Even callow young German army officers in their bright blue uniforms stopped shouldering their way ahead of me. Trainmen waved me through without looking at my ticket—unsmilingly, yes; annoyed, probably; but cowed.

After one such glorious achievement, as I thought to myself that with these dreadful new manners I could never go home again, I heard gentle laughter behind me, and it was definitely laughter from home. I tugged at my husband's arm a little to slow him down, and glanced back, and that's when we met him for the first time.

He was a young Negro soldier, a corporal, my husband told me later, and he was so obviously enjoying my drama that I was instantly charmed. Not so much because of the ham acting—this is the truth—but because I was so glad to be seen through. I didn't actually want anyone to think that was the real me!

"You an American, ma'am?" he said, still chuckling. I burst out laughing.

"How could you tell?" I asked. "Didn't I pronounce 'Bitte' right?"

"Sounded good to me," he said, as he walked along the platform with us. "Too good, I guess. You were fierce." He flashed his eyes in mock ferocity.

"It's almost the only word I know," I said, hoping not to be believed.

"Our name is Brady," my husband said. "Are you going to Heidelberg? Why don't we ride together?"

"Be glad to," he said and gave us a smile of friendliness rather than amusement, so that he suddenly looked younger and a little shy.

"I'm Jeff Potter, from Philadelphia, U.S.A., and over here I wish it was New York. You imagine what it's like explaining a word like Philadelphia to a German girl?" He looked a little startled when he heard himself say that, but I guess we didn't, because he went right on.

"I've been over here for a couple of years now, and I learned German pretty good—not to read so much, but to talk. I get along—'course I can't exactly pretend I'm German." There was an edge of irony in his laugh.

"I teach German at home," my husband said. "Maybe we can give *meine Frau* some conversation lessons on the train. If she'll talk to us."

They did, too. I mean, I can't stand to be left out of a conversation, and they were zooming along in German which I could understand very well. So I would burst in with my pidgin-German when I had to say something, which with me is fairly often, and each of these gentlemen helped me by understanding most of it, and not laughing, much.

Jeff told us some of the usual stories of the army abroad. His job had something to do with chemical warfare but he didn't talk about it in detail, and we didn't ask questions. Unlike many soldiers who are in a foreign country, he was making an effort to see the famous places, to talk with the people, to learn about the places where he was sent. For a while he had driven a jeep on some unexplained trips, and it was clear that this had been a free and golden time for him. Because I felt he wouldn't mind, I asked whether he liked this duty because it allowed him to get away from his fellow soldiers for long periods at a time. "Maybe," he said, "and just being on my own, with a car, and the country so beautiful—" He paused almost too long, and his brows wrinkled in the effort to explain.

"It just felt good, I guess," he said, and I resolved not to ask any more probing questions.

He was in Frankfurt for a few weeks now on his way to a new duty in northern Germany. Frankfurt is a way station for troops, as it is for travelers.

We always saw many servicemen in the station, where they even had their own waiting room. Jeff said it was supposed to be a good place for a leave and grinned again.

"You know, night life and all that," he said, and we said indeed we did, we walked past it every night on our way home.

"I just stick out my chin and look dignified," I declaimed in my *grande dame* voice, "and *nobody* says a *word.*"

He collapsed in laughter.

"Mrs. Brady, I believe you,"he said. "I just hope you never use that voice on me."

"I won't," I promised, in mock dejection. "You'd only laugh."

We parted good friends in Heidelberg because he was planning an all-encompassing, vigorous young tour of the city which we could never have survived, and my husband was hoping to see a few people at the University. We wrote down our name and address in Frankfurt for him, and he seemed pleased to have them, but he didn't tell us where he was staying and I don't think I really expected to see him again.

When we got back to Frankfurt that night about eight, our street had come alive. Neon lights in all colors, some of them blinking on and off, or snaking giddily back and forth and up and down—where are they in the daytime, I wondered, knowing I had never noticed them then, in their meaning-less shapes and drabness, noncommittal until the sun went down. I laughed again when I remembered the first time I saw the lights. Wum-Wum, one club was called, and another was Hazyland. I had been very tired, and sort of hanging on my husband's arm after our usual tourist's day. One always walks farther than one should, and I was cross because we had done it again. These people are crazy, I was thinking severely. Where do they *get* such silly names? But luckily my mind was stronger than my body, and it decided I hadn't been pronouncing those names Germanically.

"Voom-voom!" I said in loud delight. "Hotsy!"

"Are you all right?" my husband asked. He was tired too.

"That's the way they're *pronounced!*" I said. "That's why they *spell* them that way!"

"I know. Can you make it another block?" He's a very patient man. My discovery gave me new strength, and I went along murmuring voom-voom and hotsy-totsy under my breath. They missed a trick on that one, I thought; no totsy.

Tonight the men were out on the street — quiet, well dressed, competent-looking shills for the businesses were there, mingling with the great, uncouth public. Youngish men in ones, twos and surging groups milled cheerfully about. They looked at the nude pictures in the lighted, uncurtained windows, they pretended not to listen to the soft-spoken stories of the great things going on inside, and they argued mightily about whether to go in yet or wander around some more. Now and then a garish, bored-looking girl would appear in a doorway, but not many, and not often. Sometimes a car would go by slowly with one of them driving, looking as handsome and metallic as her car. From one place two patient German cops were helping an early casualty toward the waiting van — incongruously a Volkswagen bus. He was bleeding spectacularly from face cuts, but muttering, and able to walk.

We might not have been there. No one spoke to us, or looked at us directly. Sometimes I could feel a glance from an American soldier, or an expressionless flick of the eyes from a doorman, as I thought of them. But we walked invisibly by, and had hot baths and went to bed, perhaps to be awakened by cries in the night.

One day we spent going about Frankfurt itself, and ended grandly by going to the imposing new Opera House at night. I had just discovered that the tarnished-looking, dull rolls of metal I had seen through the glass walls during the day became magical golden clouds at night. We were standing in line waiting to buy our tickets and I was feeling unusually mellow after a fine Hungarian dinner and less walking than usual. Suddenly, an unmistakably hostile, superior voice said, *"Bitte!"* Surely, I thought, he can't be talking to me, but all my adrenalin knew better and started churning up to help me. I turned around to find my husband and Jeff already shaking hands and laughing, of course, so I did too. We got seats together and saw and heard a very good performance of "The Flying Dutchman". It was mind-wrenching and sad and unbelievable, and we went back to the Hungarian restaurant afterwards for wine and reassurance.

Jeff seemed as cheerful as before and very pleased with himself for having startled me, but he was alone again, and I thought innocently that it was too bad some of the other soldiers didn't like opera too. We reproached him gently for not having looked us up and he said he'd meant to, but just got busy.

"I went by your place once, Mrs. Brady," he told me, "But it was late at night so I didn't stop." I started to ask him what he was doing over *there* late at night, but I didn't.

He said he had six more days, and I said let's have dinner, and this time he gave us a phone number to call and I felt vaguely complimented. To give your phone number is a form of trust, isn't it? I thought. We walked the usual mile home. I soaked my feet in hot water, and took them to bed with me under the weightless, enveloping feather-bed. If there was noise that night I never heard it.

Recklessly, we planned a three-cornered trip to two smaller towns and back to Frankfurt about nine. Foolishly, we forgot that there was no decent place to eat within a mile of our hotel at that hour. And we didn't eat on the train, just because we got into an argument, very friendly all around, with two Britishers. This sounds like too much of a cliché, but they wanted to tell us what Americans were like. I did a little quiet reflection about how a cliché gets started and then helped this one carry on, saying things like Americans aren't *anything* in a lump, and how would *they* like it if *we* said, and so on.

The result was the usual fatigue plus starvation. I am cross and unreasonable when I am hungry. I refused to eat in the railroad station because the big restaurant was closed and the little platform eating places are tiny round tables which you are expected to lean on as you stand up and eat. So we walked toward the hotel. I was alert enough to see that the place where Sweet Leilani was singing (in her picture attired only in leis) seemed to be doing the best business. There were many servicemen around, and it was late enough for the sounds to be less joyful, more purposeful, more commercial. It seemed very crowded, I supposed on account of the visiting furriers. There were several police cars cruising slowly.

"Let's go to that little joint on the corner of our block," my husband said. "You know, on the other side of the street."

"Aghh!" I said.

"I know it doesn't look like much," he said, "but it's all there is, and they'll have sandwiches and tea, anyway. Maybe even some kuchen."

"That last was a bribe. I didn't believe it, but I knew there wasn't any other place, so I said all right.

We crossed over at the corner and found the little place was jumping, in a mild way. It didn't even have a name—just advertisements for various beers and wines, and it wasn't very clean, but tonight it was full of people. At first it looked as if there was no place to sit down, but an expressionless waitress said to come with her so we followed her to a booth large enough for six just around the far end of the counter. One middle-aged woman was sitting in it, but it is taken for granted in Europe that you may occupy empty seats anywhere except in grand restaurants. All of us said "Bitte" sweetly to one another and we sat down. Because it is a fine art to mind your own business when you are sharing someone's table or booth, the lady went on reading her paper and we looked around, or spoke very quietly to one another. This place was rather loud and raucous with much visiting back and forth—almost like a neighborhood tavern, but too near the center of town, and going downhill.

The waitress came back with menus and we tried to order. I saw the little lady smile as we were trying. No tea, no coffee, only beer. No dinners left, only sandwiches. That wasn't too unreasonable, considering the hour. Soup? She would see. Probably not, though. Anything else at all to drink? I asked plaintively. I don't like beer. Don't like beer? she said, almost stirred into involvement. For an instant her eyes said what are you doing here, and then went back into disinterest. She would see, she said, there might be some lemonade. I knew from experience that this wouldn't really be lemonade but some horrible carbonated drink, but I was defeated. We ordered hot sausage sandwiches and waited resignedly.

The lady, who was well-dressed and well-mannered, looked a bit out of her element too, I thought. She was picking around in a dish which looked as if it had meant to be sauerbraten. She saw me watching her and smiled.

"I got here just before they stopped serving dinners," she told us in excellent German, "but I don't think it was an advantage. This isn't at all good."

My husband told her how we had landed there, and that we were close to our hotel. She was staying at a very fine hotel about two blocks away, but its dining room was closed when she finished work, she said, and she hadn't wanted to walk farther away than this, alone and at night. She was glad we had come along to sit with her because she had been wondering what company she might acquire in that large booth.

She was a fashion reporter from Paris for a large dressmaking firm and had been looking at furs and listening to furriers all day. I started to talk French with her, while my husband talked German, and she switched effortlessly back and forth, to my boundless envy. Our food and drink came, and we consumed it, paying it as little attention as possible, but enjoying our conversation.

The noise of talk and laughter in the place was unbrokenly loud, so that when a lull came it was noticeable. We looked up to see a soldier, an American, standing in the room about five booths away, with his back to us. He was weaving gently back and forth as he stood and talked, and the sound of his voice was drunken. Not loud, not belligerent, but not in control, either. Compulsive. Repetitive. Unstoppable. What they mean by a talking jag, that's what he's on, I thought.

"Funny," I said, "I don't think there are any other soldiers in here."

"Not funny," my husband said. "There was a sign outside saying Off Limits to U. S. Armed Forces. I guess he's too drunk to know, but you'd think they'd put him out."

"*This* place Off Limits?" I scoffed, and then thought there are rooms upstairs. We were speaking English, and I turned apologetically to Mme Armand, but I could see she was understanding.

"It is too bad to be so far from home," she said slowly in English. "It is perhaps especially hard to be a Negro in Germany."

I looked at the soldier again. He *was* black, and I hadn't even noticed. Because the people in the booth where he was standing were pointedly paying no attention, he turned and came on to the next booth, his monologue moving right along with him. My husband and I stared at him helplessly, because, of course, he was Jeff.

"I came over here three years ago," he was saying in a half-whining, sing-song. "I came over and I thought oh boy now I'll get away from it. Now I'll see all those sights in Europe and get away from the North and the South, and maybe learn something and be somebody and do something different." His voice had an overlay of Southern accent that had never been apparent when he talked with us, and it seemed as if he were putting on the stereotyped Negro whine of old-time radio and vaudeville. Mind you, he was speaking in faultless German, but these characteristics were in it too, ridiculous, and to us indescribably sad. The man in the second booth spoke to him loudly and angrily and told him to move along, to stop bothering them. And he called out to the barman to get the damned black Yank out of there. The barman didn't answer.

In a walking dream Jeff went on with his story to the next booth.

"And you know what happened, man? Nothing. All the same lousy people and the same lousy life. Nothing different. White whores and black whores, and what the hell difference what language they talk? Don't need no language. The damn army is just like at home so I don't stay there. I travel around and the damn streets aren't so different either. You know how they say *Neger* at home?

They say nigger. It's all the same. One time I thought maybe—the language and the place is different—maybe the people'll be different too." He laughed harshly. They shunted him along, not too unkindly, reacting in their different ways to a drunk, as we all do, in embarrassment or amusement or anger. Some of the people tried to talk to him, but he answered no one, didn't even seem to hear anyone, cocooned in his story of mourning and despair. Dully I realized that this was an old story for him. Maybe it was the first time in this place—no one seemed to recognize him—but it was a drama doomed to be reenacted, as tragic, as inevitable as "The Flying Dutchman," and almost as unreal.

I saw that as soon as he came to the end of the row across from us, it would be our turn.

"Mme Armand, we know him," I said to the lady whose booth we shared. "I am going to try to get him to sit down."

She said nothing, just slid over to the right to make more room, as did my husband. At the same time he said quietly,

"Melissa, do you think—?"

"I don't know, but I have to try."

"All right."

Jeff turned toward us, away from the angry voices in the last booth. The disembodied monologue came on as if of its own volition.

"I've been all over, looked at all the history places, seen all the names in the history books, but it doesn't do any good. The people are here, stinking up all the old places, spoiling everything, I get so tired of 'em, so tired of listening to 'em and I got nobody to talk to." His speech was beginning to slur. He rested his hands on our table.

"Jeff," I said, not too loud, but very clearly. "Won't you sit down with us and have something to eat? Maybe a beer?" I was afraid to stop. "You remember us—Joe and Melissa Brady—we're so glad to see you again." I was babbling. I glanced at Mme Armand, at her sad eyes, at my husband's strained smile. He tried to help me.

"Sit down, man," he said to Jeff. "You need a quick one and we're having another." He even gestured to the bartender, who shook his head and walked away.

Jeff looked at us carefully. He turned his serious reddened eyes to my face and looked at me directly and completely. He didn't know me at all.

Because those eyes were looking only inward—he had not lost his mind, I thought delicately, but was lost within it. He was possessed.

The general level of noise in the cafe had risen again, and in fact there seemed to be a number of new customers coming in. I had a last, inspired idea. I was going to get through to Jeff. "Watch him, Joe," I murmured to my husband, and then I stood up next to Jeff as unobtrusively as I could, which wasn't easy as it involved squirming out of the booth. I put my hand lightly on his arm so that he would turn to face me. He was docile enough, and he was talking again.

"There's never a place to go and there never will be, and now I guess I know it but I still don't believe it, I'm too dumb to believe it, and I keep thinking..."

I can't listen to him and do this too, I thought, so I stopped listening. Stopped hearing. Then I breathed deeply, pointed my free arm to the seat beside me as forcefully as I could, and spoke directly into Jeff's sorrowing face.

"*Bitte!*" I said, in my terrible voice.

Oh god, oh god. He collapsed on his knees in the aisle, and he cried. He howled with grief, and tears ran down his face. Tears are harder to see against a black skin, my mind decided, and I think it was just trying to get away from me, who had started all this.

My husband was pulling at Jeff to get him on his feet when the Military Police arrived at our booth. Here were the "customers" I had heard earlier. The two men were not angry or rough, just bored, and doing what they had to do. I suppose the owner had called them.

I don't know how I had the strength, and they gave me that look interfering women of a certain age always get, when I said,

"Officer, we know this man. Can't we take him to a hospital or some-where until he feels better? This is my fault because I tried to talk to him—"

"We'll take care of him, ma'am," said the older of the two men, and I winced, unfairly, because his voice was Southern. Southern American, that is. My husband put his hand on my arm, and when I looked at him he shook his head. I could see why, but I couldn't feel it. The other M. P. spoke.

"This is an old story for this fellow, ma'am," he said. "We'll just take him home and let him sleep it off." Inside my head I yelled stop calling me ma'am, damn it, and what do you mean, home, he hasn't got a home—but I didn't say anything out loud. By this time Mme Armand had put *her* hand on my arm, and I had a twinge of feeling like a prisoner myself. When I looked at her, though, I knew it was as much for her own support as anything else. My husband was out of the booth now, talking earnestly with the older M. P. He came back and said,

"He says they'll take good care of him — it's just routine. They take the drunk ones off the streets so they won't get into trouble." He was quoting in a voice that was trying to believe what it was saying.

"Come along, soldier," the second man said to Jeff, still not angry, but businesslike and beginning to be impatient. Jeff looked at me, consciously this time, and he knew perfectly well who I was, and he knew what I had done. I could not look at his face for long. They started to propel him toward the door, but because the cocoon of his misery was torn and destroyed, because he knew what was happening to him now, he had to fight.

He yelled and cursed, he kicked and thrashed around and hung like a cunning corpse until he could bite the nearest hand. They had little choice. He was a bloody, quiet sack when they finally hauled him out, one dangling, pale-palmed hand hanging loose from the bundle.

— Alma Skidmore

VIGNETTES, JUST VIGNETTES

Eddie thought. And thought. Why did stories always happen to others, he wondered. "Vignettes," he said to himself, "just vignettes." At such times he would let his mind wander back. Not always in chronological order either. That's the way it always came out. In short flashes. Quick takes. Like. . . . . well like say Boxcar Betty.

Eddie had forgotten why they called her Boxcar. He always supposed that was where she had lost her virginity. Next afternoon, though, Eddie was coming up Pine Street on his way home from work and there was Boxcar coming down the street laughing and joking on the arm of her regular guy. Eddie shook his head and went inside quickly to tell everyone.

And Back-to-Back Benny. There was a guy. He got his name because whenever he was playing stud and it came to the end of the hand he would flip over his down card and say, with a chortle, "Back-to-Back." Only with Benny it came out "Beck-to-Beck." The story was (the vignette was) that Benny had lost a hundred thousand dollars and three tailor shops, lost it on the cards, horses and girls. It didn't seem to bother him, but then he had a heart attack and the doctor said there would be no more cards. Eddie found him on this winter night huddled in a chair with a blanket wrapped around him. The chair was on the street in front of the newsroom where they had "a little poker in the back" but it looked closed and the street was dark.

"What are you doing here, Back-to-Back?" Eddie asked him.

"Since the doctor told me to stay away," Benny said, "this is the closest I can get."

And there was Tom-Look-Me-Over. Eddie knew how he got his name, too. Tom came over from Italy and went to work on the route with a pick and shovel. But when prohibition came in Tom worked his way into the bootleg game and pretty soon had a Lincoln touring car and he would take his various girl friends for a ride and he would say, "Hey, girls, take a look." We are now riding over a road which I helped to build and now look-me-over." He was always saying, "Hey, look-me-over," and pretty soon he had a name. Later on Tom fell on poorer days and used the Lincoln as a flower car in funerals getting maybe eight dollars·a funeral. He lost his bankroll, but he never lost his name.

In the rooming house where Eddie lived on Pine Street was a man called "Il Ruggo" and this was because when he first came to the house, you could get a room for about four bucks a week in those days. He complained in very broken English to the landlady that his feet were very cold. He said that when he stepped on the floor in the morning he could not stand it unless he had a rug by his bed. So he got his name and all up and down the street they called him "Il Ruggo."

If you wanted to go back, Eddie thought, you could get a picture, a real picture. Eddie's parents were very strict and Victorian and his mother walked out with her hands in a muff and his father was very proper, too. And Eddie was always looking for excitement. Like the running-away bit.

So on this Saturday as his parents proudly wheeled the baby sister along Main Street nodding to this one and that who should come by and what was he doing? It was Eddie and he was on the garbage wagon sitting proudly next to Bart Dineen, the garbage man, and holding the reins.

The horror on their faces was to be repeated again. And again. Eddie went to the public beach instead of the little yacht club. He hung out with Stanco, Feinborg, and McLoughlin on the street corner. He disgraced them at a party.

He was only eight then. They were playing "Wink" and this game of "Wink" is played by having a circle of chairs with the girls sitting down and the boys behind them but one chair is empty and the boy behind the empty chair winks at the girl he wants to come and sit in his chair. If the girl really wants to go she jumps over. If the boy who has her doesn't want her to go, he holds her back. If the boy wants to get rid of her, he doesn't try to hold her. If the girl doesn't want to go, she pretends the boy is holding her back. Eddie winked at a girl. Once. Twice. Three times! Then he said, "I'm winking at you, you S.O.B." The horrified mothers sent Eddie home and he wasn't invited again.

Or the time later, when Eddie was seventeen and had been drinking a year or so and there was a carnival at the Elk's Club and everyone in town was there and Eddie and McLoughlin climbed up the ladder of the high diving act just for the lark of it and McLoughlin gave Eddie a push and he fell in the tank with the biggest splash you can make with a belly-whopper and everyone turned to look and they turned on the spotlight and Eddie climbed out.

His parents heard about that next day. When Eddie was drinking something, something in him made him want to run. When he was sixteen in Columbia, his friend Feinberg asked him to go out for cross-country just to keep him company. The coach was suspicious. "Wickham," he had said, "You're just trying to get out of physical training class."

Eddie didn't say anything; he just went to the workouts. When they ran the first race, everyone in front of Eddie got lost up in Van Cortland Park, but Eddie remembered the trail so he came in fourth. Then the coach expected big things of him every time he ran and it was always his stubborness that got him home at all. He had no ability but he could hang on when others had quit.

When he was shipped upstate after he flunked out of Columbia, he kept running every time he drank and no one could catch up with him. All of a sudden he would take off running—running.

In later years Eddie used to think that there must have been a deep psychological reason for running like that. He had a saying, "Whenever you are running away *from* something, you have to remember that you are running *toward* something else." He used that and beat it to death. Every time he wrote a skit for his dramatic group, every time he wrote a letter (well, almost every time) he would find some way to bring that in. He never got sick of saying it to himself, "Every time you are running away *from* something, you are running *toward* something else."

His stubborness always stuck by him. When he was eleven the Western Union boy just took a day aff and sent Eddie in to take his place. The manager was upset because she wasn't supposed to use anyone under twelve and so she gave Eddie three telegrams that the boy had brought back because he couldn't find the people.

It was a very hot July day on Long Island and Eddie rode and asked questions and rode and asked questions, but he would not go back; he just would not go back until he found them. The manager was suspicious; she thought he had thrown them in the harbor but she didn't know Eddie. When the other boy quit, Eddie got the job. That was how he came to hate holidays. When he came home from working on the Fourth of July, his father said it was too late to shoot off his firecrackers. Eddie never had a good holiday after that.

He remembered a very sad, sweet time, though. It brought tears of joy to his eyes when he remembered it. When Eddie lived on Pine Street, he was driving a taxi while he went to college. He would drive nights.

Christmas eve all the boys were ready to go out at 6:00 p.m. It was snowing and sleeting. It looked bad out there. Up in the balcony was Weisbard, the owner, beaming. He was beaming because he was about to give them a Christmas present.

The present was a false suede jacket. All the boys knew it hadn't cost Weisbard anything. The insurance company had given them because the boys had not had an accident in six months. This was the time of the '30s, the depression, and times were tough. Weisbard was beaming, and the jackets were passed out.

Eddie wore his like a Congressional Medal of Honor. Oh, he was proud of that jacket. It was a symbol. It meant he belonged to a group. It affected them all. One of the boys opened the door and the wind blew some sleet in and they all looked out the garage windows and all of a sudden, all of a sudden, without a word being spoken, they were all in a circle arms around each other and then they were hugging each other and making muffled sounds and Eddie didn't want anyone to see his tears . . . didn't want anyone to see until he noticed that most of the others were crying, too. It was like they didn't want anyone to have an accident tonight, either, Christmas eve with all the drunks and the ice and Weisbard beaming all this closeness like way down deep man *does* like man, something like that. A vignette.

Another Christmas in World War II, Eddie remembered when he came out of the dining hall after breakfast and the Philippine girls were there with cans. They had had French toast and syrup for breakfast and the girls would scoop off the scraps into the cans they held to take home for *their* Christmas breakfast and there he was again with tears in his eyes. He gave them a little change and they said, "Thank you, Joe." "Thank you, Joe."

The first time he caused horror Eddie remembered, at least the first time he knew about was when he was in first grade and was five years old. Miss Grummelsbacher had read them a poem by Robert Louis Stevenson and it said, "Oh, how I like to go up in a swing," and that same day Eddie called a boy a name he had heard but didn't quite know the meaning of.

Eddie's stubbornness, he always felt, he got from his maternal grandfather. John Grogan was sent out by his father to hoe the potatoes and ran away to become a drummer in the Civil War. He was sick and in the hospital and when he came out he volunteered to stand guard duty for another soldier who was sick and he fell asleep at his post and was caught.

They tried to give him a chance, so the family legend went, and asked him if he hadn't been ill. He denied it with curses and they put him in the guardhouse to be shot, but the Confederate army attacked and the Union Army retreated and as they went they opened the doors to the jails and Grandfather took off.

In later years, in later years, when Eddie had married a nurse and she called to tell him she wouldn't be home that night, Eddie understood. She said the next day, "Something told me that I could save this man's life, something just told me so I sat the night out with him, giving him hot cloths and holding his hand and giving him little sips of water. I just wanted to be there when he needed me."

She went on to say that the doctor had looked in two days ago, washed his hands of the case, given it up as lost and had gone home and hadn't been back to look in on him.

The next night Eddie's wife did the same thing, and the next, too. Then came the climax. The man took a turn for the better.

Two weeks later the man was on his way home, was being discharged and was in a wheelchair. Then he saw the doctor passing through the hall and jumped from his chair and exclaimed, "There, there's the doctor who saved my life." Eddie's wife always told it as a joke on her.

The nurse was Eddie's third wife. Eddie used to say that he was the only one he knew who had had two different wives pour a plate of spaghetti over his head. With meatballs, he would add. Even the spaghetti was just a flash in the pan, Eddie would joke. A vignette.

Nothing but a vignette.

— Darwin Skinner

STEPHANY AND THE COYOTE

Dr. Untouchable
Coyote Gulch, N.M.

Dear Dr. Untouchable:

My name is Stephany, and I am a Navaho Indian. I am sixteen, and my job is tending our flock of sheep. I am writing to you in the middle of a night because my conscience bothers me and I cannot fall asleep. I could go to my dog or to my donkey with my problem, but they would not understand. I do not want to wake up my father or my mother because I know what they would say. Cut out this foolishness; that is what they would say. And if I woke up my brother he would really get sore.

I think I could wake up my grandfther and tell him about my problem. He is very wise and good with advice; but he is old and needs rest and sleep more than I do.

So, let me tell you how it started. We keep a goat with the flock to give us milk. We all love the goat and I love her most. The goat and my dog I love like people love pets.

One day I saw a coyote with two baby coyotes in the gulch. The next day our goat disappeared and was gone. I was sure the coyotes killed the goat. My father and my brother were sure the coyotes killed the goat. I hated the coyotes with all my heart. "The only good coyote is a dead coyote," say people I know, and the more I thought of the goat the more I believed they were right. My father and brother went to the gulch with their guns and shot the old coyote dead. And I was glad.

This morning at dawn I heard a bark. I looked and there was the goat. And there was a pair of baby goats jumping up and down like a pair of little deer I saw once in the Arizona forest park. My dog was happy, my donkey was happy, the mother goat and the baby goats were happy, everybody was happy; everybody was happy but I am not. I am unhappy because I know what happened to the mother coyote and because I do not know what happened to the baby coyotes.

I like to think before I fall asleep. Tonight I cannot because I cannot stop thinking. Dr. Untouchable, of you they say that you can waken people to make them think. But can you stop a person's thoughts to make the person fall asleep?

I am your Stephany

Dear Stephany:

I am reading your story over and over, and now I cannot sleep. I am telling myself that if there never was wrong, who would know right . . . I am relating blindness mental to physical and asking myself where one blindness ends and where the other one begins.

Stephany, dear, now we both know that one has to get rid of the problem of conscience before falling asleep. But then again . . . supposing love and hate do live side by side . . . supposing the closeness of the two . . . more than the distance between heart and brain, do give a person a sense of guilt . . . what else is there on which a better deal, for you and me . . . or for the coyote can ever be built?

Thanks for thinking of me . . . . . . your Dr. Untouchable.

— *Joe Sukup*

TALE OF THE WORLDS

Once upon a time . . . TRPASLIK . . . the distant cousin of leprechauns, lived in the hollow stump of a great big cow pasture. The cow pasture used to be the wilderness where OBR, the giant, used to live till it was cleared away to make room for another cow pasture; that taking place as time went on, and as there was more and more need for milk, and less and less need for the OBR giant and for a place he could call the WORLD of his own.

After the wilderness was cleared away, TRPASLIK made his home in one big hollow dead stump at the edge of the cow pasture. A creek the cows and he drank from; cowflops for mushrooms to grow from — to live on — in short, as little as his home was, as long as he could call it the world of his own, the trpaslik was satisfied. Satisfied, even after Kristinka, the eight-year-old daughter of the pasture lot owner wrote in her school paper: "I saw a man on our pasture lot, man so small I held him in the palm of my hand. He had no teeth and looked real funny as he chewed with his gums." No offence; as long as he was good for fun, he, and the world, he thought, was his very own, was good for something worthwhile, so thought the trpaslik.

Sad to tell, the proof of ownership in the world of fables — not the same as registered in the world of unfables — one day the bulldozer came and boom, gone was the world the trpaslik thought was his own.

Homeless now, he grabbed a hold of a hunk of what was his home, a hunk that fell in the creek by the impact of the bulldozer against it, and there and then began a voyage to match many voyages in the whole of a batch. It lasted almost forever and ever, till one day the trpaslik, a sailor by now, saw his former neighbor OBR, the giant, sitting on a rock—a rock as big as an island—in the seventh sea.

Heaving to, to exchange the long time no see . . . after the small talk was over, the trpaslik sez to the obr: "Obr, a neighbor from way way back when you and I used to share the wilderness—and when I had to move every time you decided to yank a tree I was living under by the roots since both of us were driven out of the worlds—we used to think were our very own, you before me, is there anything you know that I don't, but should?"

"Anything particular?"

"Just one thing. Losing the world I thought was my own hit me hard; really hard. I am still feeling bad over the loss. You losing yours long before me, you've had more time to get over the loss. My question to you is . . . is there a way . . . is there a time . . . or is there a distance between the world lost and the world I hope to find to completely get over the loss?"

"To hope to get over the loss completely would be hoping for too much. The closest I came to getting over the loss was somewhere between the sixth and seventh seas . . . when instead of thinking big, I began to think bigger. By the time I was about to lay a claim to this huge rock, I thought of myself as the citizen of everything under me . . . and of everything in the sky above me. Once I switched my thinking to that size of the citizenship, any old place—even this island rock—was plenty good enough for me to call it the home of my own."

"You've lost me somewhere between your claim to the citizenship of this whole planet Earth—if not of the universe—as I gotcha, and this big rock you claim as your very own WORLD at the moment. And if those two claims are not too much to claim, then there is no such thing as too much."

"Well, as I gotcha, you claimed the dead stump in the pasture lot as your HOME, and the WORLD of your own, and that too was too much. So, the home on the hunk of the stump you've still got and all you need now is to start thinking bigger like I did between the sixth and the seventh sea. Now kapeesh?" sez OBR. "Me frshtej", sez TRPASLIK . . . "move over obr, pal."

There is plenty of time for rain to soften the rock—and the cycle would start over again.

— Joe Sukup

FANCY AND STAPLE GROCERIES

It was the drought combined with the glowing accounts of south Georgia that determined my grandfather to sell his farm in Missouri and set out in a covered wagon with his wife Maria, daughter Katrina, her husband Lucian Tisdel, my father, and their baby, Hazel. After disposing of the outfit in St. Louis, they proceeded by train to the small town of Fitzgerald. There they set up camp by the sawmill until there was enough lumber for Grandfather and Father to build two cabins. I remember hearing Maria tell how proud she was of her glass window, the only one in Shacktown.

Before coming to Georgia, Papa had been a clerk in a grocery store, earning a dollar a day which at the time seemed ample for supporting wife and baby. He now saw that groceries were an indispensable commodity; and since there was no grocery store in this community, one would prove to be a profitable business. With Grandpa's aid and Maria's indomitable will as a pusher, Papa built one of the first grocery stores in Fitzgerald. He had two plate glass windows installed in front on which was painted "Fancy and Staple Groceries". It was his objective to cater to those who wanted fruits and vegetables out of season as well as to supply the staples. These luxury items were sent in by express from Savannah. The elegant, imported bread, I remember, was particularly prized over the local product. "Your Grocer, L.O. Tisdel" was his slogan.

Hazel and Elsie were my older sisters, Theda, the youngest. Theda and I were allowed to play around the store, but we were told not to help ourselves to anything. If we had spent all our money then we would just have to wait until we received our next allowance. One afternoon I was in the store when the clerks had just arranged a new shipment of cookies in glass cases. How tempting they looked and they were my favorites, a whole big box of Nabiscos. We had been cautioned not to help ourselves and we knew what our punishment would be if we disobeyed. Papa, as well as Mama, was a firm believer in the rod so we didn't often take chances. Somehow I just couldn't resist the temptation to take just one Nabisco. That case was on top and I had to stand on the tips of my bare toes to look into it. Then I got to thinking Papa usually went to the bank after dinner. He was out now and perhaps that is where he was. I wanted to make sure he wasn't in sight so I went to the door and looked across the street. To the right was the post office and farther down the street to my left was the bank. I couldn't see him anywhere along that side of the street. Somehow I neglected to look along the side of the street on which our store was located. Feeling reasonably safe, I went back in the store and moving casually along the front of the cookie case so as not to arouse the curiosity of the clerks, I stood up on my toes, gently lifted the glass lid and slipped my hand down over the cookie. I was just lifting it out of the box when I felt a firm hand on my shoulder and to my horror looked up into Papa's face. It felt like my legs were filled with water and my voice had suddenly become so weak I could hardly speak. Hoping to get the situation in hand and trying to convince Papa I was only admiring the cookie display, I said lamely, "Aren't these pretty cookies, Papa?" Papa, unable to enjoy the beauty of the occasion replied, "Young lady, I'll show you how pretty they are!" Half dragging me he finally reached the back of the store where he found a thin board from a packing case and helped me to see the error of my way.

The following Saturday Papa was in Irwinville all day on business and as it was too rainy to play out, Theda and I spent most of the day at the store. As Albert was always falling for some kind of joke the other clerks were usually planning some trick to pull on him. Generally Theda and I were in on the fun and this Saturday afternoon proved to be no exception. It was planned that Burrell was to get up a bet with Albert and I was to hold the stake which was to be ten cents from each of the participants. The trick though old now was funny then. Burrell bet Albert that Albert couldn't drop a nickel from his forehead into a funnel which was inserted into the top of Albert's trousers.

Albert declared that this was an easy one and that his bet was as good as won already. Burrell produced the coin while Albert inserted the funnel. Then tipping back his head and placing the proferred nickel on his forehead he was just in the act of throwing his head forward endeavoring to deposit the coin in the funnel when Theda stepped out from behind the counter with a glass full of ice water which she poured into the funnel. Everyone was hilarious except Albert who was jumping around trying to drain the water out of his trouser leg.

We were still laughing when Miss Mabel Cummings came in the store with her grandmother. When they came in the door we saw they were both laden with luggage. Miss Mabel told us that she and her grandmother were on their way back to Minnesota as Grandma didn't like it here. It was some hours before train time so she wanted to know if her grandmother couldn't just sit with Mama upstairs until train time. Mrs. Cummings was a genial little old lady in her '80s and was in possession of most of her faculties. It was only her absent-mindedness that bothered her and Miss Mabel at times. We assured her that Mama would be glad to have them wait upstairs, and we were off in a hurry to inform Mama that she was about to have company.

Mama could make anyone feel comfortable so it wasn't long before Mrs. Cummings was telling Mama why she disliked Fitzgerald. She didn't like the heat or mosquitoes and frankly the vegetables didn't taste like those back in Minnesota. Being of a very polite nature she abruptly stopped telling about her plans and turning to Mama she began to ask about us, "Mrs. Tisdel, sometimes my memory fails me and I just can't seem to remember how many children you have." Mama laughed and said, "Yes, Mrs. Cummings, our memories do play funny tricks on us sometimes and when children come along so fast we almost lose track of them. I have four girls. Do you remember that?" Mrs. Cummings nodded her head slowly, "Yes, yes, now I do remember you told me there were four. And how old is the youngest?" she added slowly as if trying to bring to memory something that was very hazy. "The last one or the youngest is Theda and she's ten years old." Mrs. Cummings looked puzzled out of her faded blue eyes and then asked, "How many boys?" Then Mama, wishing to clear up her dilemma said, "Don't you remember Mrs. Cummings I haven't any boys."

This was too much for Grandma Cummings; she shook her head and muttered sympathetically, mostly to herself, "My, my! what a pity, ten girls and no boys."

Miss Mabel looked at her watch and saw that it was nearing train time and as she had something important to say to Mama, winked her eye at Mama and pointed toward one of the bedrooms. Mama guessed that Miss Mabel wanted to tell her something of a secretive nature so Mama called to Hazel, "Hazel, perhaps Grandma would like a little lunch before she goes to the train." Hazel came in then and Mama turned to Grandma Cummings and asked her what she would like to eat. Grandma said she'd have just a cup of tea and since she liked to make her own tea she'd just go in the kitchen and make it herself if Mama didn't object. Mama and Mabel were pleased with the turn of events as Grandma followed Hazel into the kitchen.

Mabel plunged into the problem that was bothering her. She asked Mama to look into the traveling bag Grandma was carrying. Mama was amazed to see a box neatly packed with eggs. Mabel then told her it was a setting of eggs which her grandma insisted on taking back to Minnesota. "What I would like is this, since you are very diplomatic, would you please see if you can get those eggs away from Grandma and boil them. She'll object I know, but we just can't travel that long distance with those eggs." Mama tried her best to dissuade the old lady but to no avail. Grandma was adamant. "Mabel thinks I can't get there with these eggs." After Grandma Cummings and Mabel had been gone for some time Mama received a letter from Mabel in which she said her grandma set the eggs and to her surprise, not her grandmother's though, several chickens hatched.

The store was patronized by the young as well as the old and children were very fond of the penny candies. A little toddler one day handed Papa a button and pointing to the candy case said, "I want a worth of candy." Naturally, Papa let him select what he wanted. Another little fellow on the way to buy candy lost a fifty-cent piece in the alleyway. He tearfully told Papa, "When I got home I got my business jammed."

Papa had a very genial manner and made friends easily and arranged to have the store stocked with all those things that his customers asked for and also was constantly on the lookout for new products which were continually coming on the market now. The store was kept clean, the clerks were courteous and efficient and there was such a friendly air about the place that customers met there regularly not only to buy their groceries but to chat with friends.

— Mildred Van Acker

MIRACLE IN DOMMELDANGE

Could these words be the title of a new movie with a host of featured actors and actresses? A super-special for television viewers? A smash hit Broadway stage play? Emphatically no, but they are just about the best words in my vocabulary to identify a very personal happening, a heartwarming, deeply emotional experience. It is just as vivid in my memory today as when it actually took place on Christmas Eve in December 1944. A "miracle"? I thought so then. I still think of it in the same way. That will never change.

In December of 1944, the 80th Infantry Division to which I was assigned and then under the command of General George Patton and part of the U.S. Third Army had been ordered into a rest area near Sarre Union, France, after several months of combat duty. This Christmas away from home would at least be a quiet one, I thought. A welcome relief from the hectic pace of the previous months after the Allied breakout at St. Lo, France following D Day. It didn't happen that way. The "rest period" had lasted just six days when orders were received to pack up and move out about 3:00 p.m., December 23.

The weather which had been relatively mild and sunny became progressively colder and cloudy as our truck convoy rolled on in what turned out to be a journey of about a hundred miles nonstop, which however required twenty-four hours over roads jammed with men and equipment. The snow started to fall about noon on December 24 becoming heavier as the day went on. Rumors were rampant. Fragments of information filtered down through the "Kilroy Was Here" G.I. grapevine. There was a major German counterattack underway, in force. An entire U.S. airborne division was completely cut off. Enemy troops in American uniforms, using American vehicles, were infiltrating our positions. The situation ahead was critical. The rumors proved to be all too true. It was Bastogne, Malmedy, the Ardennes Forest. It was the Battle of the Bulge.

Where were we going? Nobody seemed to know. If *they* did, *they* weren't telling us. Finally, the roadsigns began to read "Luxembourg." Where's that, someone asked, even though it didn't seem to matter to me at the time. How utterly wrong I was.

The snow now was very heavy and had begun to change the nature of the countryside, decking the splintered trees with a soft white mantle; covering the burned out vehicles which had been bulldozed into the ditches alongside the road, and the ugly, gaping ruins of what had been homes and churches and schools—the senseless destruction that is war.

Then about 4:00 p.m., on Christmas Eve, the miracle-to-be started. Unbelievingly, our convoy began to pass through a sector practically undamaged by the fighting. Finally, everything ground to a halt in the square of a small village. In the gathering dusk, to me, it was a Christmas card scene, a winter fairyland. The harsh, rasping noise of the truck motors finally was stilled and a beautiful quietness pervaded the entire scene. The griping I had done about the bone-chilling weather, the seemingly endless journey, the cold rations seemed now to be of no consequence. Gathered in the square were many of the villagers who told us we were in Dommeldange, in the Grand Duchy of Luxembourg. There was instant friendliness as they opened their hearts and homes to us. I began a friendship with Bertha and John-Pierre Bauer-Weiler and their children which endures to this day.

Later that evening, I attended Christmas Eve mass with the family in their beautiful church. Here, I thought, were people who had bravely endured four years of cruel and oppressive occupation by the Nazis. Yet, as I searched their faces, I saw only faith and hope, courage, determination and serenity. In the solitude, with the gleaming candlelight, I heard again the familiar Christmas hymns. In spirit, I was at home with family and loved ones. The familiar figures in the crib scene seemed to take on a dimension of reality. The bittersweet memories of Christmas at home, and the poignancy of the moment overwhelmed me and I wept—openly and unashamed.

The services ended and we walked back through the blacked-out streets to the little home where I was to spend the next five weeks. The newly fallen snow crunched softly underfoot and even though our conversation was hampered by my high-school conversational French, I was aware of a close bond of understanding and togetherness.

The services ended and we walked back through the blacked-out streets to the little home where I was to spend the next five weeks. The newly fallen snow crunched softly underfoot and even though our conversation was hampered by my high-school conversational French, I was aware of a close bond of understanding and togetherness.

The snowfall had ended and I was suddenly aware that there was a change taking place in the sky. It just didn't seem possible, but it was finally beginning to clear after weeks of incessant cloudiness, rain, fog, snow and very limited visibility in this particular sector. Just as we reached the door of my new friends' home, the moon began to shed its soft light, framing in muted detail the people, the streets and the rooftops where the chimneys were spiraling smoke up into the still, clear air. Then, incredibly, there were the stars, sparkling in the heavens in all their pristine glory, with the evening star gleaming brightest of all. I thought—this is how it was on that Christmas Eve in Bethlehem of Judea over two thousand years ago when shepherds watched and the herald angels, proclaiming the birth of Christ, sang, "Glory to God in the highest and on earth, peace to men of good will." If my faith had been shaken, and I would not dispute that it had been at times, it was humbly and firmly renewed at that very moment. Later, as I drifted off to sleep, I somehow knew that peace would come again and that I would be reunited with my loved ones. How long that would be didn't seem to matter any more. Some of the words of a poem I recalled seemed to sum it all up—"God's in His heaven—all's right with the world."

Eventually everything was all right—all over the world—and it can be that way again, I believe, like the ancient miracle of Christmas that gladdens the world every year.

— George Ventner

VISIT TO A CONCENTRATION CAMP
Somewhere in Germany
April 11, 1945

The story which follows took place many years ago, but the memory of that day is still crystal clear. It was an unforgettable experience. At the time I was assigned to the 80th Infantry Division, attached to the U.S. Third Army under the command of the colorful and controversial General George Patton, Jr. Due to strict security precautions I could not then be specific about names, locations, etc. However, it can now be told that my story is about a Camp Ohrdruf, near Gotha, Germany, a small unit in the chain of infamous slave labor, concentration and extermination facilities set up under the regime of Adolph Hitler to eliminate any human being, regardless of race or religious preference, who openly opposed his philosophy or was otherwise considered unsuitable to be a part of the so-called Third Reich "master race."

Come with me in spirit, back to the days of World War II. Mine is not a pretty story but, like countless other similar stories, it needs to be told and retold if necessary to substantiate the fact that "The Holocaust" did happen and to strengthen the convictions of free people everywhere that it must never be permitted to happen again.

While the details are still vivid in my mind, I'd like to give you my impression of a little trip I took today where I saw something, the like of which I have never seen before, and which I hope I shall never see again. I don't think it was just idle curiosity that prompted me to go. I rather felt that I wanted to see for myself, something about which I had heard and read a good deal, a Nazi Concentration Camp.

If you have ever visited one of our army camps in the States, you will have a good idea of what this camp looked like. Long, rambling barracks, neatly spaced, even plots of grass here and there, and a few flowers and vines. The main difference is the ten-foot high barbed wire fence which surrounds the entire place, and the many guard towers with large electric lights on them spaced here and there. Right at the entrance is a sight which gives you an inkling of what you have been told to expect. It is the body of a man, stretched at full length on the ground, in a peaceful attitude which belies the violent death he met. A closer glance at him reveals that he is well-clothed, but his chest has been exposed, and I can see ten or fifteen of the twenty-odd bullet holes which caused his death. Waste no sympathy on him, I am told, he was in charge of this place, and died a lot more easily than those over whom he exercised the power of life and death.

A short walk through the gate and I am at what appears to be one of the main yards, probably a space for exercising. At the extreme end of it, I see about twenty or thirty bodies lying in various positions on the ground. It takes a little mustering of my courage to look closer, and then I begin to notice a few particulars. These are the inmates, the slave labor, brought to this place to further a plan which in the end would rule the entire world. All the stories of starvation and mistreatment I have heard about are apparent here. Each body shows signs of malnutrition, most of them being thin to the point of emaciation. Those which are clothed, and there are many that are not, have on only a few ragged and dirty garments. If the head is not completely shaved, there is a strip about an inch and a half wide across the top. Without exception, each was killed with a bullet through the top of the head. Their positions give evidence that all did not die mercifully quick, but had to suffer a while longer, before death put an end to their misery. At first, it appears that all were older men, but a closer inspection reveals that many of them were quite young in years. The number of canes and crutches lying around is an indication that perhaps this particular group were the sick and the lame and had outlived any future usefulness. After taking a few pictures, I am content to move away, for it is not a pretty sight.

An inspection of the so-called living quarters gives an idea of the squalor and overcrowding. An attempt by some of the inmates to add a few homelike touches to the barracks only emphasized the pitiful conditions under which they existed. A bed holds the body of a man who cheated these maniacs out of a few moments of sadistic pleasure, for he apparently died of starvation.

One particular shed-like building to which we were directed held another twenty bodies. These are completely naked, and are piled criss-cross like a cord of wood. Each has some penciled information on his chest, and the bodies have been sprinkled with a limelike substance which is already helping nature in the work of decomposition. I found it was a good idea to keep my mouth and nose covered with a handkerchief while viewing this scene.

The last stop on this grisly tour is a visit to the mass burial pits. They are immense, but then they had to be so constructed to hold the thousands of bodies which are reportedly buried here. The daily death rate in this camp was said to be between twenty and thirty. One pit is still open, and as I walk along, I can see the leg of a man protruding up out of the ground. As if this wasn't enough for one day, I had yet to see probably the most gruesome sight of all—a mass crematory. Three pairs of narrow gauge railroad tracks, about twenty feet long, lie side by side, supported by logs. Within the tracks, is what at first glance, seems to be burned out wood. Unfortunately, it is the remains of the bodies that were burned there. It's impossible to mistake this, for whoever did this shameful deed wasn't quite thorough enough, and there are heads, skulls, backbones, arms, legs, ribs, and several bodies which are practically intact. A long pole with a hooked end must have been used to turn the bodies over, so that the destruction would be completed more quickly.

This brought me to the end of my visit. On the way back, though, I just couldn't help but wonder what kind of people are these. I can find no excuse for such things as this, and personally, I feel very strongly that there is none. If you could see what I did, I'm sure you would agree with me.

— George Venter

WHO SAYS PIGS CAN'T SWIM?

"It's a well known fact. Pigs can't swim."

"Their legs are too short for their weight and their pointed hooves not only cut the water, but, in their struggling, they may cut their own throats."

Two very matronly-looking women were talking, on the bus, as I was returning from work one night. If I'd dared to speak up, I'd have told them: "You're wrong. Pigs *can* swim. I've seen them do it. I saw them swim, years ago, at Brookwood, when I was only six."

It was an hour's ride home. The talk about pigs seemed to start my memory clock ticking . . . I began to dream.

How well I remember my Brookwood home. It was a big, old house, with over 300 acres of beautiful land around it. In those days, there were lots of hiding places for children . . . an attic, cellar, closets under curving stairways . . . the long banister with a low newel post allowing for an exciting slide and a mild letdown.

There were barns with haymows, and warm, friendly animals. The farm was in that part of York state country that lay along the upper Hudson Valley. The lawn lay deep in pink alsike clover. A slope to the North was a toboggan slide in winter and a wild garden of violets and adder's tongue in spring. At the foot of the hill, sycamore, butternut, and black walnut trees grew with their roots wading in the brook, where it joined the river.

High above the upper porch reached the giant, thorny branches of the honey-locust trees, swinging their dark, curling pods, full of brown beans that rattled in the wind.

There were a few pear and sour cherry trees, but it was in the big apple orchard where I spent most of my time. An orchard is beautiful in any season. We children named all the trees, because they "belonged" to us. In our imaginations they became apartments, places of business . . . whatever the occasion or the owner demanded.

It was a part of this orchard that became a pasture for our pigs. It was my Dad's idea. Dad was a frustrated farmer at heart. He had worked in a bank all his adult life and he hated it. Whenever he saved any money, it went into land, tools, and books about farming.

"Pigs aren't naturally dirty—no more so than people," my father insisted. "And pigs, like people, need room . . . Where do you usually find pigs?"

"In a pigpen," we children shouted.

"Exactly . . . jammed together and unhappy. Crowd any of God's creatures together and they, and their surroundings, become filthy."

It's true. Our pigs, free to roam, never looked any dirtier than our cows or horses—not as dirty as we kids did at the end of a day of tree-climbing and mud pies.

But for Dad and Mom, this freedom presented a new problem. Give pigs a big space in which to root and feed on timothy grass, clover, and apples, and they get thirsty. So our pigs went to the river for a long drink.

"Pigs like to play in the water. They're like children. They splash and snort, and fool around, and—all of a sudden—they're beyond the fence." It was my mother talking. Mom was no farmer either. She'd grown up in Brooklyn, but she loved the country.

"Saturday morning they were out front, eating locust pods. Then, later, out back, eating the pear windfalls. Monday they enjoyed the clover on the lawn, and yesterday, they followed the shore line. I thought they'd been lost until I found them by the brook, rooting under water for butternuts and walnuts."

My father threw back his head and laughed heartily. Mother did not join in. She continued.

"But each time, Ed, I have to persuade them to leave their newfound food and freedom and driving them back takes a great deal of time from my housework."

"We help, don't we, Mom?" asked Marion.

"Yes, often you do. But *today,* I had to drive those squealing porkies out of our garden!"

Father's laughing stopped very suddenly.

"They like melons and corn and squash even better than they like apples!" Mother added.

So Dad got out his carpenter's tools. First he put a chicken wire fence around the garden. Then he built a floating fence of heavy wire and wood. He put on his swim trunks and we children were allowed to watch from the old, flat-bottomed boat, while Dad swam out into deep water and fastened the off-shore end of the fence into the riverbed with iron stakes and stone anchors.

"There! That should keep them in. I have been told that pigs don't swim well in deep water." Dad was pleased with his work. That was on Friday.

Saturday, at the dinner table, we heard Mom say, "Well, Daddy, pigs *do* swim well, don't they? This time the whole crowd swam around the entire floating fence, and, when they couldn't get into the garden, they ran straight back to their gate and squealed to get back in the orchard again. They missed their apples, I guess."

"And, Dad, before you got home," Jim added, "All of us were in the orchard and saw them swim around the fence."

Mary joined in, "They swim as well as our dogs do—better than I do."

"They sure had a good time," I added, "They were laughing about it all morning."

So Dad had to build a floating corral—a big one—because pigs need lots of room, and *his* pigs weren't going to be dirty!"

— Margaret A. Wheeler

Beavers repairing their lodge.

From original by: Sister Mary Charles Lilly

About the editors

Florence Boochever is a graduate of Cornell University, Phi Beta Kappa, and of the School of Library Service at Columbia Univesity, and a member of Beta Phi Mu. She is former editor of *The Bookmark,* monthly publication of the New York State Library; served as copy writer at the Macmillan Company, Publishers, and did editing and promotion work in New York City. She has had articles, book reviews and light verse published in newspapers and professional journals, and is included in the 1963 edition of "Who's Who of American Women."

Raymond H. Jackson who assisted in editing this anthology is a native of Kentucky. He was graduated from Knoxville College and earned a Master's degree at the University of Michigan. He studied also at Indiana University. Throughout his long career, he has taught English. As Dean of a small college in South Carolina, his duties included freshman and sophomore English courses. At Tuskegee Institute, he taught courses at all levels from 1961 through 1965, when he was appointed to an administrative position. He continued to teach at least one English course until his retirement in 1976. The following year, he taught writing courses as an adjunct instructor at the University of Cincinnati.

About the artist

Sister Mary Charles Lilly has been a teacher in various schools of the Albany Catholic Diocese. She holds a Master's degree in history from Siena College, a Bachelor's degree in mathematics, chemistry and physics from State University of New York at Albany, and studied art at the Marywood College in Scranton Pennsylvania.

INDEX OF CONTRIBUTORS

About the book designer

Robert L. Ewell is graphic artist-designer for Albany Public Library. He recently returned to Albany (his home town) after working on the West Coast as graphic artist, instructor and free lance graphic designer.

The book was printed at Crest Litho, Inc. on 60 lb. White Wove Offset. The type style is 12 point Claro Condensed, set 14.